www.EZmethods.com

EZ SOLUTIONS

TEST PREP SERIES

MATH REVIEW

LOGIC & STATS

EZ SIMPLIFIED SOLUTIONS – THE BREAKTHROUGH IN TEST PREP!

LEADERS IN TEST PREP SOLUTIONS – WE MAKE IT EZ FOR YOU!

AUTHOR: PUNIT RAJA SURYACHANDRA

EZ Solutions
P O Box 10755
Silver Spring, MD 20914
USA

EZ SOLUTIONS
P.O. Box 10755
Silver Spring, MD 20914
USA

Conceived, conceptualized, written, and edited by:
Punit Raja SuryaChandra, EZ Solutions

PRINTED AND MANUFACTURED IN THE UNITED STATES OF AMERICA

TABLE OF CONTENTS

summary of some important points. Moreover, they assume that you already know everything, or at least most of the concepts.

However, if you are using our EZ modules to prepare for your test, it's the opposite case, you don't need to refer or consult any other book or text or any other source for assistance. On the contrary, we, in fact, discourage you from referring to any other book, just because there is absolutely no reason to. Our EZ modules contain everything that you need to know in order to do well on your test. We haven't left anything out, and we don't assume anything. Even if you don't know anything, you will find everything in our modules from topics that are frequently tested to topics that are rarely tested, and everything in between. The only topics that you won't find in our books are the topics that will probably never appear on your test!

Frequently Tested: Included in our review – topics that are repeatedly tested on your test, on a regularly basis
Occasionally Tested: Included in our review – topics that are sometimes tested on your test, every now and then
Rarely Tested: Included in our review – topics that are seldom tested on your test, very infrequently
Never Tested: Not included in our review – since these topics are never tested on your test, we don't even mention them anywhere in our review

The bottom line is, if something can be on your test, you'll find it in our modules; and if something is not going to be on your test, it's not going to be in our modules. Each and every math concept that even has the slightest possibility to be on the test can be found in our modules.

THE OFFICIAL REAL PRACTICE TESTS:

Although we don't suggest you refer to any other book, the only time we recommend using other books is for practicing previously administered tests to exercise your skills. The best resources for actual practice tests are the official guides published by the test makers that have several actual previously administered tests. One can **replicate** these tests as closely as one can, but no one other than the test administrators can **duplicate** them, and have the ability to reproduce or publish them. Therefore, to get the maximum effect of our approach, you must practice the actual tests from the official guide. You can also take a free online practice test by going to their website. EZ's practice tests are also based upon the most recently administered tests, and include every type of question that can be expected on the actual exam.

HOW OUR BOOKS CAN HELP YOU:

Our books are designed to help you identify your strengths and the areas which you need to work on. If you study all our modules, you will be fully equipped with all the tools needed to take your test head-on. Moreover, you'll also have the satisfaction that you did all you possibly could do to prepare yourself for the test, and you didn't leave any stone unturned. The amount of content covered in our books is far more than what you would learn by studying all the other test-prep books that are out there, put together, or by even taking an online or an actual prep course, and of course, spending thousands of dollars in the process. This will give you an idea of how material we have covered in our books.

STRUCTURE OF OUR MODULES:

All our modules are **structured in a highly organized and systematic manner**. The review is divided into different modules. Each module is divided into units. Each unit is further subdivided into chapters. Each chapter covers various topics, and in each specific topic, you are given all that you need to solve questions on that topic in detail – explaining key concepts, rules, and other EZ unique features. Also included in some topics are test-taking strategies specific to the topics discussed. Following each topic are solved sample examples with comprehensive explanations, which are exclusively based on that topic, and utilizing the concepts covered in that topic and section. Finally, there are practice exercises with thorough explanations containing real test-like questions for each topic and section, which are very similar to actual test questions. All units, chapters, and topics are chronologically numbered for easy reference.

Moreover, the modules, units, chapters, and topics are all arranged in sequence so that later modules, units, chapters, and topics assume familiarity with the material covered in earlier modules, units, chapters, and topics. Therefore, the best way to review is to work through from the beginning to the end.

SERIES > MODULES > UNITS > CHAPTERS > TOPICS > SUB-TOPICS > SOLVED EXAMPLES > PRACTICE EXERCISES

THE EZ DIFFERENCE:

DIFFERENCE BETWEEN EZ SOLUTIONS' PUBLICATIONS AND OTHER BOOKS:

Most of the other test-prep books suggest that your exam only tests your ability to take the test, and it does not test any actual content knowledge. In other words, they claim that your test is all about knowing the test-taking strategies, and it has very little to do with the actual knowledge of content; others claim that your test is all about knowing a few most commonly tested topics. While we have great respect for these books and the people who write or publish them, all these books have one thing in common: they all want to give their readers a quick shortcut to success. They actually want their readers to believe that just by learning a few strategies and memorizing some key formulas, they'll be able to ace their test. We are not sure if it's the fault of the people who write these books or the people who use them; but someone is definitely trying to fool someone – either those test-prep books for making the readers believe it, or the readers for actually believing it (no pun intended).

With a test as vast as this, it's simply not possible to cover the entire content in just a few pages. We all wish; however, in life, there really aren't any shortcuts to success, and your test is no exception to this rule. Nothing comes easy in life, and that is also precisely the case with your test. You have to do it the hard way by working your way through. Unfortunately, there is no magic potion, which we can give you to succeed in math! Therefore, if you want to do well on your test – be mentally, physically, and psychologically prepared to do some hard work. In this case, efforts and results are directly proportional, that is, greater the efforts you make, better your results are going to be.

While most test-preparation books present materials that stand very little resemblance to the actual tests, EZ's publication series present tests that accurately depict the official tests in both, degree of difficulty and types of questions.

Our EZ books are like no other books you have ever seen or even heard of. We have a completely different concept, and our books are structured using a totally different model. We have *re-defined the way test-prep books should be*.

STRATEGIES SEPARATED FROM CONTENT:

What we have done in our modules is, *separated the actual content-knowledge from the test-taking strategies*. We truly believe that a test-prep program should be more than just a *cheat-sheet of tricks, tips, and traps*. The test you are preparing for is not a simple game that you can master by learning these quick tactics. What you really need to do well on your test is a program that builds true understanding and knowledge of the content.

PERFECT EQUILIBRIUM BETWEEN STRATEGIES AND CONTENT:

In our modules, we've tried our best to present a *truly unique equilibrium* between two competing and challenging skills: test-taking strategies and comprehensive content-knowledge. We have *blended* the two most important ingredients that are essential for your success on your test. We have *enhanced* the old traditional approach to some of the most advanced forms of test-taking strategies. To top all this, we have *refined* our solved examples with detailed explanations to give you hands-on experience to real test-like questions before you take your actual test.

Other Books: Most of the other test-prep books primarily concentrate on teaching their readers how to *guess* and *use the process of elimination,* and they get so obsessed with the tactics that in the process they completely ignore the actual content. Majority of the content of these books consists of pages of guessing techniques.

EZ Books: With our EZ Content-Knowledge Modules, you'll find *100% pure content* that has a highly organized and structured approach to all the content areas, which actually teaches you the content you need to know to do well on your test. Therefore, if you are looking to learn more than just guessing by process of elimination, and if you are serious about developing your skills and confidence level for your exam, then our highly organized and structured test-prep modules is the solution. By studying our books, you'll learn a systematic approach to any question that you may see on your test, and acquire the tools that will help you get there.

EZ Solutions' publications are packed with important information, sophisticated strategies, useful tips, and extensive practice that the experts know will help you do your best on your test.

You should use whichever concept, fact, or tip from that section that you think is appropriate to answer the question correctly in the least possible time. If you've mastered the material in our review modules and strategy modules, you should be able to answer almost all (99.99%) of the questions.

LEARN BACKWARDS AND MOVE FORWARD: Smart students are the ones who make an honest attempt to learn what they read, and also learn from their mistakes, but at the same time, who moves ahead. Therefore, you should learn backwards, that is, learn from your past experiences, and move forward, that is, keep moving ahead without looking back!

ONE CONCEPT, EZ MULTIPLE METHODS:
Our books often give you a *choice of multiple methods* of answering the same question – you can pick the method that seems easiest to you. Our goal is not to *prescribe* any *hard-and-fast* method for taking the test, but instead, to give you the *flexibility and tools you can use to approach your test with confidence and optimism*.

STRATEGIES OR CONTENT?

In order to do well on your test, it is absolutely essential that you have a pretty good grasp of all the concepts laid out in our review modules. Our review modules contain everything you need to know, or must know to crack your test. They cover everything from basic arithmetic to logical reasoning, and everything in between. Nonetheless, that's not enough. You should be able to use these concepts in ways that may not be so familiar or well known to you. This is where our EZ Strategies kick in.

CONTENT VERSUS STRATEGIES:

There is a *succinct* difference between knowing the math content and knowing the math strategies.

Hypothetically speaking, let's assume there is a student named Alex, who learns only the test-taking strategies; and there is another student named Andria, who learns only the math-content. Now when the test time comes, Andria who learns only the math-content is extremely likely to do a lot better than Alex, who learns only the test-taking strategies.

The truth is that someone who has the knowledge of all the math content, but doesn't know anything about the strategies, will almost always do better on the test than someone who knows all the strategies but doesn't know the content properly.

Now let's assume there is another student named Alexandria, who learns both, the test-taking strategies and the math-content. Yes, now we are talking! This student, Alexandria, who knows both the strategies and the content, is guaranteed to do a lot better than Alex, who only knows the strategies, or Andria who only knows the content.

This brings us to our conclusion on this topic: don't just study the strategies, or just the content; you need to know both simultaneously – the strategies and the content, in order to do well on your test. How quickly and accurately you can answer the math questions will depend on your knowledge of the content and the strategies, and that will have an overall effect on your success on the test.

Hence, the equation to succeed on your test is: **Strategies + Content = Success!**

We are confident that if you study our books on test-taking strategies along with our books on content-knowledge, you'll have everything you possibly need to know in order to do well on your test, in fact, to ace your test, and come out with flying colors!

The good thing is that you made the smart decision to buy this book, or if you are reading this online, or in a bookstore, or in a library, you are going to buy one soon!

CONTENT-KNOWLEDGE REVIEW MODULES:

THOROUGH IN-DEPTH REVIEW:
Most other test-prep books briefly touch upon some of the concepts sporadically. On the other hand, our books start from the basics, but unlike other books, they do not end there – *we go deep inside, beyond just touching up the surface* – all the way from fundamental skills to some of the most advanced content that many other prep books choose to ignore. *Each concept is first explained in detail, and then analyzed for most effective understanding* – each and every concept is covered, and we haven't left any stone unturned. Overall, our program is more challenging – you simply get the *best-of-the-best*, and you get more of everything!

COMPREHENSIVE REVIEW:
Our Content-Knowledge Review Modules provide the *most comprehensive and complete review* of all the concepts, which you need to know to excel in your test. Each module is devoted to one of the main subject areas so that you can focus on the most relevant material. The ideal way to review our modules is to go through each topic thoroughly, understand all the solved examples, and work out all of the practice exercises. You must review each topic, understand every solved example, and work out all of the practice exercises. If you don't have enough time, just glimpse through a section. If you feel comfortable with it, move on to something else that may potentially give you more trouble. If you feel uncomfortable with it, review that topic more thoroughly.

Moreover, if you carefully work through our review, you will probably find some topics that you already know, but you may also find some topics that you need to review more closely. You should have a good sense of areas with which you are most comfortable, and in which areas you feel you have a deficiency. Work on any weaknesses you believe you have in those areas. This should help you organize your review more efficiently. Try to give yourself plenty of time and make sure to review the skills and master the concepts that you are required and expected to know to do well on your test. Of course, the more time you invest preparing for your test and more familiar you are with these fundamental principles, the better you will do on your test.

There is a lot of content reviewed in our modules. Although the amount of material presented in our books may appear to be overwhelming, it's the most complete review to get prepared for your test. To some of you, this may seem like a great deal of information to assimilate; however, when you start reviewing, you'll probably realize that you are already comfortable with many concepts discussed in our review modules. We also suggest that you spread your use of our modules over several weeks, and study different modules at your own pace. Even if you are sure you know the basic concepts, our review will help to warm you up so that you can go into your test with crisp and sharp skills. Hence, we strongly suggest that you at least touch up on each concept. However, depending on your strengths and weaknesses, you may be able to move quickly through some areas, and focus more on the others that seem to be troublesome to you. You should develop a plan of attack for your review of the wide range of content. Work on your weaknesses, and be ready to take advantage of your strengths.

Finally, our main objective in the content review modules is to refresh your knowledge of key concepts on the test and we attempt to keep things as concrete and concise as possible.

PRACTICE MODULES:

BASIC WORKBOOK:
Our math practice basic workbook contains a variety of questions on each and every topic that is covered in our review modules. The best way is to first learn all the concepts from our review modules and then apply your skills to test your knowledge on the actual test-like questions in our basic workbook.

ADVANCED WORKBOOK:
Our math practice advanced workbook also contains a variety of questions on each and every topic that is covered in our review modules. Once you become comfortable with the questions in our basic workbook, you should try your hands on our advanced workbook so that you can gain more experience with some of the most difficult questions. For students who are aiming for a very high score, practicing from our advanced workbook is very important. For students who are aiming for a mediocre score, practicing from our advanced workbook is not so important.

·ABOUT THIS BOOK

In order to excel on your test, it's important that you master each component of your test. That's why we have broken the entire test into different sections and each book focuses only on only one component. It's important to learn the art of tackling the questions you'll see on the test; nevertheless, it's equally important to get a strong hold of the mathematical fundamentals and principles. Apparently it's not enough to only know the test taking strategies, you also need to have a solid knowledge of the math content, and know how to solve the problems mathematically. This book is exclusively dedicated to the **Logic & Stats** that apply to the math section of your test.

WHAT'S COVERED IN THIS BOOK:

In this book, you will learn everything related to **Logic & Stats** content that can be used on different types of questions throughout the math section. Mastering the content of this book will not only improve your performance on the math section, but will also make you a smarter and wiser test-taker. In this book, you'll learn all the strategies and the content related to logic and stats, so that you can solve the logic and stats quickly, correctly, and more efficiently. In fact, being able to solve logic and stats is one of the most important factors to succeed on the math section.

WHAT'S NOT COVERED IN THIS BOOK:

This book does not cover any content other than Logic and Stats – to learn about other content areas, you must refer to the other books in the series.

PRE-REQUISITES FOR THIS BOOK:

The pre-requisite for this book is your thorough familiarity with arithmetic and algebraic principles and concepts. Hence, when you go through this book, you are already expected to know the content covered in some of the other books in the series.

RELATED MODULES FOR THIS BOOK: You will get the best out of this book if you use it in conjunction with some of the other related books in the series that are listed below.

List of related modules for this book:
- EZ Solutions – Test Prep Series – Math Strategies
- EZ Solutions – Test Prep Series – Math Review – Arithmetic
- EZ Solutions – Test Prep Series – Math Review – Algebra
- EZ Solutions – Test Prep Series – Math Review – Applications
- EZ Solutions – Test Prep Series – Math Review – Geometry
- EZ Solutions – Test Prep Series – Math Review – Word Problems
- EZ Solutions – Test Prep Series – Math Review – Logic & Stats
- EZ Solutions – Test Prep Series – Math Practice – Basic Workbook
- EZ Solutions – Test Prep Series – Math Practice – Advanced Workbook

Note: Look at the back of the book for a complete list of EZ books

PART 0.0: INTRODUCTION TO LOGICAL REASONING:

In simple words, *"logical reasoning"* problems are special type of math problems that **necessitate** logic or at least **accentuate** logical thinking. What needs to be figured out is how to draw conclusions from a given set of facts. Solving these problems takes more than just knowing all of the math formulas. You have to think about what math skills and tools you need to apply to the questions in order to reason your way through to the correct answer.

Generally, almost all of the questions on the math test (even some of the verbal ones) require some kind of logical reasoning. In fact, most standardized tests are nothing but a form of a reasoning test.

Logical Reasoning questions are the few questions on the math section that do not fit in any of the standard math topics. These questions require *"logical reasoning"* as opposed to the knowledge of just a particular fact, formula, or technique from arithmetic, algebra, or geometry. It's surprising to know that many of these problems don't even involve any numbers or geometric figures. Some of the logical reasoning problems can be solved by simple arithmetic, while others require some use of strategies and systematically making a list. Sporadically, it helps to know the counting principles and other techniques that we will review in this book.

It's fairly easy to spot logical reasoning questions. Some of the logical reasoning questions begin with the phrase: "How many…" In these problems, you are simply being asked to count something, such as: how many apples can John buy, how many dollars did Mary spend, how many pages did Tom read, how many people are between Monika and Susan, how many numbers satisfy a certain property, how many ways are there to complete a particular task, what is the likelihood of picking a red ball, etc.

In this book, we will present a variety of concepts and examples to illustrate the types of logical reasoning questions that you may encounter on your test.

THIS PAGE HAS BEEN INTENTIONALLY LEFT BLANK

PART 1.0: PURE LOGIC:

TABLE OF CONTENTS:

1.1: SIMPLE LOGIC:

1.1.1: QUESTIONS THAT REQUIRE ONLY LOGICAL REASONING:

There are a few logical reasoning questions that do not require the use of any formula, all they need is *"simple logic"*. Following are a few examples of such type of problems:

Example #1: How many different ways can 2 people be seated in a row of 4 empty chairs, such that there is always at least one empty chair between the two people?

Solution: We are asked to find the number of different ways in which 2 students can be seated in a row of 4 empty chairs, so that there is always at least one empty chair between the students and they are not sitting next to each other side by side.

Let's refer to the two people be X and Y and the four chairs as 1, 2, 3, and 4, in that order.

Now, let's start seating the two people keeping in mind that there should always be at least one empty chair between the two people.

Since there are two people and four chairs, in order to have at least one empty chair between the two students, there can be either one empty chair between the two people or two empty chairs between the two people.

Seating Options when there are 2 empty chairs in between $\Rightarrow$ X in #1 and Y in #4 $\Rightarrow X - - Y$
$\Rightarrow$ Y in #4 and X in #1 $\Rightarrow Y - - X$

Seating Options when there is 1 empty chair in between $\Rightarrow$ X in #1 and Y in #3 $\Rightarrow X - Y -$
$\Rightarrow$ Y in #3 and X in #1 $\Rightarrow Y - X -$
$\Rightarrow$ X in #2 and Y in #4 $\Rightarrow - X - Y$
$\Rightarrow$ Y in #4 and X in #2 $\Rightarrow - Y - X$

Therefore, there are 6 different ways in which 2 people be seated in a row of 4 chairs, such that there is always at least one empty chair between the two people.

Example #2: A certain party has 10 tables that can seat up to 5 people each. If a total of 20 people needs to be seated on these tables, and NO tables can be empty, what is the greatest possible number of tables that could be filled with 5 people?

Solution: Total No. of people who needs to be seated $\Rightarrow$ 20
No. of tables $\Rightarrow$ 10
Since, none of the tables can be empty, let's first seat 1 person in each of the 10 tables.
This would seat 10 of the 20 people, and 10 would still be standing.
Now, let's see how many tables we can seat 5 people.
Let's seat the first two tables with 5 people each, this leaves 2 people still standing.
Now these two people can be seated on any of the remaining 8 tables, it doesn't really matter where they sit.
In all we have 2 tables with 5 people each, 1 table with 3 people, and 7 tables with 1 person each.
$\Rightarrow$ 2(5) + 1(3) + 7(1) = 10 + 3 + 7 = 20
Therefore, the greatest possible number of tables that could be filled with 5 people is 2.

Example #3: How many people must be in a group in order to ensure that at least 2 people in the group have last names that begin with the same alphabet?

Solution: Whenever we have to ensure something, we must consider the worst-case scenario, which in this case is that every person's last name starts with a different alphabet. For instance, the first person's last name begins with A, the second with B, and so on.
From A to Z, we'll have 26 people, all with last names that start with a different alphabet.
Now, the 27th person's last name will have to begin with an alphabet that we already have in our list, no matter what the alphabet is.
Therefore, there must be at least 27 people in the group in order to ensure that at least 2 people in the group have last names that begin with the same alphabet.

Example #4: A certain club has 100 members, 40 men and 60 women, of whom 30 are married and 70 are unmarried. What is the minimum possible number of unmarried men in the club?

Solution: In the club, there are 40 men and 60 women of whom 30 are married and 70 are unmarried. Since we want to find the minimum possible number of unmarried men, we must find the maximum possible number of women who are unmarried. So, let's assume, all of the 60 women are unmarried. There are

a total 70 unmarried members, of whom we assumed 60 to be unmarried. This leaves only 10 unmarried members who could be men.
Therefore, the minimum possible number of unmarried men in the club is 10.

Example #5:   In a certain job interview, a total of 20 applicants were interviewed. If 2 applicants went for the interview before John, who went before George, and 5 applicants went after George, how many applicants went for the interview between John and George?

Solution: Total No. of Applicants $\Rightarrow$ 20

$\Rightarrow$ No. of Applicants before John	$\Rightarrow$ John	$\Rightarrow$ George	$\Rightarrow$ No. of applicants after George
$\Rightarrow$ 2	$\Rightarrow$ 1	$\Rightarrow$ 1	$\Rightarrow$ 5

No. of Applicants between John and George $\Rightarrow$ 20 – 2 – 1 – 1 – 5 = 11

Example #6:   In a certain arena, the front row has 50 seats. Each row behind the first row has 8 more seats than the row in front of it. If there are 76 rows, what is the total number of seats in the arena?

Solution: No. of seat in: 1st. Row $\Rightarrow$ 50
                            2nd. Row $\Rightarrow$ 50 + 8
                            3rd. Row $\Rightarrow$ 50 + 8 + 8
                            4th. Row $\Rightarrow$ 50 + 8 + 8 + 8
                            5th. Row $\Rightarrow$ 50 + 8 + 8 + 8 + 8

Total No. of Seat in the Arena $\Rightarrow$ 50 + 58 + 64 + 72 + 80…618 + 626 + 634 + 642 + 650
It would be ridiculous to manually count, instead, think logically, and apply the following method:
No. of seats in the first row $\Rightarrow$ 50
No. of seats in the 76th rows $\Rightarrow$ 50 + 75(8) = 650

Total No. of Seats in all 76 rows $\Rightarrow$ (50 + 650) $\dfrac{76}{2}$ = 26,600

1.1.2: BEST CASE VS WORST CASE SCENARIO:

There are certain logical reasoning questions that have two ways of doing a certain thing, the quickest and *"best-case scenario"* or the slowest and *"worst-case scenario"*. The Important thing to realize is that in order to be ensured of something, you must consider the worst-case scenario and not the best-case scenario.

Example #7:   A drawer contains 6 red socks and 6 blue socks. What is the least number of socks that must be drawn from the drawer to be assured of having a pair of red socks?

Solution: To be assured of something, we have to consider the worst-case scenario. We have to find the least number of socks that must be drawn from the drawer to be assured of having a pair of red socks.

     Best-case scenario $\Rightarrow$ The best-case scenario would be to think that the first two socks you draw are red socks – this is possible, but may not always happen. However, to be assured of having a pair of red socks, let's consider the worst-case scenario.

     Worst-case scenario $\Rightarrow$ The worst-case scenario would be that the first 6 socks drawn are all blue, which leaves only red socks in the drawer. If you draw two more socks, they have to be red socks. Of course, it is possible that two red socks could be drawn earlier, but with 8 drawings, we are assured of a pair of red socks.

     Therefore, to be assured of having a pair of red socks, we have to draw at least 8 socks.

Example #8:   A drawer contains 500 red socks and 500 blue socks. What is the least number of socks that must be drawn from the drawer to be assured of having a pair of socks with the same color?

Solution: To be assured of something, we have to consider the worst-case scenario. We have to find the least number of socks that must be drawn from the drawer to be assured of having a pair of socks with the same color.

     Best-case scenario $\Rightarrow$ The best-case scenario would be to think that the first two socks you draw are the same color socks, i.e., both red or both blue – this is possible, but may not always happen. However, to be assured of having a pair of socks with the same color, let's consider the worst-case scenario.

     Worst-case scenario $\Rightarrow$ The worst case scenario would be that the first sock drawn is red and the second one is blue, or the first is blue and the second is red, which gives us with a pair of socks with different colors, one red and the other blue. Now when you draw the third sock, it has to be either red or blue, in both cases you will either have a red or blue pair of socks. If you draw three socks, there has to be a pair of socks with the same color. Of course, it is possible that two red or two blue socks could be drawn earlier, but with three drawings, we are assured of a pair of socks with the same color. Therefore, to be assured of having a pair of socks with the same color, we have to draw at least 3 socks.

Example #9:   A jar contains 27 marbles: 7 red, 9 green, and 11 blue. If you randomly remove 1 marble at a time, what is the minimum number of marbles that you must remove to be certain that you have at least 1 marbles of each color?

Solution: To be assured of something, we have to consider the worst-case scenario. We have to find the least number of marbles that must be removed from the jar to be assured of having two marbles of each color.

Best-case scenario ⇒ The best-case scenario would be to think that the first three marbles you remove are one of each color – this is possible, but may not always happen. However, to be assured of having one marble of each color, let's consider the worst-case scenario.

Worst-case scenario ⇒ The worst-case scenario would be that the first 11 marbles removed are all blue, and the next 9 marbles removed are all green, which leaves only red marbles in the jar. At this point we would have 20 marbles, and you still wouldn't have even 1 red. However, since the jar now only contains red marbles, the next marble removed, must be red. So, we have to remove a minimum of 21 marbles to be assured of having one marble of each color. Of course, it is possible that these three marbles, one of each color, could be drawn earlier, but with 21 we are assured of one of each color.

Therefore, to be assured of having one marble of each color, we have to draw at least 21 marbles.

Example #10:   In a certain jar, there are 11 red balls, 15 blue balls, 16 green balls, and 18 yellow balls. How many balls must be taken out in order to ensure that 7 balls of the same color are taken out?

Solution: To be assured of something, we have to consider the worst-case scenario. We have to find the least number of balls that must be drawn from the jar to be assured of having 7 balls of the same color.

Best-case scenario ⇒ The best-case scenario would be that the first 7 balls drawn are of the same color – this is possible, but may not always happen. However, to be assured of having 7 balls of the same color, let's consider the worst-case scenario.

Worst-case scenario ⇒ The worst-case scenario would be that 6 balls of each of the four colors are drawn but still there aren't 7 balls of the same color. Now after drawing 6 balls of each of the four colors, the next ball drawn has to be one of the four colors and we'll have 7 balls of the same color.

Total Numbers of balls drawn ⇒ $(6 \times 4) + 1 = 24 + 25$

Of course, it is possible that 7 balls of the same color could be drawn earlier, but with 25 drawings, we are assured of 7 balls of the same color.

Therefore, to be assured of having 7 balls of the same color, we have to draw at least 25 balls.

1.2: SIMPLE COUNTING:

1.2.1: RULES IN SIMPLE COUNTING:

The **"simple counting"** problems involve figuring out how many integers there are between any two given integers. The key to solving such problems is to be able to determine whether the first and last numbers are **"inclusive"** or **"exclusive"**. In order to count how many integers there are between any two given integers, apply one of the following three rules:

EZ RULE #1: When Exactly One Endpoint is Inclusive $\Rightarrow$ subtract the two values.

SET UP: To count the number of integers from "A" to "B" $\Rightarrow B - A$

For Example: If Monika enters a store with $75 dollars for some grocery shopping, and when she leaves, she has only $15 left with her, how much did she spend in the store for grocery shopping?

Solution: Since, exactly one of the endpoints is included, subtract $\Rightarrow$ $75 – $15 = $60
Therefore, Monika spent $60 in grocery shopping.

EZ TIP: If you ever forget this rule, just pick two easy numbers, such as, 10 and 15. If you go into a store with $15 and come out with $10 $\Rightarrow$ you spent 11th, 12th, 13th, 14th, and 15th dollar $\Rightarrow$ $5 $\Rightarrow$ so you just have to subtract $10 from $15 $\Rightarrow$ $15 – $10 = $5. Notice that only one extreme (15) must be counted; when you merely subtract (15 – 10 = 5), you are already including the last extreme (15); hence, there is no need to add or subtract anything else.

EZ RULE #2: When Both Endpoints are Inclusive $\Rightarrow$ subtract the two values, and then add 1.

SET UP: To count the number of integers from "A" to "B" $\Rightarrow B - A + 1$

For Example: If Susan read page number 15 through page number 75 of a book, how many pages did she read?

Solution: Since, both endpoints are included, subtract, and then add 1 $\Rightarrow$ (75 – 15) + 1 = 60 + 1 = 61
Therefore, Susan read 61 pages.

EZ TIP: If you ever forget this rule, just pick two easy numbers, such as, 10 and 15. If you read page 10 through page 15 $\Rightarrow$ you read 10th, 11th, 12th, 13th, 14th, and 15th page $\Rightarrow$ 6 pages $\Rightarrow$ so you just have to subtract 10 from 15 and add 1 $\Rightarrow$ 15 – 10 + 1 = 6. Notice that both extremes (10 & 15) must be counted; when you merely subtract (15 – 10 = 5), you are forgetting to include the first extreme (10), as it has been subtracted away along with others; hence, you need to add 1 more.

EZ RULE #3: When Neither Endpoint is Inclusive $\Rightarrow$ subtract the two values, and then subtract 1 more.

SET UP: To count the number of integers from "A" to "B" $\Rightarrow B - A - 1$

For Example: If Monika is the 15th person in a line, and Susan is the 75th person in the same line, how many people are in between Monika and Susan?

Solution: Since, neither endpoint is included, subtract, and then subtract 1 more $\Rightarrow$ (75–15)–1=60–1 = 59
Therefore, there are 59 people in between Monika and Susan.

EZ TIP: If you ever forget this rule, just pick easy numbers, such as, 10 and 15. If you are the 10th person in line and your friend is the 15th person in line $\Rightarrow$ there's 11th, 12th, 13th, and 14th person in between $\Rightarrow$ 4 people $\Rightarrow$ you just have to subtract 10 from 15 and subtract 1 $\Rightarrow$ 15 – 10 – 1 = 4. Note that neither extremes (10 & 15) must be counted; when you just subtract (15 – 10 = 5), you are also including the last extreme (15); hence, you need to subtract 1 more.

COUNTING BETWEEN TWO QUANTITIES: When you have to count the number between two items or quantities:

For Example: Several people are standing in a straight line. Starting at one end of the line John is counted as the 7th person, and starting at the other end he is counted as the 12th person. How many people are there altogether in the line?

Solution: You can answer this question by careful reasoning, or you can draw it out and count. Either way, be careful that you don't leave John out or count him twice.
John is the 7th person from one end of the line $\Rightarrow$ there are 6 people (not counting John) between him and that end of the line.
John is the 12th person from the other end of the line $\Rightarrow$ there are 11 people (not counting John) between him and that end of the line.
$\Rightarrow$ 6 people between John and one end + 11 people between John and the other end + John
$\Rightarrow$ 6 + 11 + 1 = 18
Therefore, there are 18 people altogether in the line.

1.2.2: ALTERNATE METHODS IN SIMPLE COUNTING:

LOGICAL COUNTING: To solve some counting problems, you don't need to know any rules or formulas; all you need to apply is logic and common sense.

For Example: In a certain school, Naomi is both the 11th tallest and the 11th shortest student in the school. If everyone in the school is of a different height, how many students are in the school?

Solution: Since Naomi is the 11th tallest student in the school, there are 10 students who are shorter than her. Since Naomi is the 11th shortest student in the school, there are 10 students who are taller than her. Therefore, total number of students in the school ⇒ 10 + 10 + 1 (for Naomi) = 21

MANUAL COUNTING: Sometimes it may just be easier to manually count the terms instead of applying any counting method, especially when counting number of terms in a consecutive pattern. First, list the terms, and then, count them. Be careful, as one or both of the extremes may or may not be included.

For Example: How many multiples of 8 are there from 1 to 56, inclusive?

Solution: First, list all the multiples of 8 that are there from 1 to 56, inclusive ⇒ 8, 16, 24, 32, 40, 48, 56 Next, count the number of terms ⇒ there are 7 multiples of 8 that are there from 1 to 56, inclusive.

SYSTEMATIC LIST COUNTING: When the numbers in a problem are small, it is often better to systematically list all of the possibilities than to risk making an error in arithmetic. For instance in the example below, after subtracting the number of pages, instead of contemplating about whether or not to add 1 or subtract 1, you can just make a systematic list and then count them. The concept explained above can be used in more complex problems like the one given below.

For Example: From 1:09 to 1:15, John read pages 109 through 115 in his Math book. What was his rate of reading, in pages per minute?

Solution A: **By Applying the Counting Rules:**
Apply the Simple Counting Rule #2: Since John read both pages 109 and 115
⇒ No. of pages John read = 115 – 109 + 1 = 7 pages
Apply the Simple Counting Rule #1: Since John started reading during the minute that started at 1:09 (and ended at 1:10) and stopped reading at 1:15, he did not read during the minute that began at 1:15 (and ended at 1:16),
⇒ No. of minutes John spent reading = 1:15 – 1:09 = 6 minutes
Therefore, John read at the rate of 7/6 pages per minute.

Solution B: **By Making a Systematic List:**
John read: Page 109, 110, 111, 112, 113, 114, 115 ⇒ that's a total of 7 pages
John reads from Start of 1:09 to end of 1:09   ⇒ 1 minute
Start of 1:10 to end of 1:10   ⇒ 1 minute
Start of 1:11 to end of 1:11   ⇒ 1 minute
Start of 1:12 to end of 1:12   ⇒ 1 minute
Start of 1:13 to end of 1:13   ⇒ 1 minute
Start of 1:14 to end of 1:14   ⇒ <u>1 minute</u>
Total No. of minutes   ⇒ <u>6 minutes</u>
Therefore, John read at the rate of 7/6 pages per minute.

EZ TIP: However, if the numbers are bigger, like the example given below, then the only option to solve it is to apply the counting formulas.

For Example: From 1:09 to 1:59, John read pages 109 through 159 in his Math book. What was his rate of reading, in pages per minute?

Solution A: **By Applying the Counting Rules:**
Apply the Counting Rule #2: Since John read both pages 109 and 159
⇒ No. of pages John read = 159 – 109 + 1 = 51 pages
Apply the Counting Rule #1: Since John started reading during the minute that started at 1:09 (and ended at 1:10) and stopped reading at 1:59, he did not read during the minute that began at 1:59 (and ended at 2:00),
⇒ No. of minutes John spent reading = 1:59 – 1:09 = 50 minutes
Therefore, John read at the rate of 51/50 pages per minute.

Solution B: **By Making a Systematic List:**
Not feasible.

PRACTICE EXERCISE – QUESTIONS AND ANSWERS WITH EXPLANATIONS: PURE LOGIC:

Question #1: A drawer contains 25 pairs of matching socks. If 11 individual socks are randomly taken out from the drawer, what is the greatest number of pairs of matching socks that can be made from the remaining socks in the drawer?

Solution: From the 11 individual socks that are taken out from the drawer, the lowest number of pairs that can be made from these 11 individual socks is 5 full pairs and 1 sock from the sixth pair.
Therefore, the greatest number of pairs of matching socks that can be made from the remaining socks in the drawer is $25 - 6 = 19$

Question #2: In a certain job interview, a total of n applicants were interviewed. If p applicants went for the interview before John, who went before George, and q applicants went after George, how many applicants went for the interview between John and George?

Solution: Total No. of Applicants $\Rightarrow n$
Make the following grid:

$\Rightarrow$ No. of Applicants before John	$\Rightarrow$ John	$\Rightarrow$ George	$\Rightarrow$ No. of applicants after George
$\Rightarrow p$	$\rightarrow 1$	$\Rightarrow 1$	$\Rightarrow q$

No. of Applicants between John and George $\Rightarrow n - p - 1 - 1 - q = n - p - q - 2$

Question #3: Due to malfunctioning of a calculation, the multiplication and division buttons are reversed. A person presses: "÷" "5" "=" and the calculator displays 625. What answer should have been displayed if the calculator was functioning correctly?

Solution: When the calculator is malfunctioning, the multiplication (×) and division (÷) buttons are reversed:
This is what is pressed and displayed $\Rightarrow$ N ÷ 5 = 625
This is what the calculator does $\Rightarrow$ N × 5 = 625
$\Rightarrow$ Therefore $N = 625 \div 5 = 125$
When a calculator is functioning properly, the multiplication (×) & division (÷) buttons should be correct:
This is what should have been pressed and displayed $\Rightarrow 125 \div 5 = 25$
Therefore, If the calculator was functioning correctly, it should have displayed 25

Question #4: While doing the calculations for a problem, in the final step, Susan accidentally divided by 100 instead of multiplying by 100. If she erases the whole calculation and starts from scratch, it would take her too long. So, to correct the error, what should she do to her answer?

Solution: First, undo the error; then, apply the correct operation:
Undo the Error $\Rightarrow$ Multiplying the incorrect answer by 100 would undo the final division Susan made. Now, she is at the point at which she should have multiplied by 100.
Apply the Correct Operation $\Rightarrow$ To apply the correct operation, she must multiply again by 100.
Therefore, in all, she must multiply by $100 \times 100 = 10,000$

Question #5: A person was born on July 11, 1890, and dies on June 22, 1969. What was his age in years, at the time of his death?

Solution: That person's last birthday was in July 1968
His age at death was $1968 - 1890 = 78$ years.

Question #6: A class of 80 students is to be divided into smaller groups. If each group is to contain 3, 4, or 5 people, what is the largest number of groups possible.

Solution: Total No. of Students = 80
Since we want to form the largest number of groups possible, we should try to make the groups as small as possible. So, we want as many groups as possible to have only 3 students.
When we divide 80 into 3 to find the number of 3-people groups, we get 26 with a remainder or leftover of 2.
Now, since each student has to be in a group, we can throw in both of the remaining 2 students in any one of the other groups, which will make it 25 groups of 3-people and 1 group of 5-people; or both in any two of the groups, which will make it 24 groups of 3-people and 2 groups of 4-people.
In either case, we get a total of 26 groups.

Question #7: How many positive integers less than 100 have a remainder of 2 when divided by 11?

Solution: To have a remainder of 2 when divided by 11, an integer must be 2 more than a multiple of 11. For instance, when 112 is divided by 11, the quotient is 10 and the remainder is 2: 112 = 10 × 11 + 2. So, just take the multiples of 11 and add 2:

$\Rightarrow 0 \times 11 + 2 = 2$
$\Rightarrow 1 \times 11 + 2 = 13$
$\Rightarrow 2 \times 11 + 2 = 24$
$\Rightarrow 3 \times 11 + 2 = 35$
$\Rightarrow 4 \times 11 + 2 = 46$
$\Rightarrow 5 \times 11 + 2 = 57$
$\Rightarrow 6 \times 11 + 2 = 68$
$\Rightarrow 7 \times 11 + 2 = 79$
$\Rightarrow 8 \times 11 + 2 = 90$

Therefore, there are 9 positive integers less than 100 that have a remainder of 2 when divided by 11.

Question #8: On a certain occasion, if Natasha buys 5 equally priced cups, she would have exactly $2 left over. If instead, she buys 9 equally priced plates, she would have exactly $7 left over. If the prices of both cups and plates are integers, then what is the least amount of money that Natasha could be carrying?

Solution: If 5 equally priced cups are bought, and there are $2 left over $\Rightarrow$ this means that the total number of dollars could be any multiple of 5 plus 2, such as, 7, 12, 17, 22, 27, 32, 37, 42, 47, 52, 57, etc.

If 9 equally priced plates are bought, and there are $7 left over $\Rightarrow$ this means that the total number of dollars could be any multiple of 9 plus 7, such as, 16, 25, 34, 43, 52, 61, etc.

Since we are looking for the least number of dollars, the smallest number that works for both is 52, which works for both, the 5 equally priced cups with remainder 2 and 9 equally priced plates with remainder 5. Therefore, the least amount of money that Natasha could be carrying is $52.

Question #9: A jar contains 24 marbles: 6 red, 8 green, and 10 blue. If you randomly remove 1 marble at a time, what is the minimum number of marbles that you must remove to be certain that you have at least 2 marbles of each color?

Solution: To be assured of something, we have to consider the worst-case scenario. We have to find the least number of marbles that must be removed from the jar to be assured of having two marbles of each color.

Best-case scenario $\Rightarrow$ The best-case scenario would be to think that the first six marbles you remove are two of each color – this is possible, but may not always happen. However, to be assured of having two marbles of each color, let's consider the worst-case scenario.

Worst-case scenario $\Rightarrow$ The worst-case scenario would be that the first ten marbles removed are all blue, and the next eight marbles removed are all green, which leaves only red marbles in the jar. At this point we would have 18 marbles, and you still wouldn't have even 1 red. However, since the jar now only contains red marbles, the next two marbles removed, must both be red. So, we have to remove a minimum of 20 marbles to be assured of having two marbles of each color. Of course, it is possible that these six marbles, two of each color, could be drawn earlier, but with 20 we are assured of a pair of two of each color.

Therefore, to be assured of having two marbles of each color, we have to draw at least 20 marbles.

Question #10: In a certain jar, there are 15 red balls, 20 blue balls, and 25 green balls. How many balls must be taken out in order to ensure that 19 balls of the same color are taken out?

Solution: To be assured of something, we have to consider the worst-case scenario. We have to find the least number of balls that must be drawn from the jar to be assured of having 19 balls of the same color.

Best-case scenario $\Rightarrow$ The best-case scenario would be that the first 19 balls drawn are of the same color – this is possible, but may not always happen. However, to be assured of having 19 balls of the same color, let's consider the worst-case scenario.

Worst-case scenario $\Rightarrow$ The worst-case scenario would be that first 15 balls drawn are all red balls, the next 18 balls drawn are all blue balls, and the next 18 balls drawn are all green balls. Until this point, 15 + 18 + 18 = 51 balls are drawn, and there still aren't 19 balls of the same color. Now the next ball drawn has to be either blue of green, and there will be 19 balls of the same color. Note that it's not possible to get 19 red balls because there are only 15 red balls in the jar; however, the red balls must be considered as they may be drawn first.

Total Numbers of balls drawn $\Rightarrow$ 15 (red) + 18 (blue) + 18 (green) + 1 (blue or green) = 52
Of course, it is possible that 19 balls of the same color could be drawn earlier, but with 52 drawings, we are assured of 19 balls of the same color.
Therefore, to be assured of having 19 balls of the same color, we have to draw at least 52 balls.

Question #11: If a woman enters a store with $90 for some grocery shopping, and when she leaves, she has only $70 left with her, how much did she spend in the store for grocery shopping?
Solution: Since, exactly one of the endpoints is included, subtract $\Rightarrow$ $90 – $70 = $20
Therefore, the woman spent $20 in grocery shopping.

Question #12: If a family goes on a weekend getaway with $7,750, and when they come back, they only have $2,625 left with them, how much did they spend on their weekend getaway?
Solution: Since, exactly one of the endpoints is included, subtract $\Rightarrow$ $7,750 – $2,625 = $5,125
Therefore, the family spent $5,125 on their weekend getaway.

Question #13: If a woman read page number 70 through page number 90 of a book, how many pages did she read?
Solution: Since, both endpoints are included, subtract and then add 1 $\Rightarrow$ (90 – 70) + 1 = 20 + 1 = 21
Therefore, the woman read 21 pages of the book.

Question #14: If a woman read page number 112 through page number 177 of a book, how many pages did she read?
Solution: Since, both endpoints are included, subtract and then add 1 $\Rightarrow$ (177 – 112) + 1 = 65 + 1 = 66
Therefore, the woman read 66 pages of the book.

Question #15: If Ricky is the 90th person in a line, and John is the 70th person in the same line, how many people are in between Ricky and John?
Solution: Since, neither endpoint is included, subtract and then subtract 1 more $\Rightarrow$ (90 – 70) –1 = 20 – 1 = 19
Therefore, there are 19 people in between Ricky and John in the line.

Question #16: If a boy is the 199th person in a line, and his little brother is the 111th person in the same line, how many people are in between the two brothers?
Solution: Since, neither endpoint is included, subtract and then subtract 1 more $\Rightarrow$ (199 – 111) – 1 = 88 – 1 = 87
Therefore, there are 87 people in between the two brothers in the line.

Question #17: Several people are standing in a straight line. Starting at one end of the line John is counted as the 9th person, and starting at the other end he is counted as the 16th person. How many people are there altogether in the line?
Solution: You can answer this question by careful reasoning, or you can draw it out and count. Either way, be careful that you don't leave John out or count him twice.
John is the 9th person from one end of the line $\Rightarrow$ there are 8 people (not counting John) between him and that end of the line.
John is the 16th person from the other end of the line $\Rightarrow$ there are 15 people (not counting John) between him and that end of the line.
$\Rightarrow$ 8 people between John & one end + 15 people between John & the other end + John
$\Rightarrow$ 8 + 15 + 1 = 24
Therefore, there are 24 people altogether in the line.

Question #18: In a certain club, Jackie is both the 96th heaviest and the 96th lightest student in the school. If everyone in the school is of a different weight, how many students are in the school?
Solution: Since Jackie is the 96th heaviest student in the school, there are 95 students who are lighter than her.
Since Jackie is the 96th lightest student in the school, there are 95 students who are heavier than her.
Therefore, total number of students in the school $\Rightarrow$ 95 + 95 + 1 (for Jackie) = 191

THIS PAGE HAS BEEN INTENTIONALLY LEFT BLANK

PART 2.0: PERMUTATION & COMBINATION:

TABLE OF CONTENTS:

2.1: BASICS ABOUT PERMUTATION & COMBINATION:

The **"permutation and combination"** problems involve figuring out how many different ways one can select or arrange members of same or different groups, such as, letters of the alphabets, numbers, menu selections, etc. The main similarity between such questions is that they all ask to find the total different number of possibilities that can occur for a given situation. Technically speaking, permutation and combination is a branch of mathematics that especially deals with advanced counting principles.

Although some of these problems may sound like simple counting problems, some of them can be very tricky and confusing. No matter what, permutation and combination problems are almost always difficult and are going to be some of the most difficult problems on your test. The good news is that you won't see more than a few of these problems on your test. If you are shooting for a perfect score or even a very high score, we recommend you master this section; however, if you are aiming for a mediocre score, this would be a great section to just browse through or even skip altogether.

EZ SPOT: It's easy to spot permutation and combination problems. These problems contain one of the following buzz words/phrases: permutation, combination, variation, alternative, arranged, options, choices, ways, etc.

HOW TO COUNT THE NUMBER OF POSSIBILITIES WITHOUT USING PERMUTATION & COMBINATION:
In some of the easier problems, it is possible to solve them without applying any permutation and combination formulas. In such problems, the number of possibilities are generally so small that the best approach is to list them out in a systematic order, and then count them. Be systematic and organized so that you don't miss any options.

Example #1: How many three-digit numbers can be formed with the digits 1, 5, and 7?
Solution: First, list all the possibilities in a systematic order:

157	517	715
175	571	751

Finally, count the number of possibilities $\Rightarrow$ 6

Example #2: There are three hockey teams, *A*, *B*, and *C*, which play in a league against each other. By the end of the championship, how many different ways could the three teams end up ranked against each other?
Solution: First, list all the possibilities in a systematic order:

ABC	BAC	CAB
ACB	BCA	CBA

Note: First, list all the possibilities with *A* in the first place, then *B* in the first place, and then *C* in the first place
Finally, count the number of possibilities $\Rightarrow$ 6

Example #3: There are five members in a hockey team. Supposing each member shakes hands with every other member of the team before the game starts, how many handshakes will there be in all?
Solution: Let the five players be: *A*, *B*, *C*, *D*, and *E*.
Now let's make a list of all possible pair of handshakes:

AB	BC	CD	DE
AC	BD	CE
AD	BE
AE

Therefore, there should be a total of 10 handshakes.

Example #4: How many four-digit numbers can be formed with the digits 1, 5, 7, and 9?
Solution: First, list all the possibilities in a systematic order:

1579	5179	7159	9157
1597	5197	7195	9175
1759	5719	7519	9517
1795	5791	7591	9571
1957	5917	7915	9715
1975	5971	7951	9751

Finally, count the number of possibilities $\Rightarrow$ 24

WITH CONDITION: Some problems set up conditions or restrictions that somewhat limits the number of possibilities. They may ask for the number of distinct possibilities, that is, if the same combination shows up more than once in different forms, you should count them only once.

Example #5:   If n is a number generated by multiplying a number from Set-A by a number from Set-B, how many distinct possible values of n are there?
Set-A: {1, 2, 3, 4, 5}
Set-B: {1, 2, 3, 4}

Solution: First, make a systematic list of all the possibilities paring off each number in the first set with each number in the second set, so that every combination is included only once. Make sure to write down the possibilities in a systematic manner as you organize them, so that you can count them accurately, and so that you don't count the same combination more than once.

$1 \times 1 = 1$	$2 \times 1 = 2$	$3 \times 1 = 3$	$4 \times 1 = 4$	$5 \times 1 = 5$
$1 \times 2 = 2$	$2 \times 2 = 4$	$3 \times 2 = 6$	$4 \times 2 = 8$	$5 \times 2 = 10$
$1 \times 3 = 3$	$2 \times 3 = 6$	$3 \times 3 = 9$	$4 \times 3 = 12$	$5 \times 3 = 15$
$1 \times 4 = 4$	$2 \times 4 = 8$	$3 \times 4 = 12$	$4 \times 4 = 16$	$5 \times 4 = 20$

Next, count the number of value of n:
$\Rightarrow$ 1, 2, 3, 4, 2, 4, 6, 8, 3, 6, 9, 12, 4, 8, 12, 16, 5, 10, 15, and 20 $\Rightarrow$ that's a total of twenty values
Although there are twenty values for n, seven of them are the same (2 and 2), (3 and 3), (4, 4, and 4), (6 and 6), (8 and 8) and (12 and 12)
Therefore, there are only $20 - 7 = 13$ different values of n, and not 20 values.
Note: In this problem, it would have been very easy to pick twenty as the correct answer and not paid attention to the fact that these values had to be distinct. So, make sure that you read the question carefully and consider every possibility before picking your answer.

Example #6:   If n is a number generated by multiplying a number from Set-A by a number from Set-B, how many distinct possible values of n are greater than 5?
Set-A: {1, 2, 3, 4, 5}
Set-B: {1, 2, 3, 4}

Solution: First, make a systematic list of all the possibilities paring off each number in the first set with each number in the second set, so that every combination is included only once. Make sure to write down the possibilities in a systematic manner as you organize them, so that you can count them accurately, and so that you don't count the same combination more than once.

$1 \times 1 = 1$	$2 \times 1 = 2$	$3 \times 1 = 3$	$4 \times 1 = 4$	$5 \times 1 = 5$
$1 \times 2 = 2$	$2 \times 2 = 4$	$3 \times 2 = 6$	$4 \times 2 = 8$	$5 \times 2 = 10$
$1 \times 3 = 3$	$2 \times 3 = 6$	$3 \times 3 = 9$	$4 \times 3 = 12$	$5 \times 3 = 15$
$1 \times 4 = 4$	$2 \times 4 = 8$	$3 \times 4 = 12$	$4 \times 4 = 16$	$5 \times 4 = 20$

Next, count the number of value of n that are greater than 5:
$\Rightarrow$ 6, 8, 6, 9, 12, 8, 12, 16, 10, 15, and 20 $\Rightarrow$ that's a total of eleven values
Although there are eleven values for n that are greater than 5, three of them are the same (6 and 6), (8 and 8), and (12 and 12)
Therefore, there are $11 - 3 = 8$ different values of n that are greater than 5, and not 11 values.
Note: In this problem, it would have been very easy to pick eleven as the correct answer and not paid attention to the fact that these values had to be distinct. So, make sure that you read the question carefully and consider every possibility before picking your answer.

EZ NOTE: If you come across anything more complex than the two examples given above, we recommend that you apply permutation and combination formulas explained in the following section.

2.2: FUNDAMENTAL COUNTING PRINCIPLE (FCP):

There are often some useful alternative methods for counting objects and sets of objects without actually listing the elements to be counted. The following is one of the most important and fundamental principle of counting. The *"fundamental counting principle"* is the principle by which we can figure out how many different possibilities there are for selecting members of different groups. It tests your ability to consider all possible combinations.

Fundamental Counting Principle states that – If one event can occur in "*m*" different ways, and each of the "*m*" ways is followed by a second independent event that can occur in "*n*" different ways, then the total number of ways in which the two events can happen, that is, the first event followed by the second event is "*m*" times "*n*" different ways. This is called the (FCP) *"Fundamental Principle of Counting"*.

In other words, if two jobs need to be completed and there are "*m*" ways to do the first job and "*n*" ways to do the second job, then there are *m* × *n* ways to do one job followed by the other.

A slightly different version of the same principle is generally used while picking items from different groups: If an object is to be chosen from a set of *m* objects and a second object is to be chosen from a different set of *n* objects, then there are *m* × *n* ways of choosing both objects simultaneously.

When to Apply FCP: For problems that ask you to choose a number of items to fill specific spots, when each spot is filled from a different source, all you have to do is to apply the Fundamental Counting Principle stated above, i.e., multiply the number of choices for each of the spots.

EZ TIP: If you encounter a question that involves two actions or two objects, each with a number of choices, and asks for the number of possible combinations, just remember to apply the FCP, by multiplying the different elements.

For Example:	If you have 2 types of pants and 5 types of shirts, how many different combinations of outfits consist of a pant and a shirt?
Solution:	No. of different combinations of outfits ⇒ 2 Types of Pants × 5 Types of Shirts = 2 × 5 = 10 Therefore, there are 10 different combinations of outfits, where an outfit consists of a pant and a shirt.

FCP for More than Two Events: This principle can be extended to more than just two events, to any number of events.

For Example:	If you have 2 types of pants, 5 types of shirts, and 7 types of hats, how many different combinations of outfits consist of a pant, shirt, and a hat?
Solution:	No. of different Pants ⇒ 2 No. of different Shirts ⇒ 5 No. of different Hats ⇒ 7 No. of different combinations of outfits ⇒ 2 (Pants) × 5 (Shirts) × 7 (Hats) = 70 Therefore, there are 70 different combinations of outfits, where an outfit consists of a pant, shirt, and a hat.

Example #1:	If a pizza maker offers 7 types of crusts, 20 types of toppings and 5 types of seasoning on a pizza, how many different combinations of pizza can he offer?
Solution:	No. of different combinations of pizza ⇒ 7 (types of crusts) × 20 (types of toppings) × 5 (types of seasonings) ⇒ 7 × 20 × 5 = 700 Therefore, there are 700 different combinations of pizza.

Example #2:	If a French restaurant offers a special five course meal, consisting of 2 types of soups, 5 types of salads, 8 types of beverages, 2 types of main dishes, and 7 types of desserts, how many different types of 5 course meals can one choose from?
Solution:	No. of different types of 5 course meals ⇒ 2 (types of soups) × 5 (types of salads) × 8 (types of beverages) × 2 (types of main dishes) × 7 (types of desserts) ⇒ 2 × 5 × 8 × 2 × 7 = 1,120 Therefore, there are 1,120 different types of five course meals.

Example #3:	If there are 7 different routes from Annapolis to Columbia and 8 different routes from Columbia to Baltimore, how many different routes are there from Annapolis to Baltimore that go through Columbia?

Solution:	No. of different routes from Annapolis to Columbia	$\Rightarrow 7$
	No. of different routes from Columbia to Baltimore	$\Rightarrow 8$
	No. of different routes from Annapolis to Baltimore via Columbia	$\Rightarrow 7 \times 8 = 56$

Example #4:   If there are 4 paintings, of which 1 is to be hanged in the study room and 1 in the living room, how many ways are there to choose from which painting goes in each room?

Solution: No. of ways in which a painting can be hanged in the study room $\Rightarrow 4$
No. of ways in which a painting can be hanged in the living room $\Rightarrow 4 - 1 = 3$
Total No. of ways to choose from which painting goes in each room $\Rightarrow 4 \times 3 = 12$ ways

Example #5:   A security system uses a four-digit password, but no digit including 0 can be used more than once. How many possible passwords are there?

Solution: No. of possible choices for the first digit $\Rightarrow 10$
No. of possible choices for the second digit $\Rightarrow 10 - 1 = 9$
No. of possible choices for the third digit $\Rightarrow 9 - 1 = 8$
No. of possible choices for the fourth digit $\Rightarrow 8 - 1 = 7$
Note: Since we can't use the same digit twice, number of possible choices for each subsequent digit is one less than the previous digit.
Total No. of possible choices for the passwords $\Rightarrow 10 \times 9 \times 8 \times 7 = 5,040$

Example #6:   A club has 17 members. They are electing a president and a vice-president. How many different outcomes of the elections are possible? (Assume the president and vice-president must be different members of the club.)

Solution: No. of ways to elect a president of the club $\Rightarrow 17$
No. of ways to elect a vice-president of the club $\Rightarrow 17 - 1 = 16$
Total No. of ways to choose president & vice-president $\Rightarrow 17 \times 16 = 272$ ways

FACTORIALS:

Before we get in too deeply into permutation and combination, it's important to understand the concept of factorials. Factorials are a useful tool for solving questions related to permutation and combination. Occasionally, you may even see some problems involving factorial notation. The factorial of n is the number of ways that the n elements of a group can be ordered. If "n" is an integer greater than 1, then "n" factorial, denoted by the symbol $n!$, is defined as the product of all positive integers less than or equal to n, i.e., from 1 to n. In other words, it's the product of the natural numbers up to n, including n.

Factorial Notation: $n! = n \times (n-1) \times (n-2) \times (n-3) \times (n-4) \times (n-5) \times 2 \times 1$.......until the last term becomes 1

Example #1: $0!$ $\Rightarrow 1! = 1$ (this is by definition)
Example #2: $1!$ $\Rightarrow 1$
Example #3: $2!$ $\Rightarrow 2 \times 1 = 2$
Example #4: $3!$ $\Rightarrow 3 \times 2 \times 1 = 6$
Example #5: $4!$ $\Rightarrow 4 \times 3 \times 2 \times 1 = 24$
Example #6: $5!$ $\Rightarrow 5 \times 4 \times 3 \times 2 \times 1 = 120$

Example #7: $\dfrac{8!}{6!}$ $\Rightarrow \dfrac{8!}{6!} = \dfrac{8 \times 7 \times \cancel{6!}}{\cancel{6!}} = 8 \times 7 = 56$

Example #8: $\dfrac{8!}{2! \times 6!}$ $\Rightarrow \dfrac{8 \times 7 \times \cancel{6!}}{2! \times \cancel{6!}} = \dfrac{8 \times 7}{2 \times 1} = \dfrac{56}{2} = 28$

2.3: PERMUTATIONS:

A *"permutation"* is the number of ways in which a set of terms or elements can be arranged in order or sequentially. If we select member after member from the same group, the number of possible choices will decrease by 1 for each subsequent choice. Such counting problems are called permutations.

A permutation can also be thought of as a selection process in which objects are selected one by one in a certain predefined order.

The factorials are useful for solving problems involving permutations or counting the number of ways that a set of objects can be ordered. If a set of n objects is to be ordered from 1st to nth, then there are n choices for the 1st object, $n - 1$ choices for the 2nd object, $n - 2$ choices for the 3rd object, and so on, until there is only 1 choice left for the nth object. Thus, by the fundamental counting principle, the number of ways of ordering the n object is: $n \times (n - 1) \times (n - 2).......(3)\,(2)\,(1)$.

A permutation is the number of arrangements of n objects, where each different ordering of the objects counts as one permutation. When the order does matter, you are dealing with a permutation. For instance, *AB* and *BA* are two different permutations.

EZ PERMUTATION FORMULA: The formula for the number of permutations of "n" objects is n factorial, or simply $n!$.
$\Rightarrow$ $n! = n \times (n - 1) \times (n - 2) \times (n - 3) \times (n - 4) \times (n - 5).......$until the last term becomes 1

EZ TIP: You can also apply logic to solve permutation problems, however, in some of the problems, it can sometimes get very confusing, and therefore, we recommend to use the permutation formulas.

DIFFERENT TYPES OF PERMUTATIONS:
- Permutations: Single Source, Order Matters
- Permutations: Single Source, Order Matters, But Only for a Selection

2.3.1: PERMUTATIONS: SINGLE SOURCE, ORDER MATTERS:

For problems that ask you to choose from the same source to fill specific spots, all you have to do is to multiply the number of choices for each of the spots; however, the number of choices keeps getting smaller.

The number of ways that n objects can be ordered is $n!$.
For instance, to figure out how many ways there are to arrange 6 items along a shelf $\Rightarrow$ multiply the number of possibilities for the first position times the number of possibilities remaining for the second position, and so on.
Alternatively, you can just use the formula: $6! = 6 \times 5 \times 4 \times 3 \times 2 \times 1 = 720$ ways.

For Example: There are five hockey teams that play in a league against each other. By the end of the championship, how many different ways could the five teams end up ranked against each other?

Solution: Let's try to break the problem in the following way:
Since there are a total of 5 teams, there are, in fact, 5 possible teams that could end up in the first place.
No. of Teams that could possibly end up in First Place $\Rightarrow$ 5
Now, since one team has already finished first, there are, in fact, only 4 possible teams that could end up in the second place.
No. of Teams that could possibly end up in Second Place $\Rightarrow$ 4
Now, since two teams have already finished first and second, there are, in fact, only 3 possible teams that could end up in the third place.
No. of Teams that could possibly end up in Third Place $\Rightarrow$ 3
Now, since three teams have already finished first, second, and third, there are, in fact, only 2 possible teams that could end up in the fourth place.
No. of Teams that could possibly end up in Fourth Place $\Rightarrow$ 2
Now, since four teams have already finished first, second, third, and fourth, there is, in fact, only 1 possible team that could end up in the fifth place.
No. of Teams that could possibly end up in Fifth Place $\Rightarrow$ 1

The number of different ways these teams could end up in the rankings: multiply the number of possible possibilities for each spot: multiply the number of choices for first place (in this case, 5) times the number of choices for second place (in this case, 4) times the number of choices for third place (in this case, 3) times the number of choices for the fourth place (in this case, 2) times the number of choices for the fifth place (in this case, 1)

$\Rightarrow 5 \times 4 \times 3 \times 2 \times 1 = 120$ ways

Therefore, in general, no matter how many items there are to arrange, we can figure out the number of permutations of a group of n similar objects with the permutation formula: $n! = n \times (n-1) \times (n-2) \times (n-3) \times (n-4) \times (n-5)$.......until the last term becomes 1.

In this problem, we could have just used the permutation formula and solved it in one step:

$\Rightarrow 5! = 5 \times 4 \times 3 \times 2 \times 1 = 120$ ways

2.3.2: PERMUTATIONS: SINGLE SOURCE, ORDER MATTERS, BUT ONLY FOR A SELECTION:

To find the number of ways to arrange a smaller group that's being drawn from a larger group, or to find the number of permutations of m items taken n at a time, use the following permutation formula:

PERMUTATION $= {}_mP_n \Rightarrow \dfrac{m!}{(m-n)!} = m \times (m-1) \times (m-2) \dots \times (m-n+1)$

Where: m = Number in the larger group
          n = Number you're arranging

If there are "m" different terms/elements in a set, and there are "k" available or empty spots, then there are "p" different ways of arranging them, given by the following formula $\Rightarrow p = \dfrac{m!}{k!}$

Example #1:   There are ten hockey teams that play in a league against each other. The team that comes in first, second, and third place will win gold, silver, and bronze medals, respectively. By the end of the championship, how many possible outcomes for gold, silver, and bronze medal winners are there? Or how many different ways could the top 3 teams end up in the rankings?

Solution: Let's try to break the problem in the following way:

Since there are a total of 10 teams, there are, in fact, 10 possible teams that could end up in the first place.

No. of Teams that are possibilities for the First Place $\Rightarrow 10$

Now, since one team has already occupied the first spot, there are, in fact, only 9 possible teams that could end up in the second place.

No. of Teams that are possibilities for the Second Place $\Rightarrow 9$

Now, since two teams have already occupied the first and second spot, there are, in fact, only 8 possible teams that could end up in the third place.

No. of Teams that are possibilities for the Third Place $\Rightarrow 8$

The number of different ways these teams could end up in the top 3 rankings: multiply the number of possible possibilities for each spot: multiply the number of choices for first place (in this case, 10) times the number of choices for second place (in this case, 9) times the number of choices for third place (in this case, 8)

$\Rightarrow 10 \times 9 \times 8 = 720$ ways

In other words, any of the 10 teams could come in first place, leaving 9 teams who could come in second place, leaving 8 runners who could come in third place, for a total of $10 \times 9 \times 8 = 720$ possible outcomes for gold, silver, and bronze medal winners.

Therefore, in general, no matter how many items there are to arrange, we can figure out the number of permutations of a group of m similar objects chosen from a set of n objects with the permutation formula.

Alternate Method: In this problem, we could have just used the permutation formula and solved it in one step:

Large Group $= m =$ Total No. of teams $= 10$

Small Group $= n =$ Total No. of teams to be ranked $= 3$

No. of different ways the top 3 teams could end up in the rankings:

Permutation $\Rightarrow {}_mP_n \quad \Rightarrow \dfrac{m!}{(m-n)!}$

$$\Rightarrow {}_{10}P_3 \Rightarrow \frac{10!}{(10-3)!} = \frac{10!}{7!} = \frac{10 \times 9 \times 8 \times 7!}{7!} = 10 \times 9 \times 8 = 720$$

Note: There are 7! ways in which we can rank the 7 other teams. Calculating just 10! will give us 7! times as many rankings as there really are. Since the order in which the other 7 teams are ranked is not relevant to the problem, we actually do not have to count all the different rankings of those 7 teams, hence we must divide by 7!. There are 10! types of rankings in total for 10 teams. However, since 7 of the rankings are not relevant, we must divide by 7!.

Always address irrelevant (situations in which the order does not matter) repeated terms; then, divide by the factorial of the number of irrelevant repeated terms to account for over-counting.

Example #2: A security system uses a four-letter password, but no letter can be used more than once. How many possible passwords can be formed?

Solution: Let's try to break the problem in the following way:

Since there are a total of 26 alphabets, there are, in fact, 26 possible letters that could end up in the first place of the password.

No. of Letters that are possibilities for the First Place ⇒ 26

Now, since one alphabet has already occupied the first spot and since we cannot reuse any letters, there are, in fact, only 25 possible letters that could end up in the second place. (26 minus the letter used in the first letter of the password)

No. of Letters that are possibilities for the Second Place ⇒ 25

Now, since two alphabets have already occupied the first and second spot, and since we cannot reuse any letters, there are, in fact, only 24 possible letters that could end up in the third place. (26 minus the letter used in the first and second letter of the password)

No. of Letters that are possibilities for the Third Place ⇒ 24

Now, since three alphabets have already occupied the first, second, and third spot, and since we cannot reuse any letters, there are, in fact, only 23 possible letters that could end up in the fourth place. (26 minus the letter used in the first, second, and third letter of the password)

No. of Letters that are possibilities for the Fourth Place ⇒ 23

The number of different ways these alphabets could end up in the 4 spots: multiply the number of possible possibilities for each spot: multiply the number of choices for first place (in this case, 26) times the number of choices for second place (in this case, 25) times the number of choices for third place (in this case, 24) times the number of choices for the fourth place (in this case, 23)

⇒ 26 × 25 × 24 × 23 ways

In other words, any of the 26 letters could come in first place, leaving 25 letters which could come in second place, leaving 24 letters which could come in third place, leaving 23 letters which could come in the fourth place, for a total of 26 × 25 × 24 × 23 possible outcomes for a four-letter password.

Therefore, in general, no matter how many items there are to arrange, we can figure out the number of permutations of a group of m similar objects chosen form a set of n objects with the permutation formula.

Alternate Method: In this problem, we could have just used the permutation formula and solved it in one step:

Large Group = m = Total No. of letters = 26 (since there are 26 alphabets)

Small Group = n = Total No. of letters in password = 4

No. of different ways of forming four-letter passwords:

Permutation $\Rightarrow {}_mP_n \Rightarrow \dfrac{m!}{(m-n)!}$

$$\Rightarrow {}_{26}P_4 \Rightarrow \frac{26!}{(26-4)!} = \frac{26!}{22!} = \frac{26 \times 25 \times 24 \times 23 \times \cancel{22!}}{\cancel{22!}} = 26 \times 25 \times 24 \times 23 = 358,800 \text{ ways}$$

2.4: COMBINATIONS:

So far, we have only dealt with permutation problems, where the order in which the items are arranged actually matters to the problem. For instance, the order in which ten teams can end up in the top three spots, first, second, and third, in a championship could be *ABC*, or it could be *CBA*; both are entirely different in their order. The total number of permutations is $10 \times 9 \times 8 = 720$.

A ***"combination"*** is the number of ways of choosing a given number of elements from a set, where the order of element does not matter. For instance, the order in which ten teams can end up in the top three spots, where the first, second, and third position doesn't matter, in a championship could be *ABC*, or it could be *CBA*; both are exactly the same in their order. The total number of combinations is $720 \div 3! = 120$.

The concept given above is explained in detail in the following section.

Combination problems don't care about the order of the items. Therefore, if the order in which the members are chosen makes no difference, the counting problem involves combinations. For instance, *AB* and *BA* counts as two different permutations, but only as 1 combination.

Permutation and Combination are interrelated fields. To find the combination, just divide the permutation by the common elements.

EZ TIP: When the order does not matter, you are dealing with a combination problem.

2.4.1: COMBINATIONS: SINGLE SOURCE, ORDER DOESN'T MATTER:

To find the number of ways to arrange a smaller group that's being drawn from a larger group, and if the order or arrangement of the smaller group that's being drawn from the larger group does NOT matter, we are essentially looking for the number of combinations, and for that, use the following combination formula:
The number of different subsets of n objects that can be selected from a larger set of m objects ($0 \le n \le m$), without regard to the order of selection is given by the following rule:

The number of possible complete selections of n objects is called the number of combinations of m objects taken n at a time and is represented by $_mC_n$. The value of $_mC_n$ is given by the following formula:

$$\text{COMBINATION} = {}_mC_n \Rightarrow \frac{m!}{n!(m-n)!} = \frac{m(m-1)(m-2)\ldots\ldots\times(m-n+1)}{n!} = \frac{{}_mP_n}{n!}$$

Where: m = Number in the larger group
           n = Number you're choosing

Combinations are where small groups of size n are made from a larger group of size m. It is the number of n-element subsets of a set with m elements.
For instance if there are 5 elements in a set, then the number of 2-element subsets, or the number of combinations of 5 elements taken 2 at a time is:

$$\Rightarrow {}_5C_2 = \frac{5!}{2!(5-2)!} = \frac{5!}{2!3!} = \frac{120}{(2)(6)} = 10$$

In this case, we have a large group of 5, and we want to find the number of smaller groups of 2 that we could make.

Example #1:   There are ten candidates that apply for 3 job vacancies. By the end of the recruitment process, how many different ways could the candidates be selected?

Solution: Let's try to break the problem in the following way:
             To find the number of combinations, first find the number of permutations. If 10 candidates apply for a job opening, and we want to find the top 3 candidates, then, based on the permutation formula, the number of permutations would be

$$\text{Permutation} \Rightarrow {}_mP_n \Rightarrow \frac{m!}{(m-n)!}$$

$$\Rightarrow {}_{10}P_3 \Rightarrow \frac{10!}{(10-3)!} = \frac{10!}{7!} = \frac{10 \times 9 \times 8 \times 7!}{7!} = 10 \times 9 \times 8 = 720$$

However, if we don't care about the order in which they are selected, then a bunch of these 720 permutations turn out to be duplicates.

To find the number of duplicates, let's think of one of those permutations: let's say the first three candidates were John, Tom, and Paul.

Then the number of different ways we could arrange these three candidates = 3! = 3 × 2 × 1 = 6 permutations of any 3 objects.

So, of those 720 permutations of the top 3 teams, each combination is being counted 3!, or 3 × 2 × 1 = 6 times. To find the number of combinations, we need to divide 720 by 6, which is 120.

$$\text{Combination} \Rightarrow {}_mC_n \Rightarrow \frac{{}_mP_n}{n!} = \frac{720}{3!} = 120$$

So first multiply 10 by 9 by 8 to get the number of ways of choosing 3 candidates, and then divide by 6 because each of the 3 candidates can be chosen in 6 different ways $\Rightarrow (10 \times 9 \times 8) \div 6 = 720 \div 6 = 120$

Therefore, in general, no matter how many items there are to arrange, we can figure out the number of combinations of a group of m similar objects chosen from a set of n objects with the combination formula.

Alternate Method: In this problem, we could have just used the combination formula and solved it in one step:

Large Group = m = Total No. of candidates = 10
Small Group = n = Total No. of available spots = 3
No. of different ways of picking 3 candidates from a total of 10 candidates:

$$\text{Combination} \Rightarrow {}_mC_n \Rightarrow \frac{m!}{n!(m-n)!}$$

$$\Rightarrow {}_{10}C_3 \Rightarrow \frac{10!}{3!(10-3)!} = \frac{10!}{3! \times 7!} = \frac{10 \times 9 \times 8 \times 7!}{3! \times 7!} = \frac{10 \times 9 \times 8}{3 \times 2 \times 1} = \frac{720}{6} = 120$$

Therefore, there are 120 different possible combinations.

Example #2: There are 12 candidates that apply for 2 job vacancies. By the end of the recruitment process, how many different ways could the candidates be selected?

Solution: Let's try to break the problem in the following way:

To find the number of combinations, first find the number of permutations. If 12 candidates apply for a job opening, and we want to find the top 2 candidates, then, based on the permutation formula, the number of permutations would be

$$\text{Permutation} \Rightarrow {}_mP_n \Rightarrow \frac{m!}{(m-n)!}$$

$$\Rightarrow {}_{12}P_2 \Rightarrow \frac{12!}{(12-2)!} = \frac{12!}{10!} = \frac{12 \times 11 \times \cancel{10!}}{\cancel{10!}} = 12 \times 11 = 132.$$

However, if we don't care about the order in which they are selected, then a bunch of these 132 permutations turn out to be duplicates.

To find the number of duplicates, let's think of one of those permutations: let's say the first two candidates were John and Tom.

Then the number of different ways we could arrange these two candidates = 2! = 2 × 1 = 2 permutations of any 2 objects. (John first and Tom second, or Tom first and John second)

So, of those 132 permutations of the top 2 candidates, each combination is being counted 2!, or 2 × 1 = 2 times. To find the number of combinations, we need to divide 132 by 2, which is 66.

$$\text{Combination} \Rightarrow {}_mC_n \Rightarrow \frac{{}_mP_n}{n!} = \frac{132}{2!} = 66$$

So first multiply 12 by 11 to get the number of ways of choosing a pair of candidates, and then divide by 2 because each pair of candidates can be chosen in two different ways $\Rightarrow (12 \times 11) \div 2 = 132 \div 2 = 66$

Therefore, in general, no matter how many items there are to arrange, we can figure out the number of combinations of a group of m similar objects chosen from a set of n objects with the combination formula.

Alternate Method: In this problem, we could have just used the combination formula and solved it in one step:

Large Group = m = Total No. of candidates = 12

Small Group = n = Total No. of available spots = 2
No. of different ways of picking 2 candidates from a total of 12 candidates:

$$\text{Combination} \Rightarrow {}_mC_n \Rightarrow \frac{m!}{n!(m-n)!}$$

$$\Rightarrow {}_{12}C_2 \Rightarrow \frac{12!}{2!(12-2)!} = \frac{12!}{2! \times 10!} = \frac{12 \times 11 \times \cancel{10!}}{2! \times \cancel{10!}} = \frac{12 \times 11}{2 \times 1} = \frac{132}{2} = 66$$

Therefore, there are 66 different possible combinations.

EZ HINT: The key to Permutations and Combinations is to know if the order of the term matters or not:
$\Rightarrow$ If the order does matter, you are dealing with a permutation.
$\Rightarrow$ If the order does not matter, you are dealing with a combination.

EZ TIP: Always remember to divide by $n!$ when there are n repetitions of the same term.

2.4.2: PERMUTATION/COMBINATION WITH RESTRICTIONS:
Some of the most difficult or complex permutation and combination problems include restrictions or constraints, such as, two of the people can't be seated next to each other, or if two applicants are to be chosen, both can't be females, etc. Try to solve such problems just us usual; however, you do have to take into account the affect of the given restrictions.

EZ TIP: When solving complex permutation and combination problems with restrictions, be sure to always start with the objects that are involved in the restriction and then deal with the objects that are without any restrictions.

TYPE 1: "MUST NOT" SIT NEXT TO EACH OTHER:

For Example: Seven friends, two girls, Mona and Tina, and five boys, John, Robert, Nick, Victor, and Peter have seven tickets in the seven adjacent front row seats of a theater. The two girls must not sit next to each other, but the five boys can sit anywhere. In how many different ways can the seven friends be seated?

Solution: It may be helpful to visualize the seating arrangement by drawing a diagram to show the row of 7 chairs.

$S_1 \qquad S_2 \qquad S_3 \qquad S_4 \qquad S_5 \qquad S_6 \qquad S_7$

First, Seat the Constrained People: Let's start with seating Mona and then Tina:
1st: No. of possible choices for seating Mona $\Rightarrow$ 7
      If Mona is the first one to be seated, she can sit in any one of the 7 available chairs.
2nd: No. of possible choices for seating Tina $\Rightarrow$ either 4 or 5
      Following are the two cases for seating Tina:
   (i)   If Mona has chosen to sit in one of the two extreme end seats (S_1 or S_7) $\Rightarrow$ then only one seat is restricted for Tina – i.e., the seat immediately adjacent to Mona. This leaves **5** remaining seating options for Tina.
         Hence in 2/7 of the cases, the number of possible choices for seating Tina $\Rightarrow$ 5
   (ii) If Mona has chosen to sit in one of the five middle seats (S_2, S_3, S_4, S_5, S_6), exactly two seats are restricted for Tina – i.e., the two seats on either side of Mona. This leaves 4 remaining seating options for Tina.
         Hence in 5/7 of the cases, the number of possible choices for seating Tina $\Rightarrow$ 4

Next, Seat the Non-Constrained People: Now after seating the two constrained girls, Mona and Tina, let's seat the non-constrained four boys:
3rd: No. of possible choices for seating John $\Rightarrow$ 5
      John can sit in any of the 5 remaining chairs that are not occupied by Mona or Tina.
4th: No. of possible choices for seating Robert $\Rightarrow$ 4
      Robert can sit in any of the 4 remaining chairs that are not yet occupied
5th: No. of possible choices for seating Nick $\Rightarrow$ 3
      Nick can sit in any of the 3 remaining chairs that are not yet occupied
6th: No. of possible choices for seating Victor $\Rightarrow$ 2
      Victor can sit in any of the 2 remaining chairs that are not yet occupied

7th: No. of possible choices for seating Peter $\Rightarrow$ 1

Peter must sit in the 1 remaining chair that is not yet occupied

Finally, let's compute the total number of permutations, that is, find the product of the number of choices for each of the seven people $\Rightarrow 7 \times (2/7 \times 5 + 5/7 \times 4) \times 5 \times 4 \times 3 \times 2 \times 1 = 3,600$ ways

Therefore, there are 3600 different ways of seating the seven friends with restrictions.

Alternate Method: This would have been a simple permutation problem if there were no restriction that the two girls can't sit next to each other. If we ignore the restriction for now, the number of ways in which seven people can sit in 7 chairs is given by $\Rightarrow 7! = 7 \times 6 \times 5 \times 4 \times 3 \times 2 \times 1 = 5,040$ ways

Now, we are given that two of the seven people have a restriction that they must not sit next to each other, that is 2 out of 7 have restrictions and the remaining 5 out of 7 don't have restrictions.

In order to find the total number of seating arrangements including the restrictions, let's just take the five-sevenths of the total number of arrangements $\Rightarrow 5,040 \times 5/7 = 3,600$ ways.

TYPE 2: "MUST" SIT NEXT TO EACH OTHER:

For Example: Seven friends, two girls, Mona and Tina, and five boys, John, Robert, Nick, Victor, and Peter have seven tickets in the seven adjacent front row seats of a theater. The two girls must sit next to each other, but the five boys can sit anywhere. In how many different ways can the seven friends be seated?

Solution: It may be helpful to visualize the seating arrangement by drawing a diagram to show the row of 7 chairs.

S_1 S_2 S_3 S_4 S_5 S_6 S_7

First, Seat the Constrained People: Let's start with seating the two girls, Mona and Tina who must sit next to each other:

List of 2-adjacent seat combinations $\Rightarrow S_1S_2, S_2S_3, S_3S_4, S_4S_5, S_5S_6,$ and S_6S_7

No. of 2-adjacent seat possible combinations $\Rightarrow$ 6

However, there are 2 ways of seating the two girls for each 2-adjacent seat possible combination.

Therefore, total No. of 2-adjacent seat possible combinations to seat the girls $\Rightarrow 6 \times 2 = 12$

Next, Seat the Non-Constrained People: Now after seating the two constrained girls, Mona and Tina, let's seat the non-constrained four boys:

After seating the two girls, no matter which 2-adjacent seat possible combination they use, there will be 5 seats remaining for the four boys.

Total No. of ways of seat the 5 boys on the reaming 5 seats $\Rightarrow 5! = 5 \times 4 \times 3 \times 2 \times 1 = 120$

Finally, let's compute the total number of permutations, that is, find the product of the number of choices for each of the six people $\Rightarrow 12 \times 120 = 1,440$ ways

Therefore, there are 1,440 different ways of seating the seven friends with restrictions.

Alternate Method: This would have been a simple permutation problem if there were no restriction that the two girls must sit next to each other. If we ignore the restriction for now, the number of ways in which seven people can sit in 7 chairs is given by $\Rightarrow 7! = 7 \times 6 \times 5 \times 4 \times 3 \times 2 \times 1 = 5040$ ways

Now, we are given that two of the seven people have a restriction that they must sit next to each other, that is 2 out of 7 have restrictions and the remaining 5 out of 7 don't have restrictions.

In order to find the total number of seating arrangements including the restrictions, let's just take the two-sevenths of the total number of arrangements $\Rightarrow 5,040 \times 2/7 = 1,440$ ways.

Alternate Method: This is yet another way to solve this problem.

For the time being, treat the two girls who must sit next to each other as one person. Now we have 6 people, 5 boys and the two girls that act as 1.

Total No. of Seating Options for 5 boys and two girls that act as 1 $\Rightarrow 6! = 6 \times 5 \times 4 \times 3 \times 2 \times 1 = 720$

Now, let's consider the two girls who must sit next to each other:

Total No. of Seating Options for the Two Girls $\Rightarrow 2! = 2 \times 1 = 2$

Finally, let's compute the total number of possibilities:

Total No. of Seating Options for 5 Boys and 2 Girls (who must sit together) $\Rightarrow 6! \times 2! = 720 \times 2 = 1,440$

PRACTICE EXERCISE – QUESTIONS AND ANSWERS WITH EXPLANATIONS: PERMUTATION & COMBINATION:

Question #1: If an ice cream dessert can be made with 25 types of flavors, 5 types of syrups and 5 types of toppings, how many different types of the dessert can be made?

Solution: No. of different types of dessert combinations ⇒ 25 (types of flavors) × 5 (types of syrups) × 5 (types of toppings) ⇒ 25 × 5 × 5 = 625
Therefore, there are 625 different types of desserts.

Question #2: If the first class of an airline offers a special five course meal, consisting of 2 types of soups, 6 types of salads, 7 types of beverages, 2 types of main dishes, and 9 types of desserts, then how many different types of 5 course meals can one choose from ?

Solution: No. of different types of 5 course meals combinations ⇒ 2 (types of soups) × 6 (types of salads) × 7 (types of beverages) × 2 (types of main dishes) × 9 (types of desserts) ⇒ 2 × 6 × 7 × 2 × 9 = 1,512
Therefore, there are 1,512 different types of five course meals.

Question #3: How many five-digit numbers are there that are composed of only even digits?
Solution: A five-digit number is composed of 5 digits.
No. of ways to choose the first digit   ⇒ 4 (choices: 2, 4, 6, 8)
No. of ways to choose the second digit   ⇒ 5 (choices: 0, 2, 4, 6, 8)
No. of ways to choose the third digit   ⇒ 5 (choices: 0, 2, 4, 6, 8)
No. of ways to choose the fourth digit   ⇒ 5 (choices: 0, 2, 4, 6, 8)
No. of ways to choose the fifth digit   ⇒ 5 (choices: 0, 2, 4, 6, 8)
Note: 0 is an even number, and the first digit can't be a 0.
Total No. of five-digit numbers that are composed of only even digits ⇒ 4 × 5 × 5 × 5 × 5 = 2,500

Question #4: A three-digit area code must satisfy the following condition: the first digit is different from zero and all the other digits are different from each other. How many different area codes can be generated?
Solution: List all the options for each digit:
No. of options for the first digit   ⇒ 9 (from 1 to 9)
No. of options for the second digit ⇒ 9 (from 0 to 9 minus the one used as the first digit)
No. of options for the third digit   ⇒ 8 (from 0 to 9 minus the two used as the first and second digit)
Total No. of options for three-digit codes⇒ 9 × 9 × 8 = 648

Question #5: How many different ways can the letters "XYZ" be arranged?
Solution: Total No. of terms ⇒ XYZ = 3 terms
3! ⇒ 3 × 2 × 1 = 6
Therefore, there 6 different ways of arranging letters "XYZ"

Question #6: How many different ways can 4 people be seated in an auditorium in the same row with exactly 4 empty seats in the row?
Solution: Total No. of terms ⇒ 4 terms
4! ⇒ 4 × 3 × 2 × 1 = 24
Therefore, there are 24 different ways in which 4 people can be seated in the auditorium.

Question #7: How many different ways can the letters "ABCDE" be arranged?
Solution: Total No. of terms ⇒ ABCDE = 5 terms
5! ⇒ 5 × 4 × 3 × 2 × 1 = 120
Therefore, there are 120 different ways of arranging letters "ABCDE"

Question #8: The host of a party must determine how to seat himself and 6 guests in a single row with exactly 7 empty chairs. How many different seating arrangements are possible if the host always chooses the same seat for himself?
Solution: In this case, there are 6 seats to be filled; although there are 7 people in total (including the host), the host will always take the same spot, so only six seats can be changed.

Total No. of terms $\Rightarrow 6$
$6! \Rightarrow 6 \times 5 \times 4 \times 3 \times 2 \times 1 = 720$
Therefore, there are 720 different ways in which 7 people can be seated in the auditorium.
Avoid the trap by counting the number of arrangements possible if the host does not always take the same seat.

Question #9: How many different ways can 8 books be arranged on a book shelf?
Solution: Total No. of items $\Rightarrow 8$
$8! \Rightarrow 8 \times 7 \times 6 \times 5 \times 4 \times 3 \times 2 \times 1 = 40,320$
Therefore, there are 40,320 different ways in which 8 books can be arranged on a book shelf.

Question #10: How many different ways can 7 files be filed in a file cabinet?
Solution: Total No. of items $\Rightarrow 7$
$7! \Rightarrow 7 \times 6 \times 5 \times 4 \times 3 \times 2 \times 1 = 5,040$
Therefore, there are 5,040 different ways in which 7 files can be filed in a file cabinet.

Question #11: If there are 2 empty chairs left in an auditorium but there are 8 people who need to be seated, in how many number of different ways can those 8 people be seated on 2 empty chairs?
Solution: Large Group = Total No. of people $\qquad \Rightarrow m = 8$
Small Group = Total No. of empty chairs $\quad \Rightarrow n = 2$
No. of different ways of seating 8 people on 2 empty chairs:

Permutation $\Rightarrow {}_mP_n \quad \Rightarrow \dfrac{m!}{(m-n)!}$

$\Rightarrow {}_8P_2 \quad \Rightarrow \dfrac{8!}{(8-2)!} = \dfrac{8!}{6!} = \dfrac{8 \times 7 \times 6!}{6!} = 8 \times 7 = 56$

Question #12: If there are 9 books but only 2 empty spots on a book shelf, how many number of different ways can those 9 books be arranged in 2 empty spots on the book shelf?
Solution: Large Group = Total No. of books $\qquad \Rightarrow m = 9$
Small Group = Total No. of empty spots $\quad \Rightarrow n = 2$
No. of different ways of arranging 9 books on 2 empty spots:

Permutation $\Rightarrow {}_mP_n \quad \Rightarrow \dfrac{m!}{(m-n)!}$

$\Rightarrow {}_9P_2 \quad \Rightarrow \dfrac{9!}{(9-2)!} = \dfrac{9!}{7!} = \dfrac{9 \times 8 \times 7!}{7!} = 9 \times 8 = 72$

Question #13: If there are 3 rooms, a living room, a family room, and a study room, and there are 7 different paintings that need to be hanged, how many number of different ways can those 7 paintings be hanged in the 3 rooms with only one painting in each room,?
Solution: Large Group = Total No. of paintings $\qquad \Rightarrow m = 7$
Small Group = Total No. of empty rooms $\quad \Rightarrow n = 3$
No. of different ways of hanging 7 paintings in 3 rooms:

Permutation $\Rightarrow {}_mP_n \quad \Rightarrow \dfrac{m!}{(m-n)!}$

$\Rightarrow {}_7P_3 \quad \Rightarrow \dfrac{7!}{(7-3)!} = \dfrac{7!}{4!} = \dfrac{7 \times 6 \times 5 \times 4!}{4!} = 7 \times 6 \times 5 = 210$

Question #14: If there are 9 files but only 3 empty spots in a file cabinet, how many numbers of different ways can those 9 files be filed on 3 empty spots in the file cabinet?
Solution: Large Group = Total No. of files $\qquad \Rightarrow m = 9$
Small Group = Total No. of empty spots $\quad \Rightarrow n = 3$
No. of different ways of filing 9 files in 3 spots:

Permutation $\Rightarrow {}_mP_n \quad \Rightarrow \dfrac{m!}{(m-n)!}$

$$\Rightarrow {}_9P_3 \quad \Rightarrow \quad \frac{9!}{(9-3)!} = \frac{9!}{6!} = \frac{9 \times 8 \times 7 \times 6!}{6!} = 9 \times 8 \times 7 = 504$$

Question #15: How many different ways there are to choose 2 candidates from 8 possible candidates?
Solution: Large Group = Total No. of candidates $\Rightarrow m = 8$
Small Group = Total No. of available spots $\Rightarrow n = 2$
No. of different ways of picking 2 candidates from a total of 8 candidates:

$$\text{Combination} \Rightarrow {}_mC_n \quad \Rightarrow \quad \frac{m!}{n!(m-n)!}$$

$$\Rightarrow {}_8C_2 \quad \Rightarrow \quad \frac{8!}{2!(8-2)!} = \frac{8!}{2! \times 6!} = \frac{8 \times 7 \times 6!}{2! \times 6!} = \frac{8 \times 7}{2 \times 1} = \frac{56}{2} = 28$$

Therefore, there are 28 different possible combinations.

Question #16: How many different ways there are to choose 3 candidates from 9 possible candidates?
Solution: Large Group = Total No. of candidates $\Rightarrow m = 9$
Small Group = Total No. of available spots $\Rightarrow n = 3$
No. of different ways of picking 3 candidates from a total of 9 candidates:

$$\text{Combination} \Rightarrow {}_mC_n \quad \Rightarrow \quad \frac{m!}{n!(m-n)!}$$

$$\Rightarrow {}_9C_3 \quad \Rightarrow \quad \frac{9!}{3!(9-3)!} = \frac{9!}{3! \times 6!} = \frac{9 \times 8 \times 7 \times 6!}{3! \times 6!} = \frac{9 \times 8 \times 7}{3 \times 2 \times 1} = \frac{504}{6} = 84$$

Therefore, there are 84 different possible combinations.

Question #17: How many different ways there are to choose 3 candidates from 8 possible candidates?
Solution: Large Group = Total No. of candidates $\Rightarrow m = 8$
Small Group = Total No. of available spots $\Rightarrow n = 3$
No. of different ways of picking 3 candidates from a total of 8 candidates:

$$\text{Combination} \Rightarrow {}_mC_n \quad \Rightarrow \quad \frac{m!}{n!(m-n)!}$$

$$\Rightarrow {}_8C_3 \quad \rightarrow \quad \frac{8!}{3!(8-3)!} = \frac{8!}{3! \times 5!} = \frac{8 \times 7 \times 6 \times 5!}{3! \times 5!} = \frac{8 \times 7 \times 6}{3 \times 2 \times 1} = \frac{8 \times 7 \times 6}{6} = 56$$

Therefore, there are 56 different possible combinations.

Question #18: How many different ways there are to choose 2 candidates from 9 possible candidates?
Solution: Large Group = Total No. of candidates $\Rightarrow m = 9$
Small Group = Total No. of available spots $\Rightarrow n = 2$
No. of different ways of picking 2 candidates from a total of 9 candidates:

$$\text{Combination} \rightarrow {}_mC_n \quad \Rightarrow \quad \frac{m!}{n!(m-n)!}$$

$$\Rightarrow {}_9C_2 \quad \Rightarrow \quad \frac{9!}{2!(9-2)!} = \frac{9!}{2! \times 7!} = \frac{9 \times 8 \times 7!}{2! \times 7!} = \frac{9 \times 8}{2 \times 1} = \frac{72}{2} = 36$$

Therefore, there are 36 different possible combinations.

Question #19: Six friends, two girls, Mona and Tina, and four boys, John, Robert, Nick, and Victor, have six tickets in the six adjacent front row seats of a theater. The two girls must not sit next to each other, but the four boys can sit anywhere. In how many different ways can the six friends be seated?
Solution: It may be helpful to visualize the seating arrangement by drawing a diagram to show the row of 6 chairs.
$S_1 \qquad S_2 \qquad S_3 \qquad S_4 \qquad S_5 \qquad S_6$
First, Seat the Constrained People: Let's start with seating Mona and then Tina:
1st: No. of possible choices for seating Mona $\Rightarrow 6$
  If Mona is the first one to be seated, she can sit in any one of the 6 available chairs.
2nd: No. of possible choices for seating Tina $\Rightarrow$ either 3 or 4

Following are the two cases for seating Tina:

(i) If Mona has chosen to sit in one of the two extreme end seats (S_1 or S_6) $\Rightarrow$ then only one seat is restricted for Tina – i.e., the seat immediately adjacent to Mona. This leaves 4 remaining seating options for Tina.

Hence in 2/6 or 1/3 of the cases, the number of possible choices for seating Tina $\Rightarrow$ 4

(ii) If Mona has chosen to sit in one of the four middle seats (S_2, S_3, S_4, S_5), exactly two seats are restricted for Tina – i.e., the two seats on either side of Mona. This leaves 3 remaining seating options for Tina.

Hence in 4/6 or 2/3 of the cases, the number of possible choices for seating Tina $\Rightarrow$ 3

Next, Seat the Non-Constrained People: Now after seating the two constrained girls, Mona and Tina, let's seat the non-constrained four boys:

3rd: No. of possible choices for seating John $\Rightarrow$ 4

John can sit in any of the 4 remaining chairs that are not occupied by Mona or Tina.

4th: No. of possible choices for seating Robert $\Rightarrow$ 3

Robert can sit in any of the 3 remaining chairs that are not yet occupied

5th: No. of possible choices for seating Nick $\Rightarrow$ 2

Nick can sit in any of the 2 remaining chairs that are not yet occupied

6th: No. of possible choices for seating Victor $\Rightarrow$ 1

Victor must sit in the 1 remaining chair that is not yet occupied

Finally, let's compute the total number of permutations, that is, find the product of the number of choices for each of the six people $\Rightarrow$ 6 × (1/3 × 4 + 2/3 × 3) × 4 × 3 × 2 × 1 = 480 ways

Therefore, there are 480 different ways of seating the six friends with restrictions.

Question #20: Six friends, two girls, Mona and Tina, and four boys, John, Robert, Nick, and Victor, have six tickets in the six adjacent front row seats of a theater. The two girls must sit next to each other, but the four boys can sit anywhere. In how many different ways can the six friends be seated?

Solution: It may be helpful to visualize the seating arrangement by drawing a diagram to show the row of 6 chairs.

S_1 S_2 S_3 S_4 S_5 S_6

First, Seat the Constrained People: Let's start with seating the two girls, Mona and Tina who must sit next to each other:

List of 2-adjacent seat combinations $\Rightarrow$ S_1S_2, S_2S_3, S_3S_4, S_4S_5, and S_5S_6

No. of 2-adjacent seat possible combinations $\Rightarrow$ 5

However, there are 2 ways of seating the two girls for each 2-adjacent seat possible combination.

Therefore, total No. of 2-adjacent seat possible combinations to seat the girls $\Rightarrow$ 5 × 2 = 10

Next, Seat the Non-Constrained People: Now after seating the two constrained girls, Mona and Tina, let's seat the non-constrained four boys:

After seating the two girls, no matter which 2-adjacent seat possible combination they use, there will be 4 seats remaining for the four boys.

Total No. of ways of seat the 4 boys on the reaming 4 seats $\Rightarrow$ 4! = 4 × 3 × 2 × 1 = 24

Finally, let's compute the total number of permutations, that is, find the product of the number of choices for each of the six people $\Rightarrow$ 10 × 24 = 240 ways

Therefore, there are 240 different ways of seating the six friends with restrictions.

PART 3.0: PROBABILITY:

TABLE OF CONTENTS:

3.1: BASICS ABOUT PROBABILITY:

Every now and then, there are instances in which decisions must be made even though there is no uncertainty. The decision-making process often involves the selection of a plan or course of action based on an analysis of possible outcomes. This is where probability comes into the picture.

The **"probability"** is a study that deals with predicting the outcome of an event in which one has no control over the results. It refers to the statistical **"chances,"** or **"odds"** of an event occurring (or not occurring). It is the numerical representation of the **"likelihood"** that an event or events will occur. Probability indicates how **"likely"** it is that a particular event will occur, or what are the chances that it will happen. Probability that an event will occur is a number that ranges between 0 and 1, usually written as a fraction that indicates how likely it is that the event will happen.
For example: Tossing a coin, rolling a dice, picking a card from a deck of playing cards, drawing concealed balls from a jar, etc.

Discrete probability deals with experiments that have a finite number of outcomes. Given such an experiment, an event is a particular set of outcomes.
For example: rolling a 6-sided dice is an experiment with 6 possible outcomes, 1, 2, 3, 4, 5, or 6. One event in this experiment is that the outcome is 5, denoted {5}; another event is that the outcome is an even number {2, 4, 6}; yet another event is that the outcome is a prime number {2, 3, 5}.

Note: Many of the ideas discussed in the preceding topics are important to the study of probability.

EZ SPOT: It's easy to spot Probability problems. These problems contain one of the following buzz words/phrases: probability, possibilities, likelihood, chances, odds, prospects, etc.

PROBABILITY FORMULA: If "E" is any event, then P(E), the Probability that "E" will occur is given by the following formula, assuming that all of the possible outcomes are equally likely.
Note: If the probability of each outcome is the same, then the probability of each outcome is said to be equally likely.

$$P(E) \Rightarrow \frac{\textit{Number Of Favorable Outcomes}}{\textit{Total Number Of Possible Outcomes}}$$

In other words, the probability of a particular outcome is equal to the number of ways that favorable outcome can occur divided by the total number of possible outcomes.
In general, $P(E)$ can be thought of as a number assigned to an event E which expresses the probability that E occurs.

Another way to put the same thing: The probability of an event E, or $P(E)$, is given as follows:
If E can occur in m ways out of a total of n equally likely ways, then:

$$P(E) \Rightarrow \frac{m}{n} = \frac{Number\ of\ Favorable\ Outcomes\ in\ event\ E}{Total\ Number\ of\ Possible\ Outcomes}$$

Assume that an experiment is performed. If S is the set of all possible outcomes of the experiment, and E is the set of particular outcomes of the experiment, then E is a subset of S.

DIFFERENT WAYS OF EXPRESSING PROBABILITY:

Although probability is primarily defined as a fraction, we can always express it in the following different forms:
(A) As a Fraction $\Rightarrow \frac{1}{2}$
(Must be between 0 and 1)
(B) As a Ratio $\Rightarrow$ 1:2
(Must be between 0 and 1)
(C) As a Decimal Number $\Rightarrow$ 0.5
(If the fraction is converted into a decimal by dividing – it's a number that's always between 0 & 1)
(D) As a Percent $\Rightarrow$ 50%
(If the fraction is converted into a percent by multiplying it by 100 – it's a number that's always between 0% and 100%)
For instance: An event with a probability of $\frac{1}{2}$ or 0.5 is said to be 50% probable.

Therefore, probability can be expressed in term of a fraction, ratio, decimal, or percentage, that is, probability of $\frac{1}{2}$ can be expressed in terms of ratio as 1:2, or in terms of decimal as 0.5, or in terms of percentage as 50%.

$\Rightarrow P(E) = $ ½ $= 1:2 = 0.50 = 50\%$

For instance, in tossing a coin, there are only two possible outcomes: heads or tails. The probability that coin will face heads up is $1 \div 2$ or ½ $\Rightarrow P(E) = $ ½ $= 1:2 = 0.50 = 50\%$

For example, if we roll a six-sided dice (with faces numbered one through six) one time, what is the probability that it would land with "5" side facing upward? Since there are six sides in a dice each with a different number 1 through 6, there are a total of 6 possible outcomes; however, there is only one possibility of it landing with "5" facing up. So there is a one-in-six chance. In simple words, the probability in this case is one-sixth. As we have seen, probability is usually expressed as a fraction in which, the total number of possibilities is always the denominator and the number of possibilities that match what we want is the numerator. Therefore, the probability is 1/6th.

In the above example, we can find the probability that it would land with either "2" side facing upward or the "5" side facing upward. Now, the total number of possible outcomes is still 6, so the denominator remains to be 6 however, the total number of desired possibilities are 2 now, so the numerator becomes 2 now. Hence, the probability is 2/6th or 1/3rd.

For Example: If there are 10 balls in a jar, two each of a different color of red, blue, green, yellow, and white, what is the probability that the first ball picked from the jar will be red?

Solution: No. of favorable outcomes $\Rightarrow 2$
Total No. of possible outcomes $\Rightarrow 10$

$$P(\text{Red}) \Rightarrow \frac{2}{10} = \frac{1}{5}$$

EZ CAUTION: While calculating probability, be careful – remember the total outcomes include the favorable outcomes. For instance, in the previous example, the total outcome is 10, and not 8.

REVERSE PROBABILITY:
If you know the probability of an event, it's possible to find the actual numbers:

For Example: If there are 10 balls in a jar, and the probability of picking a red ball from the jar is 1/5, how many red balls are in the jar?

Solution: Total No. of possible outcomes = 10
$P(\text{Red}) = 1/5$

$$\Rightarrow \frac{n}{10} = \frac{1}{5}$$

$\Rightarrow 5n = 10$
$\Rightarrow n = 2$
Therefore, the number of red balls = 2

RANGE OF PROBABILITY:
EZ RULE #1: Probability in all cases is always between 0 and 1, that is, $0 \le P(E) \le 1$. Probability can never be less than 0 or greater than 1. Probability is never negative.
$\Rightarrow 0 \le P(E) \le 1$

EZ RULE #2: If two or more events constitute all the possible outcomes, then the sum of their Probabilities is 1. If A and B constitutes all the possibilities, then the sum of A and B must be E.
$\Rightarrow P(E) = P(A) + P(B)$

EZ RULE #3: If E is a subset of S, then $P(E) \le P(S)$.

PROBABILITY OF LIKELIHOOD:
More Likely: The more likely it is that an event will occur, the higher its probability will be or the closer it will be to 1.
Less Likely: The less likely it is that an event will occur, the lower its probability will be or the closer it will be to 0.

USE OF PROBABILITY IN RANDOM SAMPLING:

Probability can also be used in random sampling: A probability determined by random sampling of a group of items is assumed to apply to other items in that group and in other similar groups as well.

Example #1: A random sampling of 100 items manufactured in a factory shows that 10 items are defective. Based on this random sampling, how many items of the total production lot of 50,000 can be expected to be defective?

Solution: Probability of an item being defective = $P(d) \Rightarrow 10 \div 100 = 0.10 = 10\%$
Total defective items in the production lot of 50,000 $\Rightarrow$ 10% of 50,000 = 5,000

Example #2: Find the probability of choosing an even number at random from the set:
{8, 25, 11, 17, 15, 19, 27, 23, 21, 2}

Solution: Since there are 10 numbers in the set and 2 of them are even, the probability of randomly choosing an even number is (2 out of 10) $\Rightarrow \dfrac{2}{10} = \dfrac{1}{5}$

Example #3: According to John, the probability that a certain traffic light will be green when he gets to it is 0.25. What is his best prediction of the number of times the light will be green for the next 20 times he gets to it?

Solution: A probability of 0.25 means that a green light is expected 25 out of every 100 times, or ¼th of the time.
$\Rightarrow$ Probability of 0.25 = ¼
$\Rightarrow$ ¼ × 20 = 5
Therefore, the light would probably be green 5 times out of the next 20 times he gets to it.

Example #4: A jar contains 20 balls. These balls are labeled 1 through 20. What is the probability that a ball randomly chosen from the jar has a number on it which is divisible by 5?

Solution: Total No. of balls $\Rightarrow$ 20
There are only 4 balls that has a number which is divisible by 5 $\Rightarrow$ 5, 10, 15, & 20
No. of balls that are divisible by five $\Rightarrow$ 4
Probability of picking a ball that is divisible by five $\Rightarrow \dfrac{4}{20} = \dfrac{1}{5}$

3.2: DIFFERENT TYPES OF PROBABILITIES:

TYPE #1: PROBABILITY OF AN EVENT THAT WILL NOT OCCUR:

EZ RULE: Let E be the subset of S, and $P(E)$ be the probability that it will occur; and let E' be the compliment of E, the set containing all the elements of S that are not in E, and $P(E')$ be the probability that it will not occur. Then, The Probability of an event E that it will not occur is given by the following:
Probability that event will not happen $\Rightarrow$ 1 – Probability that event will happen
$\Rightarrow P(E') = 1 - P(E)$
In other words, to calculate the probability of an event E that will not occur, just subtract the probability of the event that it will occur from 1.
Note: E" is the set of outcomes that are not the outcomes in event $E \Rightarrow E \neq E$'

For Example: If there are 5 balls in a jar each of a different color of red, blue, green, yellow and orange, what is the probability that the first ball picked from the jar will NOT be red?

Solution: No. of favorable outcomes $\Rightarrow 1$
Total No. of possible outcomes $\Rightarrow 5$

$P(\text{Red}) \Rightarrow \dfrac{1}{5}$

$P(\text{Not getting Red}) = 1 - P(\text{Red}) \Rightarrow 1 - \dfrac{1}{5} = \dfrac{4}{5}$

EZ TIP: In some cases, it is too tedious to actually solve a probability problem by determining the probability that a certain event will happen. In such cases, an easy tip can help you make the problem easier:
$\Rightarrow$ Instead of finding the probability that an event WILL happen, find the probability that an event WILL NOT happen. Once you know the probability that an event WILL NOT happen, you can subtract this probability from 1 to determine the probability that the event WILL happen:
Probability that event will happen $\Rightarrow$ 1 – Probability that event will not happen
$P(E) \Rightarrow 1 - P(E')$
Note: Sometimes it is easier to calculate the probability that an event will not happen than the probability that the event will happen.

For Example:
Solution: What is the probability that, in four throws of a single fair dice, at least one of the throws will be a six?
One way to answer this question is to list all the possible outcomes of the four throws of a dice and then figure out how many of them have at least one six; however this would be too tedious of a task to do.
Alternately, we can calculate the probability that not one of the throws will yield a 6

Probability that on 1 throw, the dice will not yield a six $\Rightarrow \dfrac{5}{6}$

Probability that on all 4 throws, the dice will not yield a six $\Rightarrow \dfrac{5}{6} \times \dfrac{5}{6} \times \dfrac{5}{6} \times \dfrac{5}{6} = \dfrac{625}{1296}$

Probability that at least one of the throws will be a six $\Rightarrow$ 1 – Probability that on all 4 throws the dice will not yield a six

Probability that at least one of the throws will be a six $\Rightarrow 1 - \dfrac{625}{1296} = \dfrac{671}{1296}$

Note: The probability that at least one of the throws will be a 6 includes every outcome, except when four consecutive non-sixes are rolled.

EZ NOTE: The above two equations also give us the following equation:
Probability that event will happen + Probability that event will not happen = 1
$\Rightarrow P(E) + P(E') = 1$

TYPE #2: GREATEST PROBABILITY IS 1: PROBABILITY OF AN EVENT THAT IS CERTAIN TO OCCUR:

EZ RULE: Let E be a subset of S, and let $P(E)$ be the probability that it will occur.
Then, The Probability of an event E that is certain to occur is 1.

$\Rightarrow P(E) = 1$ or 100%
In other words, if $P(E) = 1$, it is certain that E must occur, and $E = S$, all the elements in S are also in E.

For Example: If there are 5 balls in a jar, each of which is of color red, what is the probability that the first ball picked from the jar will be red?

Solution: No. of favorable outcomes $\Rightarrow 5$
Total No. of possible outcomes $\Rightarrow 5$

$P(\text{Red}) \Rightarrow \dfrac{5}{5} = 1$

TYPE #3: PROBABILITY OF AN EVENT THAT IS UNCERTAIN TO OCCUR:

EZ RULE: Let E be a nonempty and non-equal subset of S, and let $P(E)$ be the probability that it is possible but uncertain that it will occur.
Then, the Probability of an event E that is possible but uncertain to occur is between 0 and 1, exclusive:
$\Rightarrow 0 < P(E) < 1$

TYPE #4: LOWEST PROBABILITY IS 0: PROBABILITY OF AN EVENT THAT IS IMPOSSIBLE TO OCCUR:

EZ RULE: Let E be a subset of S, and let $P(E)$ be the probability that it will occur.
Then, the Probability of an event E that is impossible to occur is 0.
$\Rightarrow P(E) = 0$ or 0%
In other words, if $P(E) = 0$, it is impossible that "E" can occur, it's an empty/null set.

For Example: If there are 5 balls in a jar each of a different color of red, blue, green, yellow and orange, what is the probability that the first ball picked from the jar will be purple?

Solution: No. of favorable outcomes $\Rightarrow 0$
Total No. of possible outcomes $\Rightarrow 5$

$P(\text{Purple}) \Rightarrow \dfrac{0}{5} = 0$

"AND" & "OR" PROBABILITIES:

"AND" PROBABILITY: PROBABILITY THAT ONE EVENT WILL OCCUR "AND" THAT ANOTHER EVENT WILL ALSO OCCUR:

EZ RULE: If an experiment is done two (or more) times, then the probability that first event will occur, and then a second event will also occur, is the product of all the individual probabilities
$\Rightarrow P(A \text{ and } B) = P(A) \times P(B)$
$\Rightarrow P(T) = P(1) \times P(2) \times P(3) \times P(4).......$
First: Figure out the probability of each individual event.
Then: Multiply the individual probabilities together.

"OR" PROBABILITY: PROBABILITY THAT ONE EVENT WILL OCCUR "OR" THAT ANOTHER EVENT WILL OCCUR:

EZ RULE: If an experiment is done two (or more times), then the probability that the first event will occur, or the second event will occur, is the sum of all the individual probabilities.
$\Rightarrow P(A \text{ or } B) = P(A) + P(B)$

EZ TIP: Another way to handle such problems is to make a list of all the possible outcomes. However, if you choose to list the outcomes, you should abbreviate them.

DIFFERENT BETWEEN "AND" & "OR" PROBABILITIES:
Probabilities involving "and" & "or" are often confused by even some of the expert students. The following explanation will clear the concept in your mind without any confusion.

"AND" PROBABILITY: When two events have to occur together, an "and" is used.
Statement A1:   I will be happy if I see a flying bird and a running tiger around the town center.

⇒ In the above statement, the "and" indicates that both events, "flying bird" and "running tiger" must occur simultaneously in order to be happy.

⇒ In this case, your chances of seeing a flying bird may be relatively higher than seeing a running tiger around the town center; however, when you combine both events, where you want to see a flying bird and a running tiger, your chances of being happy becomes slimmer.

Statement A2:   I will win a million dollars if both, horse A and horse B wins the race.

⇒ In the above statement, the "and" indicates that both, "horse A" and "horse B" must win the race in order to win a million dollars.

⇒ In this case, the odds of horse A to win the race may be one thing and odd of horse B to win the race may be another; however, when you combine both events, where you want both horses to win the race, your odds of winning a million dollar becomes slimmer.

Formula: $P(A \text{ and } B) = P(A) \times P(B)$

Odds: Probability of A and B < Individual Probability of A or B

⇒ $P(A \text{ and } B) =$ Lower than $P(A)$ or $P(B)$

EZ HINT: Odds of something to occur are slimmer with fewer options

⇒ Multiplying probabilities that are less than 1 always result is a smaller probability than the individual probabilities.

"OR" PROBABILITY: When two events do no necessarily have to occur together, an "or" is used.

Statement B1:   I will be happy if I see a flying bird or a running tiger around the town center.

⇒ In the above statement, the "or" indicates that both events, "flying bird" and "running tiger" do not necessarily have to occur simultaneously in order to be happy.

⇒ In this case, your chances of seeing a flying bird may be relatively higher than seeing a running tiger around the town center; however, when you want either one of the events to occur, where you want to see a flying bird or a running tiger, your chances of being happy becomes better.

Statement B2:   I will win a million dollars if either, horse A or horse B wins the race.

⇒ In the above statement, the "or" indicates that both, "horse A" and "horse B" do not necessary have to win the race in order to win a million dollars.

⇒ In this case, the odds of horse A to win the race may be one thing and odds of horse B to win the race may be another; however, when you want either one of the events to occur, where you want horse A to win the race or horse B to win the race, your odds of winning a million dollar becomes better.

Formula: $P(A \text{ or } B) = P(A) + P(B)$

Odds: Probability of A or B > Individual Probability of A or B

⇒ $P(A \text{ or } B) =$ Higher than $P(A)$ or $P(B)$

EZ HINT: Odds of something to occur are better with more options

⇒ Adding probabilities that are less than 1 always result is a greater probability than the individual probabilities.

⇒ Multiplying probabilities that are less than 1 always result is a smaller probability than the individual probabilities.

3.3: MULTIPLE-EVENT PROBABILITY:

The odds of multiple events are usually much smaller than single events. To figure out the probability of something happening over a series of events is actually not that difficult. Some of the probability questions involve finding the probability of a certain outcome after multiple events, such a coin being tossed several times, picking a card from a deck of cards, etc.

Probability of multiple events or a series of events, usually involve multiplication or addition. You must either multiply or add the probabilities of each of the individual events. The key to successfully solve such probability problems is to understand when you must multiply and when you must add.

These types of probability questions come in two forms: those in which each individual event must occur a certain way, and those In which individual events can have different outcomes.

3.3.1: INDIVIDUAL EVENTS HAVE SAME NO. OF POSSIBLE OUTCOMES:

In this scenario of a multiple-event probability, each individual event has the same number of total possible outcomes. In other words, the number of possible outcomes remain the same for any number of individual events.

INDEPENDENT AND DEPENDENT EVENTS:

You may be asked to find the probability that two (or more) events will occur. To answer such a question, you need to understand the difference between independent and dependent events.

Independent Events: Two events are independent events if and only if the probability of one event is not influenced by whether the other event has or has not occurred. In other words, if the probability of one event does not change after the other has occurred, then the two events are independent events. For instance, event B is independent of event A if and only if the probability of event B is not influenced by whether A has or has not occurred. If the probability of B changes after A has occurred, then A and B are dependant events.
Examples of independent events: Coin tosses, since they cannot affect each other's probabilities; the probability of each toss is independent of a previous toss and will always be ½. Throwing a dice, the probability of each throw is independent of any other throw and will always be 1/6. Separate drawings from a deck of cards are independent events if you put the cards back.

Dependant Events: Two events are dependent events if and only if the probability of one event is influenced by whether the other event has or has not occurred. In other words, if the probability of one event does changes after the other has occurred, then the two events are dependant events. For instance, event B is dependent of event A if and only if the probability of event B is influenced by whether A has or has not occurred. If the probability of B does not change after A has occurred, then A and B are independent events.
Examples of dependant events: Drawing a card form a deck of cards but not returning it; the probability of every subsequent event is affected by the prior events. By drawing a card and not returning the card, you've decreased the number of cards in the deck by 1, and you've decreased the number of whatever kind of card you drew. For instance, if you draw an ace of spades, there are 1 fewer aces and 1 fewer spades.

3.3.1.1: INDEPENDENT EVENTS:

WHEN THE TOTAL NUMBER OF POSSIBLE OUTCOMES FOR EACH SUBSEQUENT EVENT REMAINS SAME:

Two events are said to be independent events if the occurrence or nonoccurrence of either one in no way affects the occurrence of the other, i.e., outcome of either event has no effect on the other. In other words, neither event affects the probability of the other events.
For instance, flipping a fair coin – no matter how many times we flip a coin, it will always have two possible outcomes – heads or tails. For instance, rolling a fair six-sided dice – no matter how many times we roll a dice, it will always have six possible outcomes – number 1 through 6.
For example, if we toss a nickel, it has a probability ½ of landing heads. If we then toss a dime, it has probability ½ of landing heads. So, neither event affects the probability of the other.

EZ RULE #1: FOR INDEPENDENT EVENTS;

> If event A and event B are independent events; then to determine the probability that event A and event B will BOTH occur together: MULTIPLY the probabilities of two individual events together.

⇒ If events A and B are independent events, then the set of outcomes in both A and B:
$P (A \cap B) = P(A \text{ and } B) \Rightarrow P(A) \times P(B)$
For example, in the previous situation, the odds of the nickel landing heads and the dime also landing heads is ½ × ½ = ¼.

Example #1:   If a fair coin is flipped 4 times, what is the probability that the coin will land as heads each time it's flipped?

Solution: We are asked to find the probability that the coin will land as heads on all 4 flips.
No. of favorable outcomes   ⇒ 1
Total No. of possible outcomes   ⇒ 2

$P(\text{Heads})$ $\Rightarrow \dfrac{1}{2}$

$P(\text{Heads each time for 4 times})$ $\Rightarrow \dfrac{1}{2} \times \dfrac{1}{2} \times \dfrac{1}{2} \times \dfrac{1}{2} = \dfrac{1}{16}$

Note: What you get on the first flip of the coin is independent of what you get, on the second, or any subsequent flips.

Example #2:   If a fair six-sided dice is rolled 2 times, what is the probability that the dice will land with the "5" side facing up each time it's rolled?

Solution: We are asked to find the probability that the dice will land with the "5" side up on both rolls.
No. of favorable outcomes   ⇒ 1
Total No. of possible outcomes   ⇒ 6

$P(\text{side "5"})$ $\Rightarrow \dfrac{1}{6}$

$P(\text{side "5" each time for 2 times})$ $\Rightarrow \dfrac{1}{6} \times \dfrac{1}{6} = \dfrac{1}{36}$

Note: What you get on the first roll of the dice is independent of what you get, on the second, or any subsequent rolls.

Example #3:   If a fair coin is flipped and a fair six-sided dice is rolled, what is the probability of getting a head on the coin and the number "1" on the dice?

Solution: We are asked to find the probability of getting a head on the coin and the number "1" on the dice.
For Coin: For Dice:
⇒ No. of favorable outcomes = 1   ⇒ No. of favorable outcomes = 1
⇒ Total No. of possible outcomes = 2   ⇒ Total No. of possible outcomes = 6
⇒ Probability of getting a head = 1 out of 2   ⇒ Probability of getting the number "1" = 1 out of 6

⇒ $P(H) = \dfrac{1}{2}$ ⇒ $P(\text{"1"}) = \dfrac{1}{6}$

Probability of getting a head on the coin AND the number "1" on the dice:

→ $P(H) \text{ and } P(\text{"1"}) = \dfrac{1}{2} \times \dfrac{1}{6} = \dfrac{1}{12}$

Note: What you get on the coin is completely independent of what you get on the dice.

Example #4:   Someone draws a card at random out of a deck, replaces it, and then draws another card at random. What is the probability that the first card is an ace of hearts and the second card is a heart (any heart)?

Solution: For Ace   For Hearts
⇒ No. of favorable outcomes = 1   ⇒ No. of favorable outcomes = 13
⇒ Total No. of possible outcomes = 52   ⇒ Total No. of possible outcomes = 52
⇒ Probability of getting an ace in the first draw Probability of getting a hearts in the second draw

⇒ 1 out of 52 $\Rightarrow \dfrac{1}{52}$ ⇒ 13 out of 52 $\Rightarrow \dfrac{13}{52} = \dfrac{1}{4}$

Probability of getting an ace in the first draw AND a hearts in the second draw

⇒ $P(\text{Ace}) + P(\text{Hearts}) \Rightarrow \dfrac{1}{52} \times \dfrac{1}{4} = \dfrac{1}{208}$

EZ RULE #2: FOR INDEPENDENT AND MUTUALLY EXCLUSIVE EVENTS:

If event A and event B are independent events and that, they are mutually exclusive, then, to determine the probability that event A or event B will occur: ADD the two probabilities together.

$\Rightarrow$ If events A and B are independent and mutually exclusive events, then:

"A or B" is the set of outcomes in A or B or both, that is, $P(A \text{ or } B) = P(A \cup B) \Rightarrow P(A) + P(B)$

Mutually Exclusive Events: Two events are said to be mutually exclusive if the occurrence of either one rules out the occurrence of the other, that is, the two events, A and B, cannot both occur simultaneously in one run of the experiment. In other words, if events A and B are mutually exclusive, then the event, "A and B" is impossible, i.e., the intersection of the two sets is empty, $A \cap B$ has no outcome $\Rightarrow P(A \text{ and } B) = A \cap B = 0$. They are disjoint sets.

Example #1:   If a fair coin is flipped once, what is the probability that the coin will land as heads or tails?
Solution: We are asked to find the probability that the coin will land as heads or tails.
No. of favorable outcomes = 1 or 1
Total No. of possible outcomes = 2

The probability that the coin will land as heads is 1 out of 2 $\Rightarrow P(Head) = \dfrac{1}{2}$

The probability that the coin will land as tails is 1 out of 2 $\Rightarrow P(Tail) = \dfrac{1}{2}$

Probability that the coin will land as heads or tails:

$\Rightarrow P(\text{Heads or Tails}) = \dfrac{1}{2} + \dfrac{1}{2} = \dfrac{2}{2} = 1$

Note: What you get on the first flip of the coin is independent and mutually exclusive of what you get, on the second, or any subsequent flips.

Example #2:   If a fair six-sided dice is rolled once, what is the probability that the dice will land with either the "5" side facing up or the "6" side facing up?
Solution: We are asked to find the probability that the dice will land with either the "5" side up or the "6" side up
No. of favorable outcomes = 1 or 1
Total No. of possible outcomes = 6

The probability that the dice will land as 5- side-up is 1 out of 6 $\Rightarrow P(\text{5-side}) = \dfrac{1}{6}$

The probability that the dice will land as 6- side-up is 1 out of 6 $\Rightarrow P(\text{6-side}) = \dfrac{1}{6}$

Probability that the dice will land with either the "5" side facing up or the "6" side facing up:

$\Rightarrow P(\text{5-side or 6-side}) = \dfrac{1}{6} + \dfrac{1}{6} = \dfrac{2}{6} = \dfrac{1}{3}$

Note: What you get on the first roll of the dice is independent and mutually exclusive of what you get, on the second, or any subsequent rolls.

Example #3:   If $P(A) = 0.25$ and $P(B) = 0.60$, and the two events are mutually exclusive, then what is the $P(A \text{ or } B)$?
Solution: $P(A \text{ or } B)$ $\Rightarrow P(A) + P(B)$
$\Rightarrow 0.25 + 0.60 = 0.85$

COMBINATION OF RULE #1 AND RULE #2: COMBINATION OF "AND" & "OR" RULE:

Sometimes it's important to use both the "AND" & "OR" rules in the same problem. This usually happens when the problem involves two independent events, where the first event and the second event, both events must happen; and then two independent and mutually exclusive events, where the first event or the second event, either one must happen.

Example #1:   If a fair coin is flipped twice, what is the probability that the coin will land either as heads both times or tails both tlmes?
Solution: We are asked to find the probability that the coin will land as heads both time or tails both times.
First, find the probability that the coin will land as heads both times, First Time AND Second Time:

Probability that the coin will land as heads the first time $\Rightarrow P(Heads) = \dfrac{1}{2}$

Probability that the coin will land as heads the second time $\Rightarrow P(Heads) = \dfrac{1}{2}$

Probability that the coin will land as heads both times:
$\Rightarrow P(Heads\ Both\ Times) \Rightarrow P(Heads\ First\ Time) \times P(Heads\ Second\ Time)$

$$\Rightarrow \dfrac{1}{2} \times \dfrac{1}{2} = \dfrac{1}{4}$$

Second, find the probability that the coin will land as tails both times, First Time AND Second Time:

Probability that the coin will land as tails the first time $\Rightarrow P(Tails) = \dfrac{1}{2}$

Probability that the coin will land as tails the second time $\Rightarrow P(Tails) = \dfrac{1}{2}$

Probability that the coin will land as tails both times:
$\Rightarrow P(Tails\ Both\ Times) \quad \Rightarrow P(tails\ First\ Time) \times P(Tails\ Second\ Time)$

$$\Rightarrow \dfrac{1}{2} \times \dfrac{1}{2} = \dfrac{1}{4}$$

Finally, find the probability that the coin will land as heads both times OR tails both times:

$\Rightarrow P(Heads\ both\ time\ OR\ Tails\ both\ times) \quad \Rightarrow P(Heads\ Both\ Times) + P(Tails\ Both\ Times)$

$$\Rightarrow \dfrac{1}{4} + \dfrac{1}{4} = \dfrac{2}{4} = \dfrac{1}{2}$$

Note: In the first part of the problem, the two events are independent. In the second part of the problem, the two events are independent and mutually exclusive

EZ RULE #3: FOR INDEPENDENT AND MUTUALLY NON-EXCLUSIVE EVENTS:

If event A and event B are independent events and are mutually non-exclusive, then, to determine the probability that event A or event B will occur: ADD the probabilities that each event occurs, and then SUBTRACT the probability that both events occur together.
Note: In this case, the "or" formula is slightly different and must be adjusted for counting the common elements twice.
$\Rightarrow$ If events A and B are independent events and are not mutually exclusive, then:
The probability that "A or B" occurs is: $\Rightarrow \boldsymbol{P(A\ U\ B) = P(A) + P(B) - P(A \cap B)}$
$$\Rightarrow \boldsymbol{P(A\ or\ B) = P(A) + P(B) - P(A\ and\ B)}$$

In this case, the two events A and B are not mutually exclusive. Finding the probability for event A includes part of the probability of event B, and we must therefore subtract this "overlap" or "over-counted" probability to get the correct answer. The tricky part of this question lies in the fact that when we figure probability, we are really just counting the possible outcomes, and sometimes, we count twice. Therefore, we need to subtract this double counting.

The logic behind this formula is that when $P(A)$ and $P(B)$ are added, the occasions on which A and B both occur are counted twice. To adjust for this double counting, $P(A\ and\ B)$ must be subtracted.

Mutually Non-Exclusive Events: Two events are said to be non-mutually exclusive if the occurrence of either one does not rule out the occurrence of the other, that is, the two events, A and B, can both occur simultaneously in one run of the experiment. In other words, if events A and B are mutually non-exclusive, then the event, "A and B" is possible, i.e., the intersection of the two sets is nonempty, $A \cap B$ has an outcome $\Rightarrow P(A\ and\ B) = A \cap B \neq 0$. They are not disjoint sets.

Example #1: If a fair coin is flipped and a fair six-sided dice is rolled, what is the probability of getting a head on the coin or the number "1" on the dice?

Solution: We are asked to find the probability of getting a head on the coin or the number "1" on the dice. These two events are not mutually exclusive, since both can occur.

For Coin: For Dice:
$\Rightarrow$ No. of favorable outcomes = 1 $\Rightarrow$ No. of favorable outcomes = 1

⇒ Total No. of possible outcomes = 2   ⇒ Total No. of possible outcomes = 6

⇒ Probability of getting a head = 1 out of 2   ⇒ Probability of getting the number "1" = 1 out of 6

⇒ $P(H) = \dfrac{1}{2}$ ⇒ $P("1") = \dfrac{1}{6}$

Probability of getting a head on the coin AND the number "1" on the dice:

⇒ $P(H)$ and $P("1") = P(H \cap "1") = \dfrac{1}{6} \times \dfrac{1}{2} = \dfrac{1}{12}$ (overlap)

Probability of getting a head on the coin OR the number "1" on the dice:

⇒ $P(H)$ or $P("1") = P(H) + P("1") - P(H \text{ and } "1") = \left(\dfrac{1}{6} + \dfrac{1}{2}\right) - \dfrac{1}{12} = \dfrac{7}{12}$

Note: What you get on the coin is completely independent and mutually non-exclusive of what you get on the dice.

Example #2:   What is the probability that a card selected from a deck of cards will be either an ace or a heart?

Solution: We are asked to find the probability of getting an ace or heart. There is a possibility for a card to be both an ace and a heart. Therefore, these two events are not mutually exclusive, since both can occur.

For Aces: For Hearts:

⇒ No. of favorable outcomes = 4   ⇒ No. of favorable outcomes = 13

⇒ Total No. of possible outcomes = 52   ⇒ Total No. of possible outcomes = 52

⇒ Probability of getting an ace = 4 out of 52   ⇒ Probability of getting a heart = 13 out of 52

⇒ $P(Ace) = \dfrac{4}{52}$ ⇒ $P(Heart) = \dfrac{13}{52}$

Probability of getting an ace AND a heart:

⇒ $P(Ace)$ and $P(Heart) = P(H \cap "1") = \dfrac{4}{52} \times \dfrac{13}{52} = \dfrac{52}{52 \times 52} = \dfrac{1}{52}$ (overlap)

Probability of getting an ace or a heart:

Probability (Ace or Heart) ⇒ $P(A \text{ or } B)$ ⇒ $P(A) + P(B) - P(A \cap B)$

$$\Rightarrow \dfrac{4}{52} + \dfrac{13}{52} - \dfrac{1}{52} = \dfrac{16}{52} = \dfrac{4}{13}$$

Note: Since it is possible for a card to be an ace as well as a heart, we counted the "Ace of Hearts" twice when we found the probability of picking an ace and a heart; therefore, we must subtract this over-counting or overlap. Coincidentally, there is only one card in a deck of cards that is both an ace and a heart, and we must subtract this to get the final answer.

Alternately: This problem can also be solved by using simple probability:

No. of Favorable Outcomes   ⇒ 13 Hearts + 3 Aces

                               ⇒ 16

(Note that the 4th Ace, the "Ace of Hearts" is already counted in the Hearts)

Total No. of Outcomes   ⇒ 52

Probability (Ace or Hearts)   ⇒ $\dfrac{16}{52} = \dfrac{4}{13}$

Note, if the above problem would have asked to find the probability of picking an ace or a king from a deck of cards, the events would be mutually exclusive. There are 4 aces and 4 kings in a deck of cards. Moreover, aces and kings are independent, as there are no Aces of Kings of King of Aces. So, in this case, we don't have to worry about over-counting or any overlap and the probability can is straightforward. P = 1/13 + 1/13 = 2/13

Alternately, use simple probability, no of favorable outcome = 8, total = 52, P = 8/52 = 2/13

Example #3:   If $P(A) = 0.25$ and $P(B) = 0.60$, and the two events are mutually non-exclusive, then what is the $P(A \text{ or } B)$?

Solution: $P(A \text{ or } B)$ ⇒ $P(A) + P(B) - P(A \text{ or } B)$

                          ⇒ $0.25 + 0.60 - (0.25 \times 0.60) = 0.85 - 0.15 = 0.70$

EZ TIP: "AND" means multiply the probabilities. "OR" means add the probabilities.

3.3.1.2: DEPENDENT EVENTS:
WHEN THE TOTAL NUMBER OF POSSIBLE OUTCOMES FOR EACH SUBSEQUENT EVENT IS DIFFERENT:
Two events need not always be independent. Two events are said to be dependent events if the outcome of one event affects the probability of another event. The best way is to use logical reasoning to help figure out probabilities involving dependent events.

Don't forget to analyze events by considering whether one event affects subsequent events. The first roll of a dice or flip of a coin has no affect on any subsequent rolls or flips. However, the first pick of a card from a deck of card or a ball from a jar does affect subsequent picks.

For instance, picking a card from a fair deck of cards – with each card we pick, the total possible events for the next event will be 1 less than the one before that.
For example, if we toss a fair coin, the probability that it lands heads is ½ and the probability it lands tails is ½. But these are not independent events – if the coin lands heads, it cannot land tails at the same time or vice versa.

EZ RULE: If A and B are dependent, then the probability of A and B is given by the following formula:
$\Rightarrow P(A \text{ and } B) = P(A) \times P(B|A)$
Where: $P(B|A)$ is the conditional probability of B given A.

EZ CAUTION: Sometimes the outcome of the first event will affect the probability of a subsequent event. So be careful of situations in which the outcome of an event affects the probability of the subsequent events.

Example #1: If 2 red balls are to be picked at random from a jar containing 6 red balls and 6 blue balls, what's the probability that both balls picked will be red balls?

Solution: Let's break the problem in two parts:
First Event in the Series:
Total No. of Possibilities for the First Pick $\Rightarrow$ 12 (there are 12 balls)
Total No. of Red Balls $\Rightarrow$ 6

The probability of picking a Red Ball on the First Pick $\Rightarrow \dfrac{6}{12} = \dfrac{1}{2}$

Note: At this point, you might think that the probability would be exactly the same for the second choice (in which case you would multiply ½ × ½ = ¼, but in fact that's not true. Don't make this mistake! This solution is wrong, because it does not take into account the fact that the first event affects the second event. If a red ball is chosen on the first pick, then the number of balls now in the jar has decreased from 12 to 11. Additionally, the number of red balls now in the jar has decreased from 6 to 5. Therefore, the probability of choosing a red ball on the second pick is different from the probability of red ball on the first pick.
Second Event in the Series:
Total No. of Possibilities for the Second Pick $\Rightarrow$ 11 (1 red ball has already been picked)
Total No. of Red Balls $\Rightarrow$ 5 (1 red ball has already been picked)
So, now only 11 balls, with 5 red balls and 6 blue balls are remaining in the jar.

Probability of picking a Red Ball on the Second Pick $\Rightarrow \dfrac{5}{11}$

Probability that BOTH picks in this series of two picks will be Red Balls:

The probability of picking a Red Ball on Both Picks $\Rightarrow \dfrac{1}{2} \times \dfrac{5}{11} = \dfrac{5}{22}$

Example #2: If two cards are to be picked at random from a deck of card, what's the probability that both cards picked will be Jacks?

Solution: Let's break the problem in two parts:
First Event in the Series:
Total No. of Possibilities for the First Pick $\Rightarrow$ 52 (there are 52 cards in a deck of card)
Total No. of Jacks $\Rightarrow$ 4

The probability of picking a Jack on the First Pick $\Rightarrow \dfrac{4}{52} = \dfrac{1}{13}$

Second Event in the Series:

Total No. of Possibilities for the Second Pick $\Rightarrow$ 51 (1 card has already been picked)
Total No. of Jacks $\Rightarrow$ 3 (1 Jack has already been picked)
So, now only 3 Jacks, with 51 cards are remaining in the deck of cards.

Probability of picking a Jack on the Second Pick $\Rightarrow \dfrac{3}{51} = \dfrac{1}{17}$

Probability that BOTH picks in this series of two picks will be Jacks:

The probability of picking a Jack on Both Picks $\Rightarrow \dfrac{1}{13} \times \dfrac{1}{17} = \dfrac{1}{221}$

3.3.2: INDIVIDUAL EVENTS CAN HAVE DIFFERENT POSSIBLE OUTCOMES:

In this scenario of a multiple-event probability, each individual event has different number of total possible outcomes. In other words, the number of possible outcomes becomes different for each individual event.

EZ STEP-BY-STEP METHOD: Apply the following step(s) to solve multiple-event probability:

STEP 1: Find the total number of possible outcomes by determining the number of possible outcomes for each individual event and multiply these numbers together.

STEP 2: Find the number of desired outcomes by listing out the possibilities.

STEP 3: Finally apply the probability formula: $\dfrac{Number\ of\ Favorable\ Outcomes}{Total\ Number\ of\ Possible\ Outcomes}$

Example #1: If a fair coin is tossed 4 times, what's the probability that at least 3 of the 4 tosses will come up heads?
Solution: Possible Outcomes for Each Toss = 2 possible outcomes (heads or tails)
Possible Outcomes for 4 Tosses = 2 × 2 × 2 × 2 = 16 total possible outcomes
List out all the possibilities where "at least 3 of the 4 tosses" land-up as heads:
1st Possibility $\Rightarrow$ H, H, H, T
2nd Possibility $\Rightarrow$ H, H, T, H
3rd Possibility $\Rightarrow$ H, T, H, H
4th Possibility $\Rightarrow$ T, H, H, H
5th Possibility $\Rightarrow$ H, H, H, H
Total No. of Possible Desired Outcomes = 5
Probability that "at least 3 of the 4 tosses" will land up as heads:
$\Rightarrow \dfrac{Number\ of\ Favorable\ Outcomes}{Total\ Number\ of\ Possible\ Outcomes} = \dfrac{5}{16}$

3.4: COMPLEX PROBABILITY:

Most of the very difficult probability problems contain multiple series of complex events that can be simplified by listing the winning scenarios. Such problems usually involve a combination of both "AND" & "OR" situations.

Example #1: There is a jar full of marbles. The jar has 1 red marble, 2 blue marbles, 3 green marbles, and 4 yellow marbles. Raja picks one marble out of the jar at random. If he picks a green marble, he gets to pick one additional piece of marble and then stop. If he picks any non-green marble, he stops picking immediately. After Raja picks his marble(s), Rani gets to pick a marble from the jar. What is the probability that Rani picks a green marble?

Solution: There are multiple series of complex events. We can simplify the possible events by listing only the "winning" scenarios, or the scenarios that result in the desired outcomes. Next, calculate the probability of each of those "winning" events. Finally, find the probability of each series by multiplying the probability of each independent event since each "winning" scenario is an "AND" situation. Also keep in mind the affect of each pick on the remaining possibilities, as Raja's picks affect the number of green marbles and of the marbles in total left for Rani.

Its' best to tabulate all this information in a simplified table like the one given below:

	Raja's Pick #1	Raja's Pick #2	Rani's Pick	Probability
(i)	Green Marble $P = \dfrac{3}{10}$	Green Marble $P = \dfrac{2}{9}$	Green Marble $P = \dfrac{1}{8}$	$\Rightarrow \dfrac{3}{10} \times \dfrac{2}{9} \times \dfrac{1}{8} = \dfrac{6}{720}$
(ii)	Green Marble $P = \dfrac{3}{10}$	Non-Green Marble $P = \dfrac{7}{0}$	Green Marble $P = \dfrac{2}{0}$	$\Rightarrow \dfrac{3}{10} \times \dfrac{7}{9} \times \dfrac{2}{8} = \dfrac{42}{720}$
(iii)	Non-Green Marble $P = \dfrac{7}{10}$	N/A --	Green Marble $P = \dfrac{3}{9}$	$\Rightarrow \dfrac{7}{10} \times \dfrac{3}{9} = \dfrac{21}{90} = \dfrac{168}{720}$

The probability of either event series (1) OR (2) OR (3) occurrence is the sum of the individual probabilities

$$\Rightarrow \frac{6}{720} + \frac{42}{720} + \frac{168}{720} = \frac{216}{720} = \frac{3}{10}$$

Example #2: The table shows the distribution of a group of 50 college students by gender and class:

	Freshmen	Sophomores	Junior	Senior
Males	5	6	8	2
Females	5	9	9	6

If one student is randomly selected from this group, find the probability that the student chosen is:
(a) a Freshman
(b) not a Sophomore
(c) a Male Junior or a Female Senior
(d) a Female Junior or a Male Senior
(e) a Male or a Female Junior
(f) a Female or a Male Senior

Solution:
(a) a Freshman
$\Rightarrow$ Total No of Freshmen ÷ Total No
$\Rightarrow 10 ÷ 50 = 1/5$

(b) not a Sophomore
$\Rightarrow$ Total No of Non-Sophomores ÷ Total No
$\Rightarrow (50 − 15) ÷ 50 = 35/50 = 7/10$

(c) a Male Junior or a Female Senior
$\Rightarrow$ (Total No of Male Junior + Female Senior) ÷ Total No
$\Rightarrow (8 + 6) ÷ 50 = 14/50 = 7/25$

(d) a Female Junior or a Male Senior
$\Rightarrow$ (Total No of Female Junior + Male Senior) ÷ Total No
$\Rightarrow (9 + 2) ÷ 50 = 11/50$

(e) a Male or a Female Junior
$\Rightarrow$ (Total No of Male + Total No of Female Junior) ÷ Total No
$\Rightarrow (21 + 9) ÷ 50 = 30 ÷ 50 = 3/5$

(f) a Female or a Male Senior
$\Rightarrow$ (Total No of Female + Total No Male Senior) ÷ Total No
$\Rightarrow (29 + 2) ÷ 50 = 31/50$

3.5: GEOMETRIC PROBABILITY:

Probability is such a vast topic that it could even involve geometry. Geometric probability questions are those geometry questions that contain a final step in which you're asked to calculate a probability. At that final stage, just use the probability formula. So, some probability problems may involve geometric figures. Therefore, a probability problem might be accompanied by a geometric or some other type of figure that provides a visual display of the possibilities from which you will be asked to calculate a probability.

EZ RULE: If a point is chosen at random in a specific region of a geometrical figure, the probability that the chosen point lies in a particular region is given by:

$$\Rightarrow \frac{Area\ of\ that\ Specific\ Region}{Area\ of\ Whole\ Figure}$$

For Example: In the figure below, the big circle has a radius of 8 and the small circle has a radius of 2. If a point is chosen at random from the large circle, what is the probability that the point chosen will also be in the small circle?

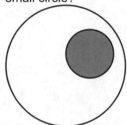

Solution: Area of Small Circle $\Rightarrow \pi r^2 = \pi(2)^2 = 4\pi$
Area of Big Circle $\Rightarrow \pi r^2 = \pi(8)^2 = 64\pi$

$$\frac{Area\ of\ Small\ Circle}{Area\ of\ Big\ Circle} \Rightarrow \frac{4\pi}{64\pi} = \frac{4}{64} = \frac{1}{16}$$

Therefore, if a point is chosen at random from the large circle, the probability that the point chosen will also be in the small circle is 1 to 16 or $\frac{1}{16}$.

3.6: MIXTURE OF PERMUTATION/COMBINATION & PROBABILITY:

Probability is such a vast topic that it could even involve Permutation and/or Combination. So, some probability problems may involve the concept of permutation/combination. The following is one such example:

Example #1: If the probability of snow on any given day in City X is 50 percent, what is the probability that it snows on exactly 5 days in a 7-day period?

Solution: Let's first determine the total number of possible outcomes of snow in City X over the 7-day period. There are two possible outcomes for each day $\Rightarrow$ either it will snow or it will not snow $\Rightarrow$ so the total number of possible outcomes for the entire 7-day period would be $2 \times 2 \times 2 \times 2 \times 2 \times 2 \times 2 = 128$ total possibilities.

Next, let's determine the total number of desired outcomes, that is, when it snows in City X.

$$\text{Combination} \Rightarrow {}_mC_n \Rightarrow \frac{m!}{n!(m-n)!}$$

$$\Rightarrow {}_7C_5 \Rightarrow \frac{7!}{5!(7-5)!} = \frac{7!}{5! \times 2!} = \frac{7 \times 6 \times 5!}{5! \times 2!} = \frac{7 \times 6}{2 \times 1} = \frac{42}{2} = 21$$

Therefore, there are a total of 21 desired outcomes.

Finally, find the probability that it snows on exactly 5 days in a 7-day period in City X:

$$\text{Probability} \Rightarrow \frac{\text{Desired Outcomes (when it snows on exactly 5 out of 7 days)}}{\text{Total Possible Outcomes}} \Rightarrow \frac{21}{128}$$

Example #2: One number is to be chosen randomly from each of the sets below. If a represents the chosen member of Set A and b represents the chosen member of Set B, what is the probability that $\frac{a}{b}$ will be an integer?

Set A: {9, 10, 11, 12}   Set B: {2, 3, 4, 5}

Solution: By the rule of combination, we know there should be a total of $4 \times 4 = 16$ combinations of $\frac{a}{b}$.

First, list all possible combinations:

$\frac{9}{2}$	$\frac{9}{3}$	$\frac{9}{4}$	$\frac{9}{5}$
$\frac{10}{2}$	$\frac{10}{3}$	$\frac{10}{4}$	$\frac{10}{5}$
$\frac{11}{2}$	$\frac{11}{3}$	$\frac{11}{4}$	$\frac{11}{5}$
$\frac{12}{2}$	$\frac{12}{3}$	$\frac{12}{4}$	$\frac{12}{5}$

Out of these 16 combinations, count the number of those combinations that result in integers:

$$\frac{9}{3} \qquad \frac{10}{2} \qquad \frac{10}{5} \qquad \frac{12}{2} \qquad \frac{12}{3} \qquad \frac{12}{4}$$

Therefore, there are 6 combinations that yield integers.

$$\text{Probability of } \frac{a}{b} \text{ to be an integer} = \frac{\text{Total Combinations}}{\text{Desired Combinations}} = \frac{6}{16} = \frac{3}{8}$$

PRACTICE EXERCISE – QUESTIONS AND ANSWERS WITH EXPLANATIONS: PROBABILITY:

Question #1: A random sampling of 100 items manufactured in a factory shows that 5 items are defective. Based on this random sampling, how many items of the total production lot of 25,000 can be expected to be defective?

Solution: Probability of an item being defective = $P(d)$ $\Rightarrow 5 \div 100 = 0.05 = 5\%$
Total defective items in the production lot of 25,000 $\Rightarrow$ 5% of 25,000 = 1,250

Question #2: Find the probability of choosing an even number at random from the set:
{8, 25, 11, 17, 15, 19, 27, 2}

Solution: Since there are 8 numbers in the set and 2 of them are even, the probability of randomly choosing an even number is (2 out of 8) $\dfrac{2}{8} = \dfrac{1}{4}$

Question #3: According to John, the probability that a certain traffic light will be green when he gets to it is 0.20. What is his best prediction of the number of times the light will be green for the next 10 times he gets to it?

Solution: A probability of 0.20 means that he would expect a green light 20 out of every 100 times, or 1/5th of the time.

$\Rightarrow$ Probability of 0.20 = $\dfrac{1}{5}$ $\Rightarrow \dfrac{1}{5} \times 10 = 2$

Therefore, the light would probably be green 2 times out of the next 10 times he gets to it.

Question #4: A jar contains 60 balls. These balls are labeled 1 through 60. What is the probability that a ball randomly chosen from the jar has a number on it that is divisible by 7?

Solution: Total No. of balls $\Rightarrow$ 60
There are only 8 balls that has a number which is divisible by 7 $\Rightarrow$ 7, 14, 21, 28, 35, 42, 49, & 56
No. of balls that are divisible by seven $\Rightarrow$ 8

Probability of picking a ball that is divisible by seven $\Rightarrow \dfrac{8}{60} = \dfrac{2}{15}$

Question #5: If there are 12 balls in a jar, two each of color red, blue, green, yellow, purple, and white, what is the probability that the first ball picked from the jar will be red?

Solution: No. of favorable outcomes $\Rightarrow$ 2   Total No. of possible outcomes $\Rightarrow$ 12

$P(\text{Red}) \Rightarrow \dfrac{2}{12} = \dfrac{1}{6}$

Question #6: If there are 12 balls in a jar, two each of color red, blue, green, yellow, purple, and white, what is the probability that the first ball picked from the jar will NOT be red?

Solution: No. of favorable outcomes $\Rightarrow$ 2   Total No. of possible outcomes $\Rightarrow$ 12

$P(\text{getting Red})$ $\Rightarrow \dfrac{2}{12} = \dfrac{1}{6}$

$P(\text{not getting Red})$ $\Rightarrow 1 - \dfrac{1}{6} = \dfrac{5}{6}$

Question #7: If there are 10 balls in a jar, each of which is of color red, what is the probability that the first ball picked from the jar will be red?

Solution: No. of favorable outcomes $\Rightarrow$ 10   Total No. of possible outcomes $\Rightarrow$ 10

$P(\text{Red}) \Rightarrow \dfrac{10}{10} = 1$

Question #8: If there are 10 balls in a jar, two each of color red, blue, green, yellow, and white, what is the probability that the first ball picked from the jar will be purple?

Solution: No. of favorable outcomes $\Rightarrow$ 0   Total No. of possible outcomes $\Rightarrow$ 10

$$P(\text{Purple}) \Rightarrow \frac{0}{10} = 0$$

Question #9:   A fair six-sided dice with faces numbered one through six is rolled three times. What is the probability that the face with the number 6 on it will NOT be facing upward on all three rolls?

Solution: The probability that the 1st roll will yield the number 6 $\Rightarrow \dfrac{1}{6}$

The probability that the 2nd roll will yield the number 6 $\Rightarrow \dfrac{1}{6}$

The probability that the 3rd roll will yield the number 6 $\Rightarrow \dfrac{1}{6}$

The probability that all 3 rolls will yield the number 6 $\Rightarrow \dfrac{1}{6} \times \dfrac{1}{6} \times \dfrac{1}{6} = \dfrac{1}{216}$

The probability that all 3 rolls will NOT yield the number 6:

$\Rightarrow$ 1 – The probability that all 3 rolls will yield the number 6 $\Rightarrow 1 - \dfrac{1}{216} = \dfrac{216}{216} - \dfrac{1}{216} = \dfrac{215}{216}$

Question #10:   Hector and Victoria are two of the nominees at an award ceremony. If there are a total of 9 men and 9 women nominees at the ceremony, and only one man and one woman are to be chosen as the recipients of the award, what is the probability that Hector and Victoria will NOT be chosen as the recipients of the award?

Solution: The probability that Hector will be chosen as the recipient of the award $\Rightarrow \dfrac{1}{9}$

The probability that Victoria will be chosen as the recipient of the award $\Rightarrow \dfrac{1}{9}$

The probability that Hector & Victoria will both be chosen $\Rightarrow \dfrac{1}{9} \times \dfrac{1}{9} = \dfrac{1}{81}$

The probability that Hector & Victoria will both NOT be chosen $\Rightarrow 1 - \dfrac{1}{81} = \dfrac{81}{81} - \dfrac{1}{81} = \dfrac{80}{81}$

Question #11:   If a fair coin is flipped 6 times, what is the probability that the coin will land as head each time it's flipped?

Solution: No. of favorable outcome $\Rightarrow$ 1   Total No. of possible outcomes $\Rightarrow$ 2

$P(\text{Head}) \Rightarrow \dfrac{1}{2}$ $P(\text{Tail})\ \Rightarrow \dfrac{1}{2}$

$P(\text{Head each time for 6 times}) \Rightarrow \dfrac{1}{2} \times \dfrac{1}{2} \times \dfrac{1}{2} \times \dfrac{1}{2} \times \dfrac{1}{2} \times \dfrac{1}{2} = \dfrac{1}{64}$

Question #12:   If a fair dice is thrown 4 times, what is the probability that the number 6 will face upwards each time?

Solution: No. of favorable outcomes $\Rightarrow$ 1   Total No. of possible outcomes $\Rightarrow$ 6

$P(\text{number 6}) \Rightarrow \dfrac{1}{6} \times \dfrac{1}{6} \times \dfrac{1}{6} \times \dfrac{1}{6} = \dfrac{1}{1296}$

Question #13:   If there are 12 balls in a jar, two each of color red, blue, green, yellow, purple, and white, what is the probability that the first ball picked from the jar will be red or blue?

Solution: No. of favorable outcomes $\Rightarrow$ 2 and 2   Total No. of possible outcomes $\Rightarrow$ 12

$P(\text{Red}) \Rightarrow \dfrac{2}{12} = \dfrac{1}{6}$ $P(\text{Blue}) \Rightarrow \dfrac{2}{12} = \dfrac{1}{6}$

$P(\text{Red or Blue})\ \Rightarrow \dfrac{1}{6} + \dfrac{1}{6} = \dfrac{2}{6} = \dfrac{1}{3}$

Question #14: If a standard deck of 52 playing cards is spread face down on a table, what is the probability of picking a heart or spade?

Solution: $P(\text{Heart}) \Rightarrow \dfrac{13}{52} = \dfrac{1}{4}$ $\qquad\qquad\qquad\qquad$ $P(\text{Spade}) \Rightarrow \dfrac{13}{52} = \dfrac{1}{4}$

$P(\text{Heart or Spade}) \quad \Rightarrow \dfrac{1}{4} + \dfrac{1}{4} = \dfrac{2}{4} = \dfrac{1}{2}$

Example #15: If a standard deck of 52 playing cards is spread face down on a table, what is the probability of picking a king or a queen?

Solution: $P(\text{King}) \Rightarrow \dfrac{4}{52} = \dfrac{1}{13}$ $\qquad\qquad\qquad\qquad$ $P(\text{Queen}) \Rightarrow \dfrac{4}{52} = \dfrac{1}{13}$

$P(\text{King or Queen}) \quad \Rightarrow \dfrac{1}{13} + \dfrac{1}{13} = \dfrac{2}{13}$

Example #16: If a standard deck of 52 playing cards is spread face down on a table, what is the probability of picking a face card (king, queen, or jack)?

Solution: $P(\text{King}) \Rightarrow \dfrac{4}{52} = \dfrac{1}{13}$ $\qquad$ $P(\text{Queen}) \Rightarrow \dfrac{4}{52} = \dfrac{1}{13}$ $\qquad$ $P(\text{Jack}) \Rightarrow \dfrac{4}{52} = \dfrac{1}{13}$

$P(\text{King, Queen, or Jack}) \Rightarrow \dfrac{1}{13} + \dfrac{1}{13} + \dfrac{1}{13} = \dfrac{3}{13}$

Alternately, we can also add all the favorable outcomes and divide that by total outcomes:

$P(\text{King, Queen, or Jack}) \Rightarrow \dfrac{12}{52} = \dfrac{3}{13}$

Question #17:
Solution: If a fair dice is thrown, what is the probability that the number facing upwards will be a 6 or a 5?

No. of favorable outcomes $\Rightarrow$ 1 and 1 $\qquad$ Total No. of possible outcomes $\Rightarrow$ 6

$P(\text{Number 5}) \Rightarrow \dfrac{1}{6}$ $\qquad\qquad\qquad\qquad$ $P(\text{Number 6}) \Rightarrow \dfrac{1}{6}$

$P(\text{Number 5 or Number 6}) \Rightarrow \dfrac{1}{6} + \dfrac{1}{6} = \dfrac{2}{6} = \dfrac{1}{3}$

Question #18: If there are 10 different flavors of candy in a packet, what is the probability that the first candy picked from the packet will be orange or lemon flavor?

Solution: No. of favorable outcomes $\Rightarrow$ 1 and 1 $\qquad$ Total No. of possible outcomes $\Rightarrow$ 10

$P(\text{Orange}) \qquad\qquad \Rightarrow \dfrac{1}{10}$ $\qquad\qquad\qquad$ $P(\text{Lemon}) \qquad\qquad \Rightarrow \dfrac{1}{10}$

$P(\text{Orange or Lemon}) \Rightarrow \dfrac{1}{10} + \dfrac{1}{10} = \dfrac{2}{10} = \dfrac{1}{5}$

Question #19: If 2 red balls are to be chosen at random from a jar with 11 red balls and 11 blue balls, what's the probability that both balls chosen will be red balls?

Solution: First event in the series:

Total No. of possibilities for the first pick $\qquad\qquad \Rightarrow$ 22 (there are 11 red and 11 blue balls in the jar)
Total No. of Red Balls $\qquad\qquad\qquad\qquad\qquad \Rightarrow$ 11

Probability of picking a red ball on the First Pick $\qquad \Rightarrow \dfrac{11}{22} = \dfrac{1}{2}$

Second event in the series:
Total No. of possibilities for the second pick $\qquad \Rightarrow$ 21 (1 ball has already been picked)
Total No. of Red Balls $\qquad\qquad\qquad\qquad\qquad \Rightarrow$ 10 (1 red ball has already been picked)
So, now only 21 balls, with 10 red balls and 11 blue balls are remaining in the jar.

Probability of picking a red ball on the Second Pick $\Rightarrow \dfrac{10}{21}$

Probability of picking a Red Ball on Both Picks $\Rightarrow \frac{1}{2} \times \frac{10}{21} = \frac{5}{21}$

Question #20: If two cards are to be picked at random from a deck of cards, what's the probability that both cards picked will be Hearts?

Solution: First event in the series:

Total No. of possibilities for the first pick $\Rightarrow 52$ (there are 52 cards in a deck of cards)

Total No. of Hearts $\Rightarrow 13$

Probability of picking a Heart on the First Pick $\Rightarrow \frac{13}{52} = \frac{1}{4}$

Second event in the series:

Total No. of possibilities for the second pick $\Rightarrow 51$ (1 card has already been picked)

Total No. of Hearts $\Rightarrow 12$ (1 Heart has already been picked)

So, now only 12 Hearts, with 51 cards are remaining in the deck of cards.

Probability of picking a Heart on the Second Pick $\Rightarrow \frac{12}{51} = \frac{4}{17}$

Probability of picking a Heart on Both Picks $\Rightarrow \frac{1}{4} \times \frac{4}{17} = \frac{1}{17}$

Question #21: There are 10 job applicants for a position, 5 men and 5 women. If two of the applicants are selected at random, what is the probability that both will be women?

Solution: First Event in the Series:

Total No. of Possibilities for the First Selection $\Rightarrow 10$ (there are 10 applicants)

Total No. of women $\Rightarrow 5$

The probability that the first person chosen will be a Woman is: $\Rightarrow P(w) = \frac{5}{10} = \frac{1}{2}$

Second Event in the Series:

Total No. of Possibilities for the Second Selection $\Rightarrow 9$ (1 applicant has already been selected)

Total No. of Women $\Rightarrow 4$ (1 woman has already been selected)

Probability that the second person chosen will be a Woman is: $\Rightarrow P(w) = \frac{4}{9}$

Probability that BOTH choices in this series of two choices will be women:

The probability that they both will be Women $\Rightarrow \frac{1}{2} \times \frac{4}{9} = \frac{4}{18} = \frac{2}{9}$

Question #22: If 2 applicants are to be selected at random from a database with 10 women and 90 men, what's the probability that both applicants selected will be women?

Solution: First Event in the Series:

Total No. of Possibilities for the First Selection $\Rightarrow 100$ (there are 100 applicants)

Total No. of women $\Rightarrow 10$

The probability that the first person chosen will be a Woman is: $\Rightarrow P(w) = \frac{10}{100} = \frac{1}{10}$

Second Event in the Series:

Total No. of Possibilities for the Second Selection $\Rightarrow 99$ (1 applicant has already been selected)

Total No. of Women $\Rightarrow 9$ (1 woman has already been selected)

Probability that the second person chosen will be a Woman is: $\Rightarrow P(w) = \frac{9}{99} = \frac{1}{11}$

Probability that BOTH choices in this series of two choices will be women:

The probability that they both will be Women $\Rightarrow \frac{1}{10} \times \frac{1}{11} = \frac{1}{110}$

Question #23: If $P(A) = 0.15$ and $P(B) = 0.60$, and the two events are mutually exclusive, then what is the $P(A \text{ or } B)$?

Solution: $P(A \text{ or } B) \Rightarrow P(A) + P(B)$

$\Rightarrow 0.15 + 0.60 = 0.75$

Question #24: If $P(A) = 0.15$ and $P(B) = 0.60$, and the two events are mutually non-exclusive, then what is the $P(A$ or $B)$?

Solution: $P(A$ or $B)$ $\Rightarrow P(A) + P(B) - P(A$ or $B)$

$\Rightarrow 0.15 + 0.60 - (0.15 \times 0.60) = 0.75 - 0.09 = 0.66$

Question #25: If a fair coin is tossed 6 times, what's the probability that at least 5 of the 6 tosses will come up heads?

Solution: Possible Outcomes for Each Toss $\Rightarrow$ 2 possible outcomes (heads or tails)

Possible Outcomes for 6 Tosses $\Rightarrow 2 \times 2 \times 2 \times 2 \times 2 \times 2 = 64$ possible outcomes

List out all the possibilities where "at least 5 of the 6 tosses" lands up as heads:

1st Possibility $\Rightarrow$ H, H, H, H, H, T

2nd Possibility $\Rightarrow$ H, H, H, H, T, H

3rd Possibility $\Rightarrow$ H, H, H, T, H, H

4th Possibility $\Rightarrow$ H, H, T, H, H, H

5th Possibility $\Rightarrow$ H, T, H, H, H, H

6th Possibility $\Rightarrow$ T, H, H, H, H, H

7th Possibility $\Rightarrow$ H, H, H, H, H, H

Total No. of Possible Desired Outcomes = 7

Probability that "at least 5 of the 6 tosses" will land up as heads:

$$\Rightarrow \frac{Number\ of\ Favorable\ Outcomes}{Total\ Number\ of\ Possible\ Outcomes} = \frac{7}{64}$$

Question #26: There is a jar full of marbles. The jar has 1 red marble, 2 blue marbles, 4 green marbles, and 8 yellow marbles. Raja picks one marble out of the jar at random. If he picks a green marble, he gets to pick one additional piece of marble and then stop. If he picks any non-green marble, he stops picking immediately. After Raja picks his marble(s), Rani gets to pick a marble from the jar. What is the probability that Rani picks a green marble?

Solution: There are multiple series of complex events. We can simplify the possible events by listing only the "winning" scenarios, or the scenarios that result in the desired outcomes. Next, calculate the probability of each of those "winning" events. Finally, find the probability of each series by multiplying the probability of each independent event since each "winning" scenario is an "AND" situation. Also keep in mind the affect of each pick on the remaining possibilities, as Raja's picks affect the number of green marbles and of the marbles in total left for Rani.

Its' best to tabulate all this information in a simplified table like the one given below:

	Raja's Pick #1	Raja's Pick #2	Rani's Pick	Probability
(i)	Green Marble	Green Marble	Green Marble	
	$P = \dfrac{4}{15}$	$P = \dfrac{3}{14}$	$P = \dfrac{2}{13}$	$\Rightarrow \dfrac{4}{15} \times \dfrac{3}{14} \times \dfrac{2}{13} = \dfrac{24}{2730}$
(ii)	Green Marble	Non-Green Marble	Green Marble	
	$P = \dfrac{4}{15}$	$P = \dfrac{11}{14}$	$P = \dfrac{3}{13}$	$\Rightarrow \dfrac{4}{15} \times \dfrac{11}{14} \times \dfrac{3}{13} = \dfrac{132}{2730}$
(iii)	Non-Green Marble	N/A	Green Marble	
	$P = \dfrac{11}{15}$	--	$P = \dfrac{4}{14}$	$\Rightarrow \dfrac{11}{15} \times \dfrac{4}{14} = \dfrac{44}{210} \times \dfrac{13}{13} = \dfrac{572}{2730}$

The probability of either event series (1) OR (2) OR (3) occurrence is the sum of the individual probabilities.

$$\Rightarrow \frac{24}{2730} + \frac{132}{2730} + \frac{572}{2730} = \frac{728}{2730} = \frac{4}{15}$$

Question #27: In the figure below, if n is an integer, what is the probability that n is an even integer?

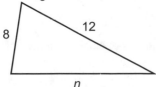

Solution: In a triangle, the measure of any side has to be less than the sum of the other two sides and greater then the difference between the other two sides.
Therefore, n has to be greater than $12 - 8 = 4$
And, n has to be less than $12 + 8 = 20$
$\Rightarrow$ n can be any integer between 4 and 20: 5, 6, 7, 8, 9, 10, 11, 12, 13, 14, 15, 16, 17, 18, 19 $\Rightarrow$ 15 total possibilities
$\Rightarrow$ No. of even integers: 6, 8, 10, 12, 14, 16, 18 $\Rightarrow$ 7 possibilities
$\Rightarrow \dfrac{Favorable\,Outcomes}{Total\,Outcomes} = \dfrac{Even\,Integers}{Total\,Integers} = \dfrac{7}{15}$

Question #28:   In the figure given below, the dartboard consists of six concentric circles, 1 though 6, as marked below, sharing the same center. The radius of the outer circle is 10, and the radius of each subsequent circle is 2 less than the next larger circle. If a dart is thrown, what is the probability that the dart will hit one of the white regions?

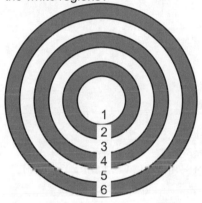

Solution: Area of Circle 6 $\Rightarrow \pi r^2 = \pi(12)^2$ $\Rightarrow 144\pi$
Area of Circle 5 $\Rightarrow \pi r^2 = \pi(10)^2$ $\Rightarrow 100\pi$
Area of Circle 4 $\Rightarrow \pi r^2 = \pi(8)^2$ $\Rightarrow 64\pi$
Area of Circle 3 $\Rightarrow \pi r^2 = \pi(6)^2$ $\Rightarrow 36\pi$
Area of Circle 2 $\Rightarrow \pi r^2 = \pi(4)^2$ $\Rightarrow 16\pi$
Area of Circle 1 $\Rightarrow \pi r^2 = \pi(2)^2$ $\Rightarrow 4\pi$
Area of 1st White Region $\Rightarrow$ Area of Circle 1 $\Rightarrow 4\pi$
Area of 2nd White Region $\Rightarrow$ Area of Circle 3 – Area of Circle 2 $\Rightarrow 36\pi - 16\pi = 20\pi$
Area of 3rd White Region $\Rightarrow$ Area of Circle 5 – Area of Circle 4 $\Rightarrow 100\pi - 64\pi = 36\pi$
Area of All White Regions $\Rightarrow 4\pi + 20\pi + 36\pi = 60\pi$
Probability of hitting the white region $\Rightarrow \dfrac{Area\,of\,White\,Re\,gion}{Total\,Area} = \dfrac{60\pi}{144\pi} = \dfrac{5}{12}$

Question #29:   If the probability of snow on any given day in City X is 50 percent, what is the probability that it snows on exactly 3 days in a 5-day period?

Solution: Let's first determine the total number of possible outcomes of snow in City X over the 5-day period.
There are two possible outcomes for each day $\Rightarrow$ either it will snow or it will not snow $\Rightarrow$ so the total number of possible outcomes for the entire 5-day period would be $2 \times 2 \times 2 \times 2 \times 2 = 32$ total possibilities.
Next, let's determine the total number of desired outcomes, that is, when it snows in City X.

Combination $\Rightarrow {}_mC_n$ $\Rightarrow \dfrac{m!}{n!(m-n)!}$

$\Rightarrow {}_5C_3$ $\Rightarrow \dfrac{5!}{3!(5-3)!} = \dfrac{5!}{3!\times 2!} = \dfrac{5\times 4\times 3!}{3!\times 2!} = \dfrac{5\times 4}{2\times 1} = \dfrac{20}{2} = 10$

Another way would be to make a systematic list of the days when it snows exactly 3 out of the 5 days.
SSSNN   SSNSN   SSNNS   SNSSN   SNSNS   SNNSS   NSSSN   NSSNS
NSNSS   NNSSS $\Rightarrow$ Therefore, there are a total of 10 desired outcomes.

Finally, find the probability that it snows on exactly 3 days in a 5-day period in City X:

Probability $\Rightarrow \dfrac{\text{Desired Outcomes (when it snows on exactly 3 out of 5 days)}}{\text{Total Possible Outcomes}} \Rightarrow \dfrac{10}{32} = \dfrac{5}{16}$

Question #30: Two integers are to be randomly selected from the two sets given below, one integer form set X and one integer form set Y. If x represent the chosen member from Set X, and y represent the chosen member from Set Y, what is the probability that $\dfrac{x}{y}$ will be an integer?

Set X: {10, 12, 15, 16}
Set Y: {1, 2, 5, 6}

Solution: Make a list of all possible combinations of $\dfrac{x}{y}$:

$\boxed{\dfrac{10}{1}}$ $\boxed{\dfrac{10}{2}}$ $\boxed{\dfrac{10}{5}}$ $\dfrac{10}{6}$

$\boxed{\dfrac{12}{1}}$ $\boxed{\dfrac{12}{2}}$ $\dfrac{12}{5}$ $\boxed{\dfrac{12}{6}}$

$\boxed{\dfrac{15}{1}}$ $\dfrac{15}{2}$ $\boxed{\dfrac{15}{5}}$ $\dfrac{15}{6}$

$\boxed{\dfrac{16}{1}}$ $\boxed{\dfrac{16}{2}}$ $\dfrac{16}{5}$ $\dfrac{16}{6}$

Note: the fractions with a square border will yield integers.
Total No. of different pairs of fractions, one form set X and one from set $Y \Rightarrow (4)(4) = 16$
Total No. of pairs that yields an integer $\Rightarrow 10$

Probability that $\dfrac{x}{y}$ will be an integer $\Rightarrow \dfrac{10}{16} = \dfrac{5}{8}$

PART 4.0: SETS:

TABLE OF CONTENTS:

4.1: BASICS ABOUT SETS:

There are special types of counting problems that require the concept of sets and Venn diagrams.

EZ SPOT: It's easy to spot Set problems. These problems contain one of the following buzz words/phrases: both, either, neither, etc.

SET: A *"set"* is a collection of well-defined things or items called elements or members of the set. Sets are represented by listing their elements.
For Example: If S is the set of numbers 1, 2, 3, 4, and 5; it can be written as: $S = \{1, 2, 3, 4, 5\}$.

ELEMENTS: The things or items contained in a set are called the *'elements"* or *"members"* of the set. A set contains only those items that can fit its definition.
For Example: The numbers 1, 2, 3, 4, and 5 are the elements of set $S = \{1, 2, 3, 4, 5\}$.
The order in which the elements are listed in a set does not matter. For instance: $\{1, 2, 5\} = \{5, 2, 1\}$.
The elements of a set are usually listed inside a pair of braces or curly brackets { }
The symbol for element is $\in$. If 1 is an element of S, then $1 \in S$.

FINITE SET: A set that contains only a finite number of elements is called a *'finite set"*.
For Example: $\{a, b, c, d, e\}$ is the finite set which contains elements a, b, c, d and e.

INFINITE SET: A set that contains an infinite number of elements is called an *"infinite set"*.
For Example: $\{1, 2, 3, 4, 5.......\}$ is an infinite set of all positive integers.

Number of Elements in a Set: If S is a set with a finite number of elements, then the number of elements is denoted by $|S|$. Such a set is usually defined by listing its elements.
For Example: $S = \{1, 2, 5, 7, 9\}$ is a set with $|S| = 5$.

SUBSET: If all the elements of one set, S, are also elements of another set, T; then the first set, S, is a *"subset"* of the second set, T.
For Example: $S = \{1, 5, 9\}$ is a subset of $T = \{1, 2, 5, 7, 9\}$.

VENN DIAGRAM: Sets can also be represented by *'Venn diagrams"*, that is, the relationship among the elements of sets is often illustrated by Venn diagrams. Venn diagram is used to graphically represent sets and solve certain sets problems that are related to counting. Venn diagram is a figure in which two or more sets are represented by circular regions that may or may not be over-lapping, usually enclosed in a rectangular plane. All the elements of the set fall within the rectangle. Venn diagrams also help in visualizing the relationship between numbers or objects of a set.
Note: None of the problems requires the use of Venn diagrams. In fact, on some problems you may even find it easier not to use one. However, even though for some problems you may not need a Venn diagram, the fact is that they can sometimes be very useful. In fact, for solving some types of problems, it is almost essential to use a Venn diagram.

IMPORTANCE OF VENN DIAGRAMS:
(A) Sometimes, you are given a Venn diagram and asked to answer a question about it.
(B) More frequently, you will come across a problem without any Venn diagram; however, you will be able to solve it more easily if you draw a Venn diagram.

OVERLAPPING SETS: Sets involve two or more given sets of data that partially intersect with each other are termed overlapping sets.

4.2: UNION & INTERSECTION OF SETS:

UNION SET: The *"union"* of two or more sets – represented by the symbol "U" – The set consisting of all the elements that exist in either one or all of the sets, i.e., the set of elements that are in either set or both of the different sets you start with. In other words, union of sets is what you get when you merge two or more sets.
$\Rightarrow n \in A \cup B$ if and only if $n \in A$ or $n \in B$

INTERSECTION SET: The *"intersection"* of two or more sets – represented by the symbol "∩" – The set consisting of all elements that exist in both the sets, i.e., the set of elements that are common in both of the different sets you start with.
$\Rightarrow m \in A \cup B$ if and only if $m \in A$ and $n \in B$

NON-DISJOINT SETS: Two sets that have elements in common are said to be *"non-disjoint"* sets, where two sets are not disjoint and neither one is a subset of the other.
For Example: Set A: {1, 2, 3, 4, 5, 6}
               Set B: {5, 6, 7, 8}
               Union of Set A and Set B $\Rightarrow A \cup B$ = {1, 2, 3, 4, 5, 6, 7, 8}
               Intersection of Set A and Set B $\Rightarrow A \cap B$ = {5, 6}

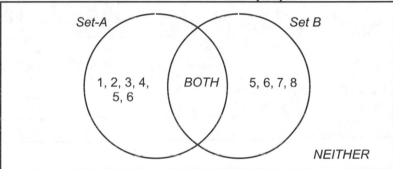

The above diagram points an important fact about any two finite sets A and B:
The number of elements in the union of two sets equals the sum of the individual numbers of elements minus the number of elements in the intersection (because the common elements are counted twice in the sum)
$\Rightarrow |A \cup B| = |A| + |B| - |A \cap B|$
This counting method is also known as the general addition rule for two sets.
The intersection $A \cap B$ is represented by the shaded region of the diagram below.

DISJOINT SETS: Two sets that have no elements in common are said to be *"disjoint"* or mutually exclusive sets.
For Example: Set A: {1, 2, 3, 4, 5, 6}
               Set B: {7, 8}
               Union of Set A and Set B: $\Rightarrow A \cup B$ = {1, 2, 3, 4, 5, 6, 7, 8}
               Intersection of Set A and Set B: $\Rightarrow A \cap B$ = {0}

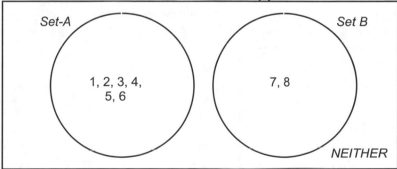

The above diagram points an important fact about any two disjoint or mutually exclusive sets A and B:
The number of elements in the union of two sets equals the sum of the individual numbers of elements
For instance: If set A and set B are disjoint, then $\Rightarrow |A \cup B| = |A| + |B|$ since $|A \cap B| = 0$.

4.3: SOLVING SETS:

TERMS USED IN SETS:
Some word problems involve two groups with overlapping members, and possibly elements that belong to neither group. It's easy to identify these types of questions because the words **"both"**, **"and"**, **"either"**, **"or"**, **"neither"** appear in the question.

"EITHER.......OR.......": Means you can take both, so items belonging to both the groups are counted among the items in either one of the group.
Note: You must avoid counting the same item twice.
Items Belonging to "Either.......Or......." $\Rightarrow$ Group$_1$ + Group$_2$ – Both
$\Rightarrow$ Group$_1$ Exclusive + Group$_2$ Exclusive + Both
$\Rightarrow$ Total – Neither

BOTH: Items in this group are the common or overlapping items that belong to both the groups. You have to subtract the number belonging to both groups since they are counted once with those in one group and counted once again with those in the other group. Recognizing overlap in sets helps us to avoid mistakenly counting certain elements twice.

NEITHER: Item in this group belongs to neither of the groups.

FORMULAS FOR SETS:

1) GROUP$_1$ EXCLUSIVE + GROUP$_2$ EXCLUSIVE + BOTH + NEITHER = TOTAL
Where: Group$_1$ Exclusive = items belonging to only Group 1
Group$_2$ Exclusive = items belonging to only Group 2
Both (Overlap) = items belonging to both Groups 1 & 2
Neither = item belonging to neither Group 1 nor 2

2) GROUP$_1$ + GROUP$_2$ – BOTH + NEITHER = TOTAL
Where: Group$_1$ = items belonging to Group-1 some of which may also belong to Group 2
Group$_2$ = items belonging to Group-2 some of which may also belong to Group 1
Both (Overlap) = items belonging to both Groups 1 & 2
Neither = items belonging to neither Group 1 nor 2

3) GROUP$_1$ EXCLUSIVE = GROUP$_1$ – BOTH
Where: Group$_1$ Exclusive = items belonging to only Group 1
Group$_1$ = items belonging to Group 1 some of which may also belong to Group 2
Both (Overlap) = items belonging to both Groups 1 & 2

4) GROUP$_2$ EXCLUSIVE = GROUP$_2$ – BOTH
Where: Group$_2$ Exclusive = items belonging to only Group 2
Group$_2$ = items belonging to Group 2 some of which may also belong to Group 1
Both (Overlap) = items belonging to both Groups 1 & 2

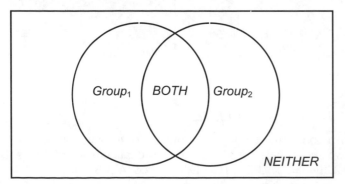

SOLVING TWO SETS PROBLEMS:

Problems that involve two overlapping sets can be easily solved by using a Venn Diagram.
While working with Venn Diagrams, the best way is to **"work from the inside out"**.

In this case, there are 3 different sections in the Venn Diagram:
1 Innermost Section: ⇒ There is one innermost section (*A*) where both circles overlap.
                                                  ⇒ This contains members who are in both groups.
2 Outermost Sections: ⇒ There are two non-overlapping outermost sections (*B* and *C*)
                                                  ⇒ These contain members who are only in one group.

STEP 1: First, fill in a number in the innermost section (*A*).
STEP 2: Next, fill in the outermost sections last (*B* and *C*).

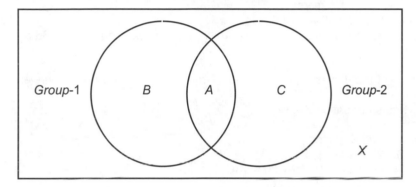

For Example: In a small music club, there are 150 members, of which, 72 members are singers, 86 members are dancers, 20 members are both singers and dancers, and 12 members are neither singers nor dancers.

We can form the following Venn diagram, which divides the rectangle into four regions, which shows the distribution of those members as singers and/or/neither dancers.

EZ TIP: Set problems are generally designed to illustrate principles of overlapping sets. The above relationships can be displayed graphically with the help of a Venn diagram.

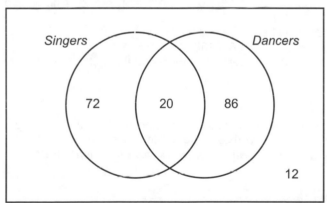

Both: The 20 written in the part of the diagram where the two circles overlap represents the 20 members who are both singers and dancers.
                   ⇒ No of students who are BOTH Singers and Dancers = 20

Group₁: The 72 written in the circle on the left represents the total 72 members who are singers, some of which may also be dancers:
                   ⇒ Number of members who are Singers, some of which may also be Dancers = 72

Group₁ Exclusive: If we subtract 20 from this group, we would get the number of members who are only singers and not dancers:
⇒ Number of members who are ONLY Singers:
⇒ Group₁ Exclusive = Group₁ − BOTH = 72 − 20 = 52
Therefore, there are 72 members who are singers, out of which, 20 are also dancers, and 52 are not dancers.

Group₂: The 86 written in the circle on the right represents the total 86 members who are dancers, some of which may also be singers.
⇒ Number of members who are Dancers, some of which may also be Singers = 86

Group₂ Exclusive: If we subtract 20 from this group, we would get the number of members who are only dancers and not singers:
⇒ Number of members who are ONLY Dancers:
⇒ Group₂ Exclusive = Group₂ − BOTH = 86 − 20 = 66
Therefore, there are 86 members who are dancers, out of which, 20 are also singers, and 66 are not singers.

Neither: The 12 written in the rectangle outside of the circles represents the 12 members who are neither singers nor dancers.
⇒ No of members who are neither singers nor dancers = 12

Either: No of students who are EITHER Singers and Dancers:
⇒ Group₁ + Group₂ − Both = (72 + 86) − 20 = 138
⇒ Group₁ Exclusive + Group₂ Exclusive + Both = 52 + 66 + 20 = 138
⇒ Total − Neither = 150 − 12 = 138

CONCLUSION: Based on the information deduced above, we can come to the following two conclusions:

Singers	+	Dancers	−	Both	+	Neither	=	Total
72	+	86	−	20	+	12	=	150

Only Singers	+	Only Dancers	+	Both	+	Neither	=	Total
52	+	66	+	20	+	12	=	150

EZ HINT: If we add members in both groups, i.e., 72 + 86 = 158 ⇒ this adds up to more than the total number of members in the club. Why so?
The reason for this is that 20 members are in both groups and so have been counted twice.
Therefore, the number of members who are singers or dancers is only 158 − 20 − 138.
And, these 138 members, together with the 12 members who are neither singers nor dancers, make up the total 150.

SOLVING THREE SETS PROBLEMS:
Sets problems may also involve three or more groups; however, the basic principles remain to be the same as for two groups. Problems that involve three overlapping sets can also be easily solved by using a Venn Diagram.
Like already mentioned earlier, while working with Venn Diagrams, the best way is to **"work from the inside out"**.

There are 7 different sections in a Venn Diagram:
1 Innermost Section: ⇒ There is one innermost section (A) where all 3 circles overlap.
⇒ This contains members who are in all three groups.
3 Middle Sections: ⇒ There are three middle sections (B, C, and D) where 2 circles overlap.
⇒ These contain members who are in two groups.
3 Outermost Sections: ⇒ There are three non-overlapping outermost sections (E, F, and G)
⇒ These contain members who are only in 1 group.

STEP 1: First, fill in a number in the innermost section (A).
STEP 2: Next, fill in numbers in the middle sections (B, C, and D).

STEP 3: Finally, fill in the outermost sections last (*E*, *F*, and *G*).

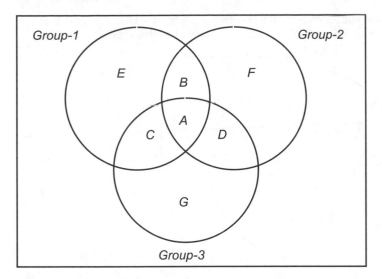

Group₁ Exclusive $\Rightarrow$ Group₁ – Any Two – All Three = $E - A - B - C$
Group₂ Exclusive $\Rightarrow$ Group₂ – Any Two – All Three = $F - A - B - D$
Group₃ Exclusive $\Rightarrow$ Group₃ – Any Two – All Three = $G - A - C - D$

Total $\Rightarrow$ Group₁ Exclusive + Group₂ Exclusive + Group₃ Exclusive + Any Two + All Three + Neither

Example #1:   In a certain sports club, members are placed in at least one of the three groups. There are 70 members in the soccer group, 80 members are in the hockey group, and 90 members are in the football group. There 7 members in both soccer and hockey group, 8 members in both hockey and football group, and 9 members in both soccer and football group. There are 2 members that are in all three groups. How many members are there in total in the sports club?

Solve the problem taking one step at a time.

First: List Member in All Three Groups: First, list the number of members who are in all three groups, this is easy as it is given in the problem.
$\Rightarrow$ No. of members who are in all three groups = 2

Second: List Member in ONLY Two Groups: Next, list the number of members in exactly two of the three groups. Here it is important to remember to subtract those members who are in all three groups. For instance, according to the problem, there are 7 members in the soccer and hockey groups. However, this includes the 2 members who are in all three groups. Therefore, in order to find the number of members who are only in soccer and hockey group, we must subtract the 2 members who are in all three groups.
$\Rightarrow$ No. of members who are ONLY in Soccer & Hockey Groups = 7 – 2 = 5
$\Rightarrow$ No. of members who are ONLY in Hockey & Football Groups = 8 – 2 = 6
$\Rightarrow$ No. of members who are ONLY in Soccer & Football Groups = 9 – 2 = 7

Third: List Members in ONLY One Group: Finally, list the number of members in exactly one of the three groups. Here it is important to remember to subtract those members who are in two groups and those members who are in all three groups. For instance, according to the problem, there are 70 members in soccer group. However, this includes the 5 members who are in both soccer and hockey groups, the 7 members who are in both soccer and football teams, and the 2 members who are in all three groups. Therefore, in order to find the number of members who are only in soccer group, we must subtract all of these members to find the number of members who are only in the soccer group.
$\Rightarrow$ No. of members who are ONLY in Soccer Group= 70 – 2 – 5 – 7 = 56
$\Rightarrow$ No. of members who are ONLY in Hockey Group   = 80 – 2 – 5 – 6 = 67

⇒ No. of members who are ONLY in Football Group   = 90 – 2 – 6 – 7 = 75

Finally: Total number of members in the sports club = All the members who are ONLY in one group + All the member who are ONLY in two groups + All the members who are in all three group
⇒ (56 + 67 + 75) + (5 + 6 + 7) + (2) = 198 + 18 + 2 = 218

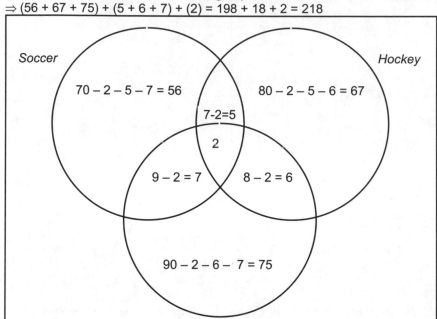

4.4: GROUP PROBLEMS:

The **"group problems"** involving either/or categories typically involve a group of members (people or items), and then involve sub-groups. Be sure not to mix-up with other word problems that involve groups with distinct "either/or" categories. The key to solving these types of problems is to organize the information in a grid.

EZ STEP-BY-STEP METHOD: Apply the following step(s) to solve group problems:

STEP 1: First, organize and fill-in the information given in the problem in the form of a grid or a double-matrix.

STEP 2: Next, complete the grid – keep on filling the remaining boxes until you find the number you are looking for.

EZ TIP: ▪ Use the totals as a guiding factor.
▪ Each row and each column sum to a total value.
▪ Both horizontal and vertical totals must sum up to the same value. So make sure that each row and each column adds-up to the corresponding totals.
▪ Both, rows and columns, must work both ways, vertically as well as horizontally.

Note: Sometimes a problem does not require completing the whole grid or matrix; however, it is recommended to complete the matrix so that the computations can be checked.

GROUP PROBLEMS WITH NUMBERS:

For Example: At a certain professional conference with 192 attendees, 116 of the attendees are opticians and the rest are optometrists. If 70 of the attendees are females, and ¼th of the optometrists in attendance are females, how many of the attendees are male opticians?

Solution: First, organize the information given in the question in the form of the following grid. Next, complete the grid – keep on filling the remaining boxes until you find the number you are looking for – in this case, you should be looking for number of male opticians. Also, make sure that each row and column adds-up to the corresponding totals.

	Opticians	Optometrists	Total
Male	**65**	57	**122**
Female	51	19	70
Total	116	**76**	192

Note: The non-bolded values in the grid are given, the bolded values are what we found out, and the cell with the double border is the answer.

After you've filled in the information from the question, fill in the remaining boxes until you get the number you are looking for. Following is how you should be looking for the missing values:

For the Horizontal Total:	Total No. of Attendees	$\Rightarrow$ 192
	No. of Opticians	$\rightarrow$ 116
	No. of Optometrists	$\Rightarrow$ 192 – 116 = 76
For the Vertical Total:	Total No. of Attendees	$\Rightarrow$ 192
	No. of Females	$\Rightarrow$ 70
	No. of Males	$\Rightarrow$ 192 – 70 = 122
For the Total Optometrists:	Total No. of Optometrists	$\Rightarrow$ 76
	No. of Female Optometrists	$\Rightarrow$ ¼ × 76 = 19
	No. of Male Optometrists	$\Rightarrow$ 76 – 19 = 57
For the Total Males:	Total No. of Male Attendees	$\Rightarrow$ 122
	No. of Male Optometrists	$\Rightarrow$ 57
	No. of Male Opticians	$\Rightarrow$ 122 – 57 = 65

Therefore, in this case, it is evident that 65 of the attendees are male opticians.

GROUP PROBLEMS WITH PERCENTS:

Complicated group problems can even involve percents. Such problems are also solved in the same way as other group problems by using a grid to organize the information given in the problem. However, since percents are always out of 100, don't forget to use 100 to represent the total.

For Example: In a certain organization, an employee is either a white-collar employee or a blue-collar employee. 75% of the employees are white-collar employees. 40% of the employees are males who are white-collar employees. If half of the employees are males, what percent of the employees are female blue-collar employees?

Solution: First, organize the information given in the question in the form of the following grid. Next, complete the grid – keep on filling the remaining boxes until you find the number you are looking for – in this case, you should be looking for number of female white-collar employees. Also, make sure that each row and column adds-up to the corresponding totals.

	White-Collar	Blue-Collar	Total
Male	40%	**10%**	**50%**
Female	**35%**	**15%**	50%
Total	75%	**25%**	100%

Note: The non-bolded values in the grid are given, the bolded values are what we found out, and the cell with the double border is the answer.

After you've filled in the information from the question, fill in the remaining boxes until you get the number you are looking for. Following is how you should be looking for the missing values:

For the Total WC Employees: Total Percent of WC Employees $\Rightarrow$ 75%
                               Percent of Male WC Employees $\Rightarrow$ 40%
                               Percent of Female WC Employees $\Rightarrow$ 75% – 40% = 35%

For the Total Male Employees: Total Percent of male Employees $\Rightarrow$ ½(100%) = 50%
                               Percent of Male WC Employees $\Rightarrow$ 40%
                               Percent of Male BC Employees $\Rightarrow$ 50% – 40% = 10%

For the Horizontal Total: Total Percent of Employees $\Rightarrow$ 100%
                               Percent of WC Employees $\Rightarrow$ 75%
                               Percent of BC Employees $\Rightarrow$ 100% – 75% = 25%

For the Vertical Total: Total Percent of Employees $\Rightarrow$ 100%
                               Percent of Male Employees $\Rightarrow$ ½(100%) = 50%
                               Percent of Female Employees $\Rightarrow$ ½(100%) = 50%

Option #1 to get the answer:
For the Total Female Employees: Total Percent of Female Employees $\Rightarrow$ ½(100%) = 50%
                               Percent of Female WC Employees $\Rightarrow$ 35%
                               Percent of Female BC Employees $\Rightarrow$ 50% – 35% = 15%

Option #2 to get the answer:
For the Total BC Employees: Total Percent of BC Employees $\Rightarrow$ 25%
                               Percent of Male BC Employees $\Rightarrow$ 10%
                               Percent of Female BC Employees $\Rightarrow$ 25% – 10% = 15%

Therefore, in this case, it is evident that 15% of the employees are female blue-collar employees.

PRACTICE EXERCISE – QUESTIONS AND ANSWERS WITH EXPLANATIONS: SETS:

Question #1: Set A, B, and C are given below. What is the set that is the result of $A \cup (B \cap C)$?
Set A: {1, 2, 3, 4, 5, 6, 7}
Set B: {6, 7, 8, 9, 10, 11}
Set C: {10, 11, 12, 13, 14, 15}

Solution: Apply PEMDAS, first solve within the parentheses, and work your way out:
Step 1: $(B \cap C)$ $\Rightarrow$ {6, 7, 8, 9, 10, 11} $\cap$ {10, 11, 12, 13, 14, 15}
$\Rightarrow$ {10, 11}
Step 2: $A \cup (B \cap C)$ $\Rightarrow$ {1, 2, 3, 4, 5, 6, 7} $\cup$ {10, 11}
$\Rightarrow$ {1, 2, 3, 4, 5, 6, 7, 10, 11}

Question #2: Set A, B, and C are given below. What is the set that is the result of $(A \cup B) \cap C$?
Set A: {1, 2, 3, 4, 5, 6, 7}
Set B: {6, 7, 8, 9, 10, 11}
Set C: {10, 11, 12, 13, 14, 15}

Solution: Apply PEMDAS, first solve within the parentheses, and work your way out:
Step 1: $(A \cup B)$ $\Rightarrow$ {1, 2, 3, 4, 5, 6, 7} $\cup$ {6, 7, 8, 9, 10, 11}
$\Rightarrow$ {1, 2, 3, 4, 5, 6, 7, 8, 9, 10, 11}
Step 2: $(A \cup B) \cap C$ $\Rightarrow$ {1, 2, 3, 4, 5, 6, 7, 8, 9, 10, 11} $\cap$ {10, 11, 12, 13, 14, 15}
$\Rightarrow$ {10, 11}

Question #3: Set A, B, and C are given below. What is the set that is the result of $A \cap (B \cup C)$?
Set A: {1, 2, 3, 4, 5, 6, 7}
Set B: {6, 7, 8, 9, 10, 11}
Set C: {10, 11, 12, 13, 14, 15}

Solution: Apply PEMDAS, first solve within the parentheses, and work your way out:
Step 1: $(B \cup C)$ $\Rightarrow$ {6, 7, 8, 9, 10, 11} $\cap$ {10, 11, 12, 13, 14, 15}
$\Rightarrow$ {6, 7, 8, 9, 10, 11, 12, 13, 14, 15}
Step 2: $A \cap (B \cup C)$ $\Rightarrow$ {1, 2, 3, 4, 5, 6, 7} $\cap$ {6, 7, 8, 9, 10, 11, 12, 13, 14, 15}
$\Rightarrow$ {6, 7}

Question #4: Set A, B, and C are given below. What is the set that is the result of $(A \cap B) \cup C$?
Set A: {1, 2, 3, 4, 5, 6, 7}
Set B: {6, 7, 8, 9, 10, 11}
Set C: {10, 11, 12, 13, 14, 15}

Solution: Apply PEMDAS, first solve within the parentheses, and work your way out:
Step 1: $(A \cap B)$ $\Rightarrow$ {1, 2, 3, 4, 5, 6, 7} $\cap$ {6, 7, 8, 9, 10, 11}
$\Rightarrow$ {6, 7}
Step 2: $(A \cap B) \cup C$ $\Rightarrow$ {6, 7} $\cap$ {10, 11, 12, 13, 14, 15}
$\Rightarrow$ {6, 7, 10, 11, 12, 13, 14, 15}

Question #5: Set A, B, and C are given below. What is the set that is the result of $A \cup (B \cup C)$?
Set A: {1, 2, 3, 4, 5, 6, 7}
Set B: {6, 7, 8, 9, 10, 11}
Set C: {10, 11, 12, 13, 14, 15}

Solution: Apply PEMDAS, first solve within the parentheses, and work your way out:
Step 1: $(B \cup C)$ $\Rightarrow$ {6, 7, 8, 9, 10, 11} $\cup$ {10, 11, 12, 13, 14, 15}
$\Rightarrow$ {6, 7, 8, 9, 10, 11, 12, 13, 14, 15}
Step 2: $A \cup (B \cup C)$ $\Rightarrow$ {1, 2, 3, 4, 5, 6, 7} $\cup$ {6, 7, 8, 9, 10, 11, 12, 13, 14, 15}
$\Rightarrow$ {1, 2, 3, 4, 5, 6, 7, 10, 11, 13, 14, 15}

Question #6: Set A, B, and C are given below. What is the set that is the result of $A \cap (B \cap C)$?
Set A: {1, 2, 3, 4, 5, 6, 7}

Set *B*: {6, 7, 8, 9, 10, 11}
Set *C*: {10, 11, 12, 13, 14, 15}

Solution: Apply PEMDAS, first solve within the parentheses, and work your way out:
Step 1: $(B \cap C)$ $\Rightarrow$ {6, 7, 8, 9, 10, 11} $\cap$ {10, 11, 12, 13, 14, 15}
                              $\Rightarrow$ {10, 11}
Step 2: $A \cap (B \cap C)$ $\Rightarrow$ {1, 2, 3, 4, 5, 6, 7} $\cap$ {10, 11}
                              $\Rightarrow$ {0}

Question #7:   If in a school of 80 students, 25 enrolled in English class and 65 enrolled in Math class, and if 5 students enrolled in neither subject, how many students enrolled in both English and Math class?

Solution: Let the No. of students enrolled in both English & Math $\Rightarrow x$
Then, No. of students enrolled in only English $\Rightarrow (25 - x)$
And, No. of students enrolled in only Math $\Rightarrow (65 - x)$
Total number of students enrolled in either English or Math $\Rightarrow 80 - 5 = 75$
EZ Problem Set-Up $\Rightarrow$ English only + Math only + English & Math = Total Students
                   $\Rightarrow (25 - x) + (65 - x) + x = 75$
                   $\Rightarrow 90 - x = 75$
                   $\Rightarrow x = 15$
Therefore, 15 students enrolled in both English and Math.

Question #8:   If in a school of 285 students, 110 enrolled in algebra class and 1%0 enrolled in geometry class, and if 15 students enrolled in neither subject, how many students enrolled in both algebra and geometry class?

Solution: Let the No. of students enrolled in both Algebra & Geometry$\Rightarrow x$
Then, No. of students enrolled in only Algebra $\Rightarrow (110 - x)$
And, No. of students enrolled in only Geometry $\Rightarrow (1\%0 - x)$
Total No. of students enrolled in either Algebra or Geometry$\Rightarrow 285 - 15 = 270$
EZ Problem Set-Up $\Rightarrow$ Algebra only + Geometry only + Algebra & Geometry = Total Students
                   $\Rightarrow (110 - x) + (1\%0 - x) + x = 270$
                   $\Rightarrow 260 - x = 270$
                   $\Rightarrow x = 10$
Therefore, 10 students enrolled in both Algebra and Geometry.

Question #9:   If in a certain group of 98 people, 56 ordered fries and 67 ordered burgers, and if 2 people ordered neither, how many people ordered both fries and burgers?

Solution: Let the No. of people who ordered both Fries & Burgers$\Rightarrow x$
Then, No. of people who ordered only Fries $\Rightarrow (56 - x)$
And, No. of people who orders only Burgers $\Rightarrow (67 - x)$
Total No. of people who ordered either Fries or Burgers$\Rightarrow 98 - 2 = 96$
EZ Problem Set-Up $\Rightarrow$ Burgers only + Fries only + Burgers & Fries = Total Students
                   $\Rightarrow (56 - x) + (67 - x) + x = 96$
                   $\Rightarrow 123 - x = 96$
                   $\Rightarrow x = 27$
Therefore, 27 people ordered both burgers and fries.

Question #10: If in a certain group of 186 people, 108 people knows how to swim and 119 people knows how to skate, and if 18 knows neither, how many people can swim and skate?

Solution: Let the No. of people who can swim & skate $\Rightarrow x$
Then, No. of people who can only swim $\Rightarrow (108 - x)$
And, No. of people who can only skate $\Rightarrow (119 - x)$
Total No. of students who can swim or skate $\Rightarrow 186 - 18 = 168$
EZ Problem Set-Up $\Rightarrow$ Swim only + Skate only + Swim & Skate = Total
                   $\Rightarrow (108 - x) + (119 - x) + x = 168$
                   $\Rightarrow 227 - x = 168$
                   $\Rightarrow x = 59$
Therefore, 59 people can swim and skate.

Question #11:   If in a school of 95 students, 50 enrolled in French class, 60 enrolled in Spanish class, and if 5 students enrolled in neither language, how many students enroll in both French and Spanish class?

Solution: Let's first draw a Venn diagram labeling all the information that is given in the problem:

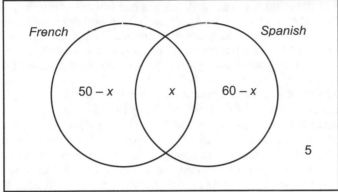

Let, the No. of students enrolled in both French & Spanish $\Rightarrow x$
Then, the No. of students enrolled in only French $\Rightarrow (50 - x)$
And, the No. of students enrolled in only Spanish $\Rightarrow (60 - x)$
EZ Problem Set-Up $\Rightarrow$ French only + Spanish only + French & Spanish + Neither = Total Students
$\Rightarrow (50 - x) + (60 - x) + x + 5 = 95$
$\Rightarrow 110 - x = 90$
$\Rightarrow x = 20$
Therefore, 20 students enrolled in French and Spanish.

Question #12:   If in a school of 95 students, 50 enrolled in French class, 60 enrolled in Spanish class, and if 20 students are enrolled in both languages, how many students enroll in neither French nor Spanish class?

Solution: Let's first draw a Venn diagram labeling all the information that is given in the problem:

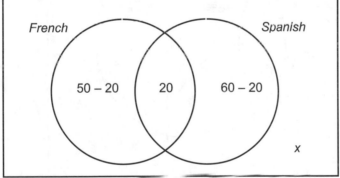

Let, the No. of students enrolled in neither French nor Spanish $\Rightarrow x$
The No. of students enrolled in only French $\Rightarrow (50 - 20) = 30$
And, No. of students enrolled in only Spanish $\Rightarrow (60 - 20) = 40$
Total No. of students $\Rightarrow 95$
EZ Problem Set-Up $\Rightarrow$ French only + Spanish only + French & Spanish + Neither = Total Students
$\Rightarrow 30 + 40 + 20 + x = 95$
$\Rightarrow 90 + x = 95$
$\Rightarrow x = 5$
Therefore, 5 students enrolled in neither French nor Spanish.

Question #13:   In a certain sports club, members are placed in at least one of the three groups. There are 75 members in the soccer group, 85 members are in the hockey group, and 95 members are in the football group. There are 8 members in both soccer and hockey group, 10 members in both hockey and football group, and 12 members in both soccer and football group. There are 2 members that are in all three groups. How many members are there in total in the sports club?

Solution: Solve the problem taking one step at a time.
First: List Members in All Three Groups: First, list the number of members who are in all three groups, this is easy as it is given in the problem.
⇒ No. of members who are in all three groups = 2
Second: List Members in ONLY Two Groups: Next, list the number of members in exactly two of the three groups. Here it is important to remember to subtract those members who are in all three groups. For instance, according to the problem, there are 8 members in the soccer and hockey groups. However, this includes the 2 members who are in all three groups. Therefore, in order to find the number of members who are only in soccer and hockey groups, we must subtract the 2 members who are in all three groups.
⇒ No. of members who are ONLY in Soccer & Hockey Groups = 8 – 2 = 6
⇒ No. of members who are ONLY in Hockey & Football Groups = 10 – 2 = 8
⇒ No. of members who are ONLY in Soccer & Football Groups = 12 – 2 = 10
Third: List Members in ONLY One Group: Finally, list the number of members in exactly one of the three groups. Here it is important to remember to subtract those members who are in two groups and those members who are in all three groups. For instance, according to the problem, there are 75 members in soccer group. However, this includes the 6 members who are in both soccer and hockey groups, the 10 members who are in both soccer and football teams, and the 2 members who are in all three groups. Therefore, in order to find the number of members who are only in soccer group, we must subtract all of these members to find the number of members who are only in the soccer group.
⇒ No. of members who are ONLY in Soccer Group= 75 – 2 – 6 – 10 = 57
⇒ No. of members who are ONLY in Hockey Group   = 85 – 2 – 6 – 8 = 69
⇒ No. of members who are ONLY in Football Group   = 95 – 2 – 8 – 10 = 75
Finally: Total No. of members in the sports club = All the member who are ONLY in one group + All the members who are ONLY in two groups + All the members who are in all three groups
⇒ (57 + 69 + 75) + (6 + 8 + 10) + (2) = 201 + 24 + 2 = 227

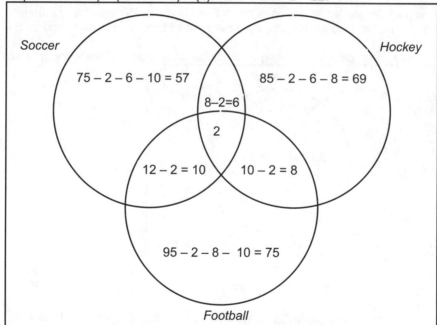

Question #14:   At a certain professional conference with 177 attendees, 127 of the attendees are opticians and the rest are optometrists. If 95 of the attendees are females, and ½ of the optometrists in attendance are females, how many of the attendees are male opticians?
Solution: First, organize the information given in the question in the form of the following grid. Next, complete the grid – keep on filling the remaining boxes until you find the number you are looking for – in this case, you should be looking for number of male opticians. Also make sure that each row and column adds up to the corresponding totals.

	Opticians	Optometrists	Total
Male	57	25	82
Female		25	95
Total	127	50	177

Therefore, 57 of the attendees are male opticians.

Question #15: In a certain organization, an employee is either a white-collar employee or a blue-collar employee. 80% of the employees are white-collar employees. 20% of the employees are males who are white-collar employees. If one-fourth of the employees are males, what percent of the employees are female blue-collar employees?

Solution: First, organize the information given in the question in the form of the following grid. Next, complete the grid – keep on filling the remaining boxes until you find the number you are looking for – in this case, you should be looking for number of female blue-collar employees. Also make sure that each row and column adds up to the corresponding totals.

	White-Collar	Blue-Collar	Total
Male	20%	5%	25%
Female	60%	15%	75%
Total	80%	20%	100%

Therefore, 15% of the employees are female blue-collar employees.

THIS PAGE HAS BEEN INTENTIONALLY LEFT BLANK

PART 5.0: SEQUENCE & PATTERNS:

TABLE OF CONTENTS:

5.1: BASIC ABOUT SEQUENCE & PATTERNS:

SEQUENCE: A series, list, collection, or group of numbers that follows a specific pattern is called a *"sequence"*. In other words, it's an ordered list of numbers. The terms of a sequence don't necessarily have to follow any specific pattern or rule, but for the purpose of your test, they always do.

PATTERN: A series of numbers or objects whose sequence is determined by a particular rule is called *"pattern"*. Patterns are like repeating sequences, except that in patterns, the terms don't necessarily have to be numbers.

For instance: 1, 3, 5, 7, 9.......is a sequence that follows the pattern "add 2" to get the next term. That is, each term in the sequence is 2 more than the one before it. The first term is 1, the second term is 3, and in general, if n is a positive integer, the nth term in the sequence is $1 + 2(n - 1)$.

TERMS: The numbers in the sequence, such as: 2, 4, 6, 8, 10 are called the *"terms"* of the sequence.
Terms in a sequence are separated by commas. The terms of the sequence can be identified by their position in the sequence $\Rightarrow$ 2 is the first term, and 10 is the fifth term in the sequence, and so on.
Dots: The *"dots"* indicate that the sequence continues indefinitely, i.e. it goes on forever.

EZ NOTE: You should be able to figure out the succeeding terms. In the example above, the sequence is the sequence of even integers, and the next term after 10 would be 12.

The patterns in a number sequence are formed by relationships involving sums, differences, products, divisions, exponents, etc., between adjacent terms.

TERMINATING OR FINITE SEQUENCE: Sequence that ends at some point.
For Example: 1, 3, 5, 7, 9.......21, 23, 25
The dots (…) in the middle indicate that the sequence continues according to the pattern as shown, but it ends with the number 25. The sequence contains odd numbers 1 through 25, where the sequence ends.

NON-TERMINATING OR INFINITE SEQUENCE: Sequence that goes on indefinitely.
For Example: 1, 3, 5, 7, 9.......
The dots (…) at the end indicate that the sequence continues according to the pattern as shown, and it goes on infinitely. The sequence contains odd numbers starting from 1 and goes on forever.

ASCENDING & DESCENDING: A sequence may be ascending, (the numbers increase), or descending (the numbers decrease).

The sequence and pattern questions do not usually ask you to figure out the rule for determining the numbers in a sequence. In fact, when a number is used in a question, you may even be told what the rule is. The most common type of sequence question presents you with a rule for finding the terms of a sequence, and then asks you for either the value of a specific term in a sequence, or the sum/average of certain terms in a sequence.

5.2: TYPES OF SEQUENCES:

5.2.1: ARITHMETIC SEQUENCE:

An **"arithmetic progression"** is a sequence of numbers in which each subsequent term in the sequence is being increased or decreased by the same number to form the next term, that is, the same number is added to each term to yield the next term. In other words, it has the property that the difference of any two consecutive numbers must always be the same. The number being added or subtracted is called the **"common difference"**. So, arithmetic sequences are sequences for which there is a common difference that exists between consecutive terms.

EZ RULE: If "d" is the common difference and "a" is the first term of an arithmetic progression, then the nth term of the arithmetic progression will be = $a + (n - 1)d$.

For Example: If an arithmetic progression's first term is 5 and the common difference is 7, then, for any positive integer n, the nth term of this sequence is $5 + (n - 1)7$.
The 9th term in the sequence $\Rightarrow 5 + 8(7) = 5 + 56 = 61$
You can check your answer, the sequence would be 5, 12, 19, 26, 33, 40, 47, 54, 61.......
Therefore, 61 is indeed the 9th term.

EZ TIP: Before answering a question involving a sequence, always write out at least the first five terms.

Example #1:   A sequence is formed as follows: the first term is 5, and every other term is 6 more than the term that precedes it. What is the 10th term in the sequence?
Solution: Write down the sequence starting with first term, which is 5, and keep adding 6 to get the next term:
$\Rightarrow$ 5, 11, 17, 23, 29, 35, 41, 47, 53, 59 (11 is 6 more than 5, 17 is 6 more than 11, etc.)
Therefore, the 10th term in sequence is 59.

Example #2:   A sequence is formed as follows: the first term is 5, and every other term is 6 more than the term that precedes it. What is the 100th term in the sequence?
Solution A: Write down the sequence starting with first term, which is 5, and keep adding 6 to get the next term:
$\Rightarrow$ 5, 11, 17, 23, 29, 35, 41, 47, 53, 59.......... (11 is 6 more than 5, 17 is 6 more than 11, etc.).
Evidently, we could continue writing out the terms, and if the question asked for the 10th term, that would be the easiest thing to do. However, we are not going to write out 100 terms.
The terms are just 1 less than the corresponding multiples of 6 (6, 12, 18, 24, 30.......):
$\Rightarrow$ 11, which is the 2nd term, is 1 less than 2 × 6
$\Rightarrow$ 29 which is the 5th term, is 1 less than 5 × 6
Now that we have found the pattern, the 100th term is 1 less than 100 × 6 $\Rightarrow$ 600 – 1 = 599.
Solution B: We can also solve this problem in one step by using our EZ Rule:
First Term $\Rightarrow a = 5$
Common Difference $\Rightarrow d = 6$
nth Term = 100th term $\Rightarrow a + (n - 1)d = 5 + (100 - 1)6 = 5 + (99)6 = 5 + 594 = 599$

ASCENDING & DESCENDING ARITHMETIC SEQUENCE:

(A) ASCENDING ARITHMETIC SEQUENCE:
Ascending Arithmetic Sequence is a sequence of numbers formed by addition.
EZ STEP-BY-STEP METHOD: Apply the following step(s) to find a missing term in an ascending arithmetic sequence:
STEP 1: Subtract any term from the one following it to find the common difference.
STEP 2: Add the common difference to the term preceding the missing term.

EZ TIP: If the missing term is the first term, it may be found by subtracting the common difference from the second term.

Method to Determine Whether a Sequence is Ascending Arithmetic: If the sequence is ascending, subtract the first term from the second, the second term from the third, and the third from the fourth, and so on. If the difference is the same in all the cases, the sequence is arithmetic.

Example #1:   5, 10, 15, 20, 25, 30, 35, 40, 45, 50.......
⇒ is an arithmetic sequence in which the common difference is 5. Add each term by 5 to get each successive term; therefore, the next term would be 50 + 5 = 55.

Example #2: 10, 15, 20, 25, 30, 35, 40, 45, 50, 55
⇒ is an arithmetic sequence in which the common difference is 5. Subtract 5 from the second term to get the first term; therefore, the first term would be 10 – 5 = 5

(B) DESCENDING ARITHMETIC SEQUENCE:
Descending Arithmetic Sequence is a sequence of numbers formed by subtraction.
EZ STEP-BY-STEP METHOD: Apply the following step(s) to find a missing term in a descending arithmetic sequence:
STEP 1: Subtract any term from the one preceding it to find the common difference.
STEP 2: Subtract the common difference from the term preceding the missing term.

EZ TIP: If the missing term is the first term, it may be found by adding the common difference to the second term.

Method to Determine Whether a Sequence is Descending Arithmetic: If the sequence is descending, subtract the second term from the first, and the third term from the second, and the fourth from the third, and so on. If the difference is the same in all the cases, the sequence is arithmetic.

Example #1:   50, 45, 40, 35, 30, 25, 20, 15, 10.......
⇒ is an arithmetic sequence in which the common difference is 5. Subtract each term by 5 to get each successive term; therefore, the next term would be 10 – 5 = 5

Example #2: 50, 45, 40, 35, 30, 25, 20, 15, 10, 5
⇒ is an arithmetic sequence in which the common difference is 5. Add 5 to the second term to get the first term; therefore, the first term would be 50 + 5 = 55.

5.2.2: GEOMETRIC SEQUENCE:
A *"geometric progression"* is a sequence of terms involving exponential growth, also known as exponential sequence, is a sequence of numbers in which each term of the sequence is being multiplied by the same number to form the next term that is, the same number is multiplied to each term to yield the next term. In other words, each successive term is the same multiple of the preceding one, that is, the ratio of consecutive terms is always the same. The number multiplied by each term or the ratio of consecutive terms is called the *"common ratio"*. So, geometric sequences are sequences for which there is a constant ratio that exists between consecutive terms.

EZ RULE: If "a_1" is the first term, and "r" is the common ratio between consecutive terms of a geometric progression, and a_n is the nth term, then the nth term of a geometric progression will be ⇒ $a_n = a_1 r^{n-1}$

For Example: 5, 10, 20, 40, 80.......
⇒ is a geometric progression in which the first term is 5 and, since: $\dfrac{10}{5} = \dfrac{20}{10} = \dfrac{40}{20} = \dfrac{80}{40} = 2$, the common ratio (multiple) is 2; therefore, the next term in the sequence would be 80 × 2 = 160. Notice that you multiple each term by 2 to obtain the next term.

For Example: If a geometric progression's first term is 5 and the common ratio is 2, then, for any positive integer n, the nth term of this sequence is $5 \times 2^{n-1}$
The 6th term of this sequence ⇒ $5 \times 2^5 = 5 \times 32 = 160$
You can check your answer, the sequence would be 5, 10, 20, 40, 80, 160.......
Therefore, 160 is indeed the 6th term of the progression.

FINDING THE FIRST TERM: Solving for the first term (a_1) when the a_n and common ratio (r) and nth term is given:
For Example: If the ninth term in a geometric sequence is 512, and the common ratio is 2, what is the first term?
First, use the formula to solve for r:
⇒ $a_n = a_1 r^{n-1}$ [Write the formula]
⇒ $512 = a_1 (2)^{9-1}$ [Substitute the value of the terms]

$\Rightarrow 512 = a_1(2)^8$ [Simplify the power]
$\Rightarrow 512 = a_1(256)$ [Solve the exponent]
$\Rightarrow a_1 = 2$ [Divide both sides by 256]
Therefore, the first term in the sequence is 2.

FINDING THE N^{TH} TERM: Solving for the nth term when the first term (a_n) and another term is given:
For Example: If the first term in a geometric sequence is 2, and the third term is 8, what is the ninth term?
$\Rightarrow a_1 = 2 \quad \Rightarrow a_3 = 8$
First, use the formula to solve for r:
$\Rightarrow a_n = a_1 r^{n-1}$ [Write the formula]
$\Rightarrow 8 = 2r^{3-1}$ [Substitute the value of the terms]
$\Rightarrow 8 = 2r^2$ [Simplify the power]
$\Rightarrow 4 = r^2$ [Divide both sides by 2]
$\Rightarrow r = 2$ [Square root both sides]
Next, using $r = 2$, solve for a_9
$\Rightarrow a_n = a_1 r^{n-1}$ [Write the formula]
$\Rightarrow a_9 = 2(2^{9-1})$ [Substitute the value of the terms]
$\Rightarrow a_9 = 2(2)^8$ [Simplify the power]
$\Rightarrow a_9 = 2(256)$ [Solve the exponent]
$\Rightarrow a_9 = 512$ [Do the multiplication]
Therefore, the tenth term in the sequence is 512.

Note: The sequence questions don't ask you to figure out the rule for determining the numbers in a sequence without giving the information in some form. For instance, in the preceding example, if you were given that the nth term of the sequence was $5 \times 2^{n-1}$, you may be asked to determine that each term after the first was 2 times the term before it. Conversely, if you were given that the first term in the sequence was 5 and that each term after the first was 2 times the term before it, you might be asked to find that the nth term of the sequence was $5 \times 2^{n-1}$.

SUM OF TERMS IN A GEOMETRIC SEQUENCE: We can easily add up the first "n" terms of a geometric progression that starts with "a" and has common ratio "r".

The formula for the sum of the first "n" terms is $= \dfrac{ar^n - a}{r - 1}$, when $r \neq 1$.

Note: If $r = 1$, then all terms are the same, so the sum is $=$ "na"

For Example: Find the sum of the first 8 terms of the sequence 5, 10, 20, 40, 80.......
Since, $\dfrac{10}{5} = \dfrac{20}{10} = \dfrac{40}{20} = \dfrac{80}{40} = 2$, the sequence is a geometric sequence with a common ratio of 2.
First term $\Rightarrow a = 5$
Common Ratio $\Rightarrow r = 2$
No. of terms $\Rightarrow n = 8$
Sum of the first 8 terms $\Rightarrow \dfrac{ar^n - a}{r - 1} \Rightarrow \dfrac{5 \times 2^8 - 5}{2 - 1} = 5(2^8 - 1) = 5(256 - 1) = 5 \times 255 = 1275$
Check: The first eight terms are 5, 10, 20, 40, 80, 160, 320, and 640.
$\Rightarrow 5 + 10 + 20 + 40 + 80 + 160 + 320 + 640 = 1275$

ASCENDING & DESCENDING GEOMETRIC SEQUENCE:

(A) ASCENDING GEOMETRIC SEQUENCE:
Ascending Geometric Sequence is a sequence of numbers formed by multiplication.
EZ STEP-BY-STEP METHOD: Apply the following step(s) to find a missing term in an ascending geometric sequence:
STEP 1: Divide any term by the one preceding it to find the common ratio.
STEP 2: Multiply the term preceding the missing term by the common ratio.
EZ TIP: If the missing term is the first term, it may be found by dividing the second term by the common ratio.

Method to Determine Whether a Sequence is Ascending Geometric: If the sequence is ascending, divide the second term by the first, the third term by the second, and the fourth by third, and so on. If the ratio is the same in all the cases and the value of each subsequent term is increasing, then the sequence is ascending geometric.

Example #1:   1, 2, 4, 8, 16, 32, 64.......
⇒ is a geometric sequence in which the common ratio is 2. Multiply each term by 2 to get the successive term; therefore, the next term would be 64 × 2 = 128.

Example #2: 2, 4, 8, 16, 32, 64, 128
⇒ is a geometric sequence in which the common ratio is 2. Divide the second term by 2 to get the first term; therefore, the first term would be 2 ÷ 2 = 1

(B) DESCENDING GEOMETRIC SEQUENCE:
Ascending Geometric Sequence is a sequence of numbers formed by division.
EZ STEP-BY-STEP METHOD: Apply the following step(s) to find a missing term in a descending geometric sequence:
STEP 1: Divide any term by the one following it to find the common ratio.
STEP 2: Divide the term preceding the missing term by the common ratio.
EZ TIP: If the missing term is the first term, it may be found by multiplying the second term by the common ratio.

Method to Determine Whether a Sequence is Descending Geometric: If the sequence is descending, divide the first term by the second, the second term by the third, the third by fourth, and so on. If the ratio is the same in all the cases and the value of each subsequent term is decreasing, then the sequence is decreasing geometric.

Example #1:   128, 64, 32, 16, 8, 4, 2.......
⇒ is a geometric sequence in which the common ratio is ½. Divide each term by 2 to get each successive term; therefore, the next term would be 2 ÷ 2 = 1

Example #2: 64, 32, 16, 8, 4, 2, 1
⇒ is a geometric sequence in which the common ratio is ½. Multiply the second term by 2 to get the first term; therefore, the first term would be 64 × 2 = 128

EZ NOTE: These sequences have real-life applications, and there may be questions in the math section using geometric sequences in contexts such as, population growth or trends. Since the *n*th term of geometric sequences can be written using exponential notation, the growth or progression of such sequences is sometimes called exponential growth.

5.2.3: MULTIPLE OPERATIONS SEQUENCE:
Mixed or multiple operation sequence is a sequence formed by the combination of arithmetic and geometric sequence. It is a sequence of numbers in which each term of the sequence is formed by applying multiple operations, such as addition, subtraction, multiplication, and/or division.

Example #1:   1, 4, 10, 22, 46, 94, 190.......
⇒ Multiply each term by 2 and then add 2 to get each successive term

Example #2:   1, 7, 19, 43, 91, 187.......
⇒ Multiply each term by 2 and then add 5 to get each successive term

Example #3:   1, 2, 4, 7, 11, 16, 22, 29.......
⇒ Add the first term by 1, second by 2, third by 3, fourth by 4, fifth by 5, and so on to get each successive term

Example #4:   27, 26, 24, 21, 17, 12, 6.......
⇒ Subtract the first term by 1, second by 2, third by 3, fourth by 4, fifth by 5, and so on to get each successive term

5.2.4: MISCELLANEOUS SEQUENCES:

If the sequence is neither arithmetic nor geometric, there can be other miscellaneous types of sequences. For instance, such sequences can be formed by using exponents or radicals, or there may be a varied pattern in the sequence that must be determined.

(A) HARMONIC SEQUENCE: Harmonic sequence is a sequence of fractions in which the numerator is 1, and the denominators form an arithmetic sequence.

For Example: $\dfrac{1}{2}$ $\dfrac{1}{7}$ $\dfrac{1}{12}$ $\dfrac{1}{17}$ $\dfrac{1}{22}$ $\dfrac{1}{27}$

(B) EXPONENTIAL SEQUENCE: SEQUENCE FORMED BY EXPONENTS: Exponential sequence is a sequence in which each term of the sequence is being raised to the power of the same number to form the next term or the same number may be first squared, then cubed, etc. Such a sequence may have each term a square or a cube, or the difference may be squares or cubes.

Example #1:   1, 4, 9, 16, 25, 36, 49, 64, 81.......
⇒ Each term is the square of 1, 2, 3, 4, 5.......

Example #2:   5, 25, 125, 625.......
⇒ The same number "5" is first raised to the power of 1, then 2, then 3, and so on to get each successive term.

(C) RADICAL SEQUENCE: SEQUENCE FORMED BY RADICALS: Radical sequence is a sequence in which each term of a sequence is being square rooted or cube rooted to form the next term or the same number may be first square rooted, then cube rooted, etc.

(D) LINEAR RELATIONSHIPS: Linear Relationships are formed when a linear pair follows a particular pattern. These patterns in a linear pair are formed by relationships involving sums, differences, products, and/or divisions between adjacent numbers.

Example #1:   (1, 6), (2, 7), (5, 10), (7, 12).......
⇒ Add 5 to the first term to get the second term in all the linear pairs.

Example #2:   (20, 18), (14, 12), (10, 8), (9, 7).......
⇒ Subtract 2 from the first term to get the second term in all the linear pairs.

Example #3:   (1, 6), (2, 12), (8, 48), (9, 54), (10, 60).......
⇒ Multiply the first term by 6 to get the second term in all the linear pairs.

Example #4:   (100, 50), (80, 40), (50, 25), (20, 10), (10, 5).......
⇒ Divide the first term by 2 to get the second term in all the linear pairs.

Example #5:   (1, 6), (5, 26), (10, 51), (15, 76), (20, 101).......
⇒ Multiply the first term by 5 and then add 1 to get the second term in all the linear pairs.

5.3: SOLVING SEQUENCE:

5.3.1: SEQUENCE RULE:

A given sequence is a collection of numbers in a set order. The order of a given sequence can be determined by a specific **"sequence rule"**. In other words, sequence is defined by **"function rules,"** where each term in the sequence is a function of its place in the sequence.

Following are some examples of sequence rules:

$\Rightarrow A_n = 7n$ $\Rightarrow$ The nth term of this sequence is defined by the given rule $7n$.
For Instance: $A_1 \Rightarrow$ The first term in the sequence = $7(1) = 7$
                   $A_2 \Rightarrow$ The second term in the sequence = $7(2) = 14$
                   $A_3 \Rightarrow$ The third term in the sequence = $7(3) = 21$
                   $A_4 \Rightarrow$ The fourth term in the sequence = $7(4) = 28$
                   First Ten Terms $\Rightarrow$ {7, 14, 21, 28, 35, 42, 49, 56, 63, 70,.......}

$\Rightarrow S_n = n^2 + 5$ $\Rightarrow$ The nth term of this sequence is defined by the given rule $n^2 + 5$.
For Instance: $S_1 \Rightarrow$ The first term in the sequence = $(1)^2 + 5 = 6$
                   $S_2 \Rightarrow$ The second term in the sequence = $(2)^2 + 5 = 9$
                   $S_3 \Rightarrow$ The third term in the sequence = $(3)^2 + 5 = 14$
                   $S_4 \Rightarrow$ The fourth term in the sequence = $(4)^2 + 5 = 21$
                   First Ten Terms $\Rightarrow$ {6, 9, 14, 21, 30, 41, 54, 69, 86, 105,.......}

Note: The rule that defines the sequence is not always given. So, if the sequence rule is not given, you'll have to figure it out yourself; it's like working backwards, from the sequence to the rule that defines it.

DEFINING RULES FOR SEQUENCES:

Generally, in sequence problems, the important thing to remember is that you must be given the rule in order to find a particular number in a sequence. It may sometimes lead to a wrong answer while trying to solve a sequence problem without the rule.
For instance: If $S_1 = 7$ and $S_2 = 8$, what is S_3 = ?
At the first glimpse, it looks like this is a sequence where the value of each term is one more than the previous one or that it's a counting sequence by 1's, so the next term or $S_3 = 9$.
So the sequence might be: 7, 8, 9, 10, 11.......
This inference is true but may not necessarily be mathematically valid, because we were not given the rule for this particular sequence.
For all we know, it could be a sequence where the second term is one more then first term, third term is two more than the second term, the fourth term is three more than the second term, and so on, where the difference between each successive term is increasing by 1
So the sequence might now be: 7, 8, 10, 13, 17, 22.......
Therefore, without the rule, there is no way to be sure.
However, there are times when a sequence rule can be determined, especially when we know that there is a constant difference between two successive terms and are given at least one term.

5.3.2: FIGURING-OUT THE PATTERN OR MISSING TERMS:

To find the rule, determine the pattern and find the missing term in sequences, you have to figure out what rule has been used by studying the terms you are given, and you often have to apply **"hit-and-try"** or **"trial-and-error"** method to find the **"pattern"** and the **"missing term(s)"**.
You have to determine what operation or sequence of operations will always result in the next term in the series. Once you are able to determine the rule that forms the pattern, you can easily find the missing terms.

Following are some of the common sequence rules:
(A) If the difference between successive terms is always constant, the rule will take the form of $kn + x$, where k and x are real numbers and k is equal to the difference between successive terms.

For Example: If the first four terms of a sequence are 14, 20, 26, 32; what is the sequence rule and what is the value of the 10th and 90th term?

Since the difference between each successive term is 6, the rule for this sequence must be in the form of $kn + x$.

First term $\Rightarrow S_1 = 14$
     $\Rightarrow Kn + x = 14$
     $\Rightarrow 6(1) + x = 14$
     $\Rightarrow x = 8$

Now that we know the rule of the sequence and also k and x, we can find any term in the sequence.

1st Term $\Rightarrow kn + x = (6)(1) + 8 = 14$
2nd Term $\Rightarrow kn + x = (6)(2) + 8 = 20$
10th Term $\Rightarrow kn + x = (6)(10) + 8 = 68$
90th Term $\Rightarrow kn + x = (6)(90) + 8 = 548$

(B) If the difference between successive terms changes in a set pattern, the rule will take the form of $an^2 + bn + c$, where a, b, and c are real numbers.

For Example: If the first four terms of a sequence are 16, 26, 38, 52; what is the sequence rule and what is the value of the 10th and 50th term?

Since the difference between each successive term is increasing by 2, the rule for this sequence must be in the form of $an^2 + bn + c$.

Using this rule, we can set up a system of three different equations with three variables:

1st Term (16) $\Rightarrow a(1)^2 + b(1) + c = a + b + c = 16$
2nd Term (26) $\Rightarrow a(2)^2 + b(2) + c = 4a + 2b + c = 26$
3rd Term (38) $\Rightarrow a(3)^2 + b(3) + c = 9a + 3b + c = 38$

Now we solve these equations simultaneously and solve for a, b, and $c \Rightarrow a = 1$; $b = 7$; $c = 8$

Finally, we can find the sequence rule $\Rightarrow n^2 + 7n + 8$

Now, we can use this rule to find any term in the sequence:

1st Term $\Rightarrow n^2 + 7n + 8 \Rightarrow (1)^2 + 7(1) + 8 = 1 + 7 + 8 = 16$
2nd Term $\Rightarrow n^2 + 7n + 8 \Rightarrow (2)^2 + 7(2) + 8 = 4 + 14 + 8 = 26$
3rd Term $\Rightarrow n^2 + 7n + 8 \Rightarrow (3)^2 + 7(3) + 8 = 9 + 21 + 8 = 38$
4th Term $\Rightarrow n^2 + 7n + 8 \Rightarrow (4)^2 + 7(4) + 8 = 16 + 28 + 8 = 52$
10th Term $\Rightarrow n^2 + 7n + 8 \Rightarrow (10)^2 + 7(10) + 8 = 100 + 70 + 8 = 178$
50th Term $\Rightarrow n^2 + 7n + 8 \Rightarrow (50)^2 + 7(50) + 8 = 2500 + 350 + 8 = 2858$

Note: You will generally not be required to derive a very complex sequence rule; however, it is important to understand that sequence rules can be derived using given terms in the sequence.

ALTERNATE METHODS:

If you are not able to determine the sequence formula as demonstrated above or if it gets too complicated, there are often easier alternate methods that you can use to solve some sequence problems.

For Example: If each term in a sequence is two more than the previous term, and the eighth term is 24, what is the value of the 100th term?

Solution: From the eighth term to the hundredth term, there are 92 terms in between. Since $92 \times 2 = 184$, there is an increase of 184 from the eighth term to the one hundredth term.

Therefore, the 100th term is $\Rightarrow 24 + 184 = 208$.

5.4: REPEATING PATTERN SEQUENCE:

HOW TO SOLVE SEQUENCE PROBLEMS WITH REPEATING TERMS:

Some sequence problems contain terms that follow a *"repeating pattern"*. In these types of sequence problems, the given terms in the sequence repeat a pattern over and over again. The problem will usually tell you the repeating pattern and ask you to find out the nth term.

The best way to solve such problems is to familiarize yourself with the following rule and make sure you understand it.

EZ RULE: When k numbers or terms form a repeating sequence or pattern, to find the nth number or term, divide n by k and take the remainder r.
         $\Rightarrow$ The rth term and the nth term represent the same value.

Example #1:   Consider the following infinite sequence: 1, 5, 2, 8, 7, 9, 6, 1, 5, 2, 8, 7, 9, 6, ..., where the seven digits 1, 5, 2, 8, 7, 9, and 6, keep on repeating in that order indefinitely. What is the 600th term of the sequence?

Solution: When 600 is divided by 7, the quotient is 85 ($7 \times 85 = 595$) and the remainder is 5.
         Therefore, the first 595 terms are just the numbers 1, 5, 2, 8, 7, 9, 6, repeated 85 times.
         The 595th term in the sequence is simply the 85th 6 in the sequence.
         After the 595th term, the pattern repeats again: the 596th term is 1, the 597th term is 5, the 598th term is 2, the 599th term is 8, and the 600th term is 7.
         Note: You must notice that in this case that since 5 is the remainder when 600 is divided by 7, the 600th term is the same as the 5th term.

Example #2:   In the sequence below, every number is ½ more than the previous number. What is half of the difference between 62nd and 68th term?
         1, 1½, 2, 2½, 3, 3½, 4, 4½, 5.......

Solution: Since the interval between successive terms is constant (½), the difference between the 62nd and 68th terms will be equal to the difference between the largest and the smallest of any seven consecutive terms. So begin with 1, and write the sequence out to six more terms, and then subtract 1 from the value of that term: (Largest of 7 terms) – (Smallest of 7 terms) = $4 - 1 = 3$. And half of 3 = $3(\frac{1}{2}) = 1.5$

5.5: SEQUENCE NOTATIONS:

HOW TO SOLVE SEQUENCE PROBLEMS WITH NOTATIONS:

Sequences are sometimes given by a rule or **"sequence notation"** that defines an entry, usually called the nth entry in terms of previous entries of the sequence. These sequence problems contain strange looking rules or notations. Don't let that strange looking notation throw you off. The notation simply defines the nth term in the sequence. In a sequence problem, the given notation in the sequence is generated by performing an operation, which will be defined for you, on either nth term or on any of the previous terms in the sequence. The best way to solve such problems is to familiarize yourself with the sequence notation and make sure you understand it.

Example #1:   What is the difference between the sixth and fifth terms in the sequence 2, 10, 30, 68.......whose nth term is $n(n^2 + 1)$?

Solution: Use the operation given to come up with the values for your terms:
Sixth Term $\Rightarrow n_6 = 6(6^2 + 1) = 6(37) = 222$
Fifth Term $\Rightarrow n_5 = 5(5^2 + 1) = 5(26) = 130$
Difference between the Sixth and Fifth terms $\Rightarrow n_6 - n_5 = 222 - 130 = 92$
Therefore, the difference between the sixth and fifth terms is $222 - 130 = 92$

Example #2:   What is the difference between the sixth and fifth terms in the sequence 0, 6, 24, 60.......whose nth term is $n(n^2 - 1)$?

Solution: Use the operation given to come up with the values for your terms:
Sixth Term $\Rightarrow n_6 = 6(6^2 - 1) = 6(35) = 210$
Fifth Term $\Rightarrow n_5 = 5(5^2 - 1) = 5(24) = 120$
Difference between the Sixth and Fifth terms $\Rightarrow n_6 - n_5 = 210 - 120 = 90$
Therefore, the difference between the sixth and fifth terms is $210 - 120 = 90$

SEQUENCE AND PATTERNS: Some sequences are often easier to look at in terms of patterns, instead of rules.

For Example: If $S_n = 2^n$, what is the units digit of S_{75}?

Solution: Since we are asked to find the value of the 75th term, no one is expected to compute 75 terms, so most likely there has to be a pattern. Let's first list the first ten terms of the sequence and try to figure out a pattern.
$\Rightarrow S_1 = 2^1 = 2$
$\Rightarrow S_2 = 2^2 = 4$
$\Rightarrow S_3 = 2^3 = 8$
$\Rightarrow S_4 = 2^4 = 16$
$\Rightarrow S_5 = 2^5 = 32$
$\Rightarrow S_6 = 2^6 = 64$
$\Rightarrow S_7 = 2^7 = 128$
$\Rightarrow S_8 = 2^8 = 256$
$\Rightarrow S_9 = 2^9 = 512$
$\Rightarrow S_{10} = 2^{10} = 1024$
Observe the pattern of the units digits in the sequence: 2, 4, 8, 6, repeating over and over again every four terms. Also note that the units digit of S_n when n is a multiple of 4, is always equal to 6 (the fourth term is 16 and eighth term is 256). We can use the multiples of 4 as benchmark points in the pattern. Since 75 is one less than 76 (which is the closest multiple of 4), the units digit of S_{75} will be 8, which always comes before 6 in the pattern. Therefore, the units digit of S_{75} is 8.

PRACTICE EXERCISE – QUESTIONS AND ANSWERS WITH EXPLANATIONS: SEQUENCE & PATTERNS:

Question #1: Find the value of n in the following sequence: 1, 7, 13, 19, n
Solution: Add 6 to each successive term $\Rightarrow n = 25$

Question #2: Find the value of n in the following sequence: 1, 3, 7, 13, 21, 31, 43, n
Solution: Add the first term by 2, second term by 4, third term by 6, fourth term by 8, and so on $\Rightarrow n = 57$

Question #3: Find the value of n in the following sequence: 57, 51, 45, 39, 33, 27, 21, n
Solution: Subtract 6 to get each subsequent term $\Rightarrow n = 15$

Question #4: Find the value of n in the following sequence: 27, 25, 21, 15, n
Solution: Subtract the first term by 2, second by 4, third by 6, fourth by 8, and so on $\Rightarrow n = 7$

Question #5: A sequence is formed as follows: the first term is 5, and every other term is 7 more than the term that precedes it. What is the 10th term in the sequence?
Solution: Write down the sequence starting with the first term, which is 5, and keep adding 7 to get the next term
$\Rightarrow$ 5, 12, 19, 26, 33, 40, 47, 54, 61, 68 (12 is 7 more than 5, 19 is 7 more than 12, etc.)
Therefore, the 10th term in sequence is 68.

Question #6: A sequence is formed as follows: the first term is 5, and every other term is 7 more than the term that precedes it. What is the 100th term in the sequence?
Solution: Write down the sequence starting with the first term, which is 5, and keep adding 7 to get the next term
$\Rightarrow$ 5, 12, 19, 26, 33, 40, 47, 54, 61, 68....... (12 is 7 more than 5, 19 is 7 more than 12, etc.)
Evidently, we could continue writing out the terms, and if the question asked for the 10th term, that would be the easiest thing to do. However, we are not, going to write out 100 terms.
The terms are just 2 less than the corresponding multiples of 7 (7, 14, 21, 28, 35.......):
$\Rightarrow$ 12, which is the 2nd term, is 2 less than 2 × 7
$\Rightarrow$ 33 which is the 5th term, is 2 less than 5 × 7
Now that we have found the pattern, the 100th term is 2 less than 100 × 7 = 700 − 2 = 698.
Alternately: We can also solve this problem in 1 step by using our EZ Rule:
First Term $\Rightarrow a = 5$
Common Difference $\Rightarrow d = 7$
nth Term = 100th term $\Rightarrow a + (n - 1)d = 5 + (100 - 1)7 = 5 + (99)7 = 5 + 693 = 698$

Question #7: Find the value of n in the following sequence: 1, 6, 36, 216, n
Solution: Multiply by 6 to get each successive term $\Rightarrow n = 1{,}296$

Question #8: Find the value of n in the following sequence: 1, 9, 81, 729, n
Solution: Multiply by 9 to get each successive term $\Rightarrow n = 6{,}561$

Question #9: Find the value of n in the following sequence: 128, 64, 32, 16, n
Solution: Divide by 2 to get each successive term $\Rightarrow n = 8$

Question #10: Find the value of n in the following sequence: 15625, 3125, 625, 125, n
Solution: Divide by 5 to get each successive term $\Rightarrow n = 25$

Question #11: If the ninth term in a geometric sequence is 1024, and the common ratio is 2, what is the first term?
Solution: First, use the formula to solve for r:
$\Rightarrow a_n = a_1 r^{n-1}$ [Write the formula]
$\Rightarrow 1024 = a_1(2)^{9-1}$ [Substitute the value of the terms]
$\Rightarrow 1024 = a_1(2)^8$ [Simplify the power]
$\Rightarrow 1024 = a_1(256)$ [Solve the exponent]
$\Rightarrow a_1 = 4$ [Divide both sides by 256]

Therefore, the first term in the sequence is 4.

Question #12: If the eighth term in a geometric sequence is 15309, and the common ratio is 3, what is the first term?

Solution: First, use the formula to solve for r:

$\Rightarrow a_n = a_1 r^{n-1}$ [Write the formula]

$\Rightarrow 15309 = a_1 (3)^{8-1}$ [Substitute the value of the terms]

$\Rightarrow 15309 = a_1 (3)^7$ [Simplify the power]

$\Rightarrow 15309 = a_1 (2187)$ [Solve the exponent]

$\Rightarrow a_1 = 7$ [Divide both sides by 2187]

Therefore, the first term in the sequence is 7.

Question #13: If the first term in a geometric sequence is 4, and the fifth term is 64, what is the ninth term?

Solution: $\Rightarrow a_1 = 4$ $\Rightarrow a_5 = 64$

First, use the formula to solve for r:

$\Rightarrow a_n = a_1 r^{n-1}$ [Write the formula]

$\Rightarrow 64 = 4r^4$ [Substitute the value of the terms]

$\Rightarrow 16 = r^4$ [Divide both sides by 4]

$\Rightarrow r = 2$ [Take the fourth root of both sides]

Next, using $r = 2$, solve for a_9

$\Rightarrow a_n = a_1 r^{n-1}$ [Write the formula]

$\Rightarrow a_9 = 4(2^{9-1})$ [Substitute the value of the terms]

$\Rightarrow a_9 = 4(2)^8$ [Simplify the power]

$\Rightarrow a_9 = 4(256)$ [Solve the exponent]

$\Rightarrow a_9 = 1024$ [Do the multiplication]

Therefore, the ninth term in the sequence is 1024.

Question #14: If the first term in a geometric sequence is 7, and the third term is 63, what is the eighth term?

Solution: $\Rightarrow a_1 = 7$ $\Rightarrow a_3 = 63$

First, use the formula to solve for r:

$\Rightarrow a_n = a_1 r^{n-1}$ [Write the formula]

$\Rightarrow 63 = 7r^2$ [Substitute the value of the terms]

$\Rightarrow 9 = r^2$ [Divide both sides by 7]

$\Rightarrow r = 3$ [square root both sides]

Next, using $r = 3$, solve for a_8

$\Rightarrow a_n = a_1 r^{n-1}$ [Write the formula]

$\Rightarrow a_8 = 7(3^{8-1})$ [Substitute the value of the terms]

$\Rightarrow a_8 = 7(3)^7$ [Simplify the power]

$\Rightarrow a_8 = 7(2187)$ [Solve the exponent]

$\Rightarrow a_8 = 15309$ [Do the multiplication]

Therefore, the eighth term in the sequence is 15309.

Question #15: Find the value of n in the following sequence: 1, 3, 7, 15, 31, 63, n

Solution: Multiply prior term by 2, and then add 1 to get each successive term $\Rightarrow n = 127$

Question #16: Find the value of n in the following sequence: 1, 8, 22, 50, 106, n

Solution: Multiply each term by 2, and then add 6 to get each successive term $\Rightarrow n = 218$

Question #17: Consider the following infinite sequence: 1, 5, 2, 8, 7, 9, 6, 1, 5, 2, 8, 7, 9, 6, ..., where the seven digits 1, 5, 2, 8, 7, 9, and 6, keep on repeating in that order indefinitely. What is the 800th term of the sequence?

Solution: When 800 is divided by 7, the quotient is 114 (7 × 114 = 798) and the remainder is 2.

Therefore, the first 798 terms are just the numbers 1, 5, 2, 8, 7, 9, 6, repeated 114 times.

The 798th term in the sequence is simply the 114th 6 in the sequence.

After the 798th term, the pattern repeats again: the 799th term is 1, and the 800th term is 5.

Note: You must notice that in this case that since 2 is the remainder when 800 is divided by 7, the 800th term is the same as the 2nd term.

Question #18: A car dealership carried cars in six colors (red, blue, green, yellow, white, and black). The cars were lined up in a long parking lot in the following order: red, blue, green, yellow, white, black, red, blue, green, yellow, white, black....... What was the color of the 800th car in the line?

Solution: When 800 is divided by 6, the quotient is 133 (6 × 133 = 798) and the remainder is 2.
Therefore, the first 798 cars are just the colors red, blue, green, yellow, white, and black, repeated 133 times.
The 798th car in the sequence is simply the 133rd black car in the sequence.
After the798th car, the pattern repeats again: the 799th car is red, and the 800th car is blue.
Note: You must notice that in this case that since 2 is the remainder when 800 is divided by 6, the 800th car is the same as the 2nd term.

Question #19: For any positive integer n: the first term of the sequence S_n is n, and every term after that is 1 less than twice the preceding term. What is the value of greatest term of S_5, that is less than 100?

Solution: Sequence S_5 proceeds as follows: 5, 9, 17, 33, 65, 129.......
So the greatest term smaller than 100 is 65

Question #20: For any positive integer n: the first term of the sequence S_n is n, and every term after that is 1 more than twice the preceding term. What is the units digit of the 100th term of S_9?

Solution: Obviously we are not going to write 100 terms, so let's first write the first few terms of the sequence:
Sequence S_9 proceeds as follows: 9, 19, 39, 79, 159.......
As you can observe, the unit's digit of every term is 9, so the unit's digit of the 100th term will also be 9.

Question #21: What is the difference between the sixth and fifth terms in the sequence 2, 12, 36, 80.......whose nth term is $n^2(n + 1)$?

Solution: Use the operation given to come up with the values for your terms:
Sixth Term $\Rightarrow n_6 = 6^2(6 + 1) = 36(7) = 252$
Fifth Term $\Rightarrow n_5 = 5^2(5 + 1) = 25(6) = 150$
Difference between the sixth and fifth terms $\Rightarrow n_6 - n_5 = 252 - 150 = 102$
Therefore, the difference between the sixth and fifth terms is $252 - 150 = 102$

Question #22: What is the difference between the sixth and fifth terms in the sequence 0, 4, 18, 48.......whose nth term is $n^2(n - 1)$?

Solution: Use the operation given to come up with the values for your terms:
Sixth Term $\Rightarrow n_6 = 6^2(6 - 1) = 36(5) = 180$
Fifth Term $\Rightarrow n_5 = 5^2(5 - 1) = 25(4) = 100$
Difference between the sixth and fifth terms $\Rightarrow n_6 - n_5 = 180 - 100 = 80$
Therefore, the difference between the sixth and fifth terms is $180 - 100 = 80$

PART 6.0: MISCELLANEOUS PROBLEMS:

TABLE OF CONTENTS:

6.1: CLOCK PROBLEMS:

6.1.1: ANALOG CLOCKS:

The *"analog clock"* problems involve the concept of how analog clocks function. Analog clock problems can often be solved with simple logic. The face of an analog clock or watch is a circle that consists of hands and time spaces.

There are Two Hands in Every Clock: ⇒ Hour Hand (H. H.): Also known as the Short Hand
⇒ Minute Hand (M. H.): Also known as the Long Hand

Note: Some clocks also have a second-hand, but that's not in the scope of our discussion here.

The Face of a Clock is Divided into Two Parts: ⇒ 12 Hour Spaces, and
⇒ 60 Minute Spaces

In 1 Hour: The hour-hand goes over 1 hour-space or 5 minute-space where as the minute-hand passes over 60 minute-spaces or 12 hour-spaces.
That is, in 1 hour or 60 minutes, the minute-hand gains 55 minutes on the hour-hand.

In 24 Hours: The hour-hand goes over 24 hour-space or 120 minute-spaces where as the minute-hand passes over 1,440 minute-spaces or 288 hour-spaces.

Every Hour: ⇒The two hands coincide once.
⇒The two hands are twice at right angles. (In this position, the hands are 15 minute-spaces apart)
⇒The two hands point in opposite directions once. (In this position, the hands are 30 minute-spaces apart)
Note: The hands are in the same straight line when they are coincident or opposite to each other.

Too Fast or Too Slow:
Too Fast: If a clock indicates 7:10, when the correct time is 7:00, it is said to be 10 minutes too fast
Too Slow: If a clock indicates 6:50, when the correct time is 7:00, it is said to be 10 minutes too slow.

Example #1:   If the minute hand of a clock moves 90 degrees, how many minutes of time have elapsed?
Solution: Every hour   ⇒ Minute Hand completes a whole revolution
⇒ Minute Hand moves 360°, every 60 minutes
Now since 90° is ¼ of 360°, the time it takes to move 90° will be ¼ of 60 minutes, which is 15 minutes.

Alternately, we can also form a proportion ⇒ $\dfrac{60}{n} = \dfrac{360}{90}$

$$\Rightarrow n = \dfrac{60 \times 90}{360}$$

$$\Rightarrow 15 \text{ minutes}$$

Example #2:   If the hour hand of a clock moves 90 degrees, how many hours of time have elapsed?
Solution: Every 12 hours   ⇒ Hour Hand completes a whole revolution
⇒ Hour Hand moves 360°, every 12 hours
Now since 90° is ¼ of 360°, the time it takes to move 90° will be ¼ of 12 hours, which is 3 hours.

Alternately, we can also form a proportion ⇒ $\dfrac{12}{n} = \dfrac{360}{90}$

$$\Rightarrow n = \dfrac{12 \times 90}{360}$$

$$\Rightarrow 3 \text{ hours}$$

Example #3:   What is the degree measure of the smaller angle formed by the hour hand and minute hand of a clock at 1:50?
Solution: First thing to do is to draw the following diagram of a clock that shows 1:50, and label it.

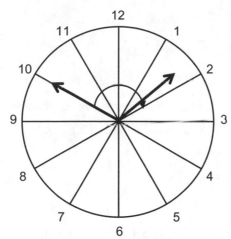

At 1:50 ⇒ Minute hand is pointing exactly at 10 (as shown above)
        ⇒ Hour Hand is point between 1 and 2 (as shown above)
        ⇒ The hour hand is not pointing exactly at 1; it was pointing exactly at 1 at 1:00.
Since the measure of each of the 12 central angles from one-hour number to the next hour number on the clock is 30° ⇒ Angle between the Minute Hand and hour of 1 = 30° × 3 = 90°
During the 50-minute between 1:00 and 1:50, the hour hand moved five-sixth of the way from 1 to 2. Since the measure of the angle between 1 and 2 is 30°, at 1:50 the hour hand has moved 25° from 1 toward 2 and still has 5° to go before it touches 2.

Precisely, the hour hand has gone $\dfrac{50}{60} = \dfrac{5}{6}$ of the way from 1 to 2.

Angle between the hour of 1 and Hour Hand ⇒ $\dfrac{5}{6}$ × 30° = 25°

Total Degree Measure of Angle between Minute Hand and Hour Hand ⇒ 90° + 25 ° = 115°

Example #4:   What is the degree measure of the smaller angle formed by the hour hand and minute hand of a clock at 1:15?

Solution: First thing to do is to draw the following diagram of a clock that shows 1:15, and label it.

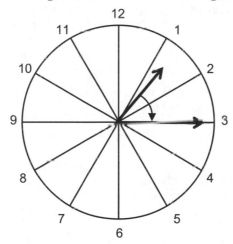

At 1:15 ⇒ Minute hand is pointing exactly at 3 (as shown above)
        ⇒ Hour Hand is pointing between 1 and 2 (as shown above)
        ⇒ The hour hand is not pointing exactly at 1, it was pointing exactly at 1 at 1:00.
Since the measure of each of the 12 central angles from one-hour number to the next hour number on the clock is 30° ⇒ Angle between the Minute Hand and hour of 2 = 30° × 1 = 30°
During the quarter-hour between 1:00 and 1:15, the hour hand moved one-fourth of the way from 1 to 2. Since the measure of the angle between 1 and 2 is 30°, at 1:15 the hour hand has moved 7.5° from 1 toward 2 and still has 22.5° to go before it touches 2.

Precisely, the hour hand has yet to go $\dfrac{22.5}{30} = \dfrac{3}{4}$ of the way from 1 to 2.

Angle between the hour of 2 and Hour Hand $\Rightarrow \dfrac{3}{4} \times 30° = 22.5°$

Total Degree Measure of Angle between Minute Hand and Hour Hand $\Rightarrow 30° + 22.5° = 52.5°$

Example #5:   If it is now 7:10, what time will it be when the hour hand has moved through the angle of 10°

Solution: The angle by which the hour hand moves every hour $\Rightarrow \dfrac{1}{12}$ of 360° = 30°

In other words, the hour hand moves 30° every hour

Therefore, it will move 10° in $\dfrac{1}{3}$ of an hour or 20 minutes.

Now, 20 minutes after 7:10 is 7:30

Example #6:   If it is now 9:15, what time will it be when the hour hand has moved through the angle of 20°

Solution: The angle by which the hour hand moves every hour $\Rightarrow \dfrac{1}{12}$ of 360° = 30°

In other words, the hour hand moves 30° every hour.

Therefore, it will move 20° in $\dfrac{2}{3}$ of an hour or 40 minutes.

Now, 40 minutes after 9:15 is 9:55

GAINING OR LOSING TIME: Some clocks/watches do not run at the speed at which they are supposed to run. Due to this, they either run too fast or too slow, which results in gain of time or loss of time.

Example #7:   A watch gains 9 minutes and 10 seconds every 5 days. If the rate of gain is constant, how much does the watch gain in one day?

Solution: Amount of gain in 5 days $\Rightarrow$ 9 minutes & 10 seconds $\qquad \Rightarrow 9(60) + 10 = 540 + 10 \Rightarrow 550$ sec
Amount of gain in 1 day $\Rightarrow$ 550 seconds ÷ 5 $\qquad \Rightarrow 110 = 60 + 50$ sec $\qquad \Rightarrow$ 1 min & 50 sec

Example #8:   A watch loses 7 minutes and 6 seconds every 6 days. If the rate of loss is constant, how much does the watch lose in one day?

Solution: Amount of loss in 6 days $\Rightarrow$ 7 minutes & 6 seconds $\qquad \Rightarrow 7(60) + 6 = 420 + 6 \qquad \Rightarrow 426$ seconds
Amount of loss in 1 day $\Rightarrow$ 426 seconds ÷ 6 $\qquad \Rightarrow 71 = 60 + 11$ seconds $\Rightarrow$ 1 min & 11 sec

6.1.2: DIGITAL CLOCKS:

The **"digital clock"** problems involve the concept of how digital clocks function. Digital clock problems can often be solved with simple logic. The face of a digital clock or watch consists only of digits.

Example #9:   When a digital clock displays 5:22, the sum of the digits is 9. How many minutes after 5:22 will the sum of the digits be 20 for the first time?

Solution: In a digital clock, the largest possible sum of the digits for the minutes is 14, when it is 59 minutes after the hour. Therefore, the first time that the sum of all the digits can be 20 occurs when the hour is 6, at exactly 6:59, this is when we have the sum of the digits: 6 + 5 + 9 = 20.
The time lag between 6:59 and 5:22 $\Rightarrow$ 1 hour and 37 minutes = 60 + 37 = 97 minutes.
Therefore, the sum of 20 will occur after 97 minutes.

Example #10:   When a digital clock displays 7:11, the sum of the digits is 9. How many minutes after 7:11 will the sum of the digits be 22 for the first time?

Solution: In a digital clock, the largest possible sum of the digits for the minutes is 14, when it is 59 minutes after the hour. Therefore, the first time that the sum of all the digits can be 22 occurs when the hour is 9, at exactly 8:59, this is when we have the sum of the digits: 8 + 5 + 9 = 22.
The time lag between 8:59 and 7:11 $\Rightarrow$ 1 hour and 48 minutes = 60 + 48 = 108 minutes.
Therefore, the sum of 22 will occur after 108 minutes.

6.2: ALPHANUMERIC PROBLEMS:

An **"alphanumeric"** problem is an arithmetic problem in which some or all of the digits have been replaced by alphabets, and you are required to determine what numbers the alphabets represent. Typically, there are no formulas to solve such problems. The best method to solve these problems is to use a little logic, some trial-and-error, and reason through the problem one-step at a time. The easiest way to explain this is by showing a few examples.

6.2.1: BASED ON SUM:

Example #1: In the correctly worked out addition problem given below, if each letter represents a distinct digit, what is the value of A?

$$\begin{array}{r} AB \\ + \ AB \\ \hline BCC \end{array}$$

Solution: Since any two-digit number is always less than $100 \Rightarrow AB < 100$

Since sum of any two two-digit number is always less than $200 \Rightarrow AB + AB < 200 \Rightarrow BCC < 200$

It implies that BCC is some number that is between 100 and 199. No matter what, B has to be "1".
Now let's go back to our addition problem and rewrite it, replacing each B with a "1":

$$\begin{array}{r} A1 \\ + \ A1 \\ \hline 1CC \end{array}$$

Now, since $1 + 1 = 2$, let's go back to our addition problem and rewrite it, replacing both C's with 2's.

$$\begin{array}{r} A1 \\ + \ A1 \\ \hline 122 \end{array}$$

Value of $A \Rightarrow A + A = 12 \quad \Rightarrow 2A = 12 \qquad \Rightarrow A = 6$

EZ TIP: If the sum of two two-digit numbers is a three-digit number, the first digit of the sum is 1. Similarly, if the sum of two three-digit numbers is a four-digit number, the first digit of the sum is 1.

6.2.2: BASED ON PRODUCT:

Example #2: In the correctly worked out multiplication problem given below, each letter represents a different digit. What is the value of $A \times B \times C \times D$?

$$\begin{array}{r} ABA \\ \times \quad A \\ \hline CBD5 \end{array}$$

Solution: The first step in the multiplication is to multiply $A \times A$, which is A^2. Since 5 is the only digit whose square ends in 5, A must be 5, so replace each A with 5. The problem now looks like this:

$$\begin{array}{r} 5B5 \\ \times \quad 5 \\ \hline CBD5 \end{array}$$

Since $5 \times 500 = 2500$ and $5 \times 600 = 3000$, the product $CBD5$ is somewhere in between.

Therefore, $C = 2$ and $B \geq 5$. Rewrite the problem, replacing C with 2:

$$\begin{array}{r} 5B5 \\ \times \quad 5 \\ \hline 2BD5 \end{array}$$

Since A is 5, B can't be 5, so B is at least 6. Notice that the second digit of $5B5$ and the second digit of $2BD5$ are the same. But $5 \times 5\underline{6}5 = 2\underline{8}25$, which doesn't work; so B must be at least 8: $5 \times 5\underline{8}5 = 2\underline{9}25$, which also doesn't work, but $5 \times 5\underline{9}5 = 2\underline{9}75$, which does work:

$$\begin{array}{r} 595 \\ \times \quad 5 \\ \hline 2975 \end{array}$$

Then, $B = 9$ and $D = 7$:
Therefore, $A = 5$, $B = 9$, $C = 2$, and $D = 7$
Value of $A \times B \times C \times D \Rightarrow 5 \times 9 \times 2 \times 7 = 630$

PRACTICE EXERCISE – QUESTIONS AND ANSWERS WITH EXPLANATIONS: MISCELLANEOUS PROBLEMS:

Question #1: If the minute hand of a clock moves 45 degrees, how many minutes of time have elapsed?

Solution: Every hour $\Rightarrow$ Minute Hand completes a whole revolution
$\Rightarrow$ Minute Hand moves 360°, every 60 minutes
Since 45° is 1/8 of 360°, the time it takes to move 45° will be 1/8 of 60 minutes, that is, 7.5 minutes.

Alternately, we can also form a proportion $\Rightarrow \dfrac{60}{n} = \dfrac{360}{45}$

$$\Rightarrow n = \frac{45 \times 60}{360} = \frac{15}{2}$$

$$\Rightarrow 7.5 \text{ minutes}$$

Question #2: If the hour hand of a clock moves 45 degrees, how many hours of time have elapsed?

Solution: Every 12 hours $\Rightarrow$ Hour Hand completes a whole revolution
$\Rightarrow$ Hour Hand moves 360°, every 12 hours
Now since 45° is 1/8 of 360°, the time it takes to move 45° will be 1/8 of 12 hours, that is, 1.5 hours.

Alternately, we can also form a proportion $\Rightarrow \dfrac{12}{n} = \dfrac{360}{45}$

$$\Rightarrow n = \frac{12 \times 45}{360}$$

$$\Rightarrow 1.5 \text{ hours}$$

Question #3: What is the degree measure of the smaller angle formed by the hour hand and minute hand of a clock at 11:20?

Solution: First thing to do is to draw the following diagram of a clock that shows 11:20, and label it.

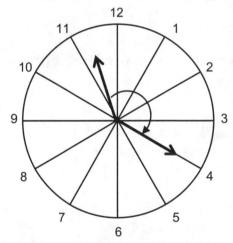

At 11:20 $\Rightarrow$ Minute hand is pointing exactly at 4 (as shown above)
$\Rightarrow$ Hour Hand is pointing between 11 and 12 (as shown above)
$\Rightarrow$ The hour hand is not pointing exactly at 11; it was pointing exactly at 11 at 11:00.
Since the measure of each of the 12 central angles from one-hour number to the next hour number on the clock is 30° $\Rightarrow$ Angle between the Minute Hand and hour of 12 = 30° × 4 = 120°
During the one-third-hour between 11:00 and 11:20, the hour hand moved one-third of the way from 11 to 12. Since the measure of the angle between 11 and 12 is 30°, at 11:20 the hour hand has moved 1/3 of 30°, or 10°, from 11 toward 12 and still has 20° to go before it touches 12.

Precisely, the hour hand has yet to go $\dfrac{20}{30} = \dfrac{2}{3}$ of the way from 11 to 12.

Angle between the hour of 12 and Hour Hand $\Rightarrow \dfrac{2}{3} \times 30° = 20°$

Total Degree Measure of Angle between Minute Hand and Hour Hand $\Rightarrow 120° + 20° = 140°$

Question #4: What is the degree measure of the smaller angle formed by the hour hand and minute hand of a clock at 10:10?

Solution: First thing to do is to draw the following diagram of a clock that shows 10:10, and label it.

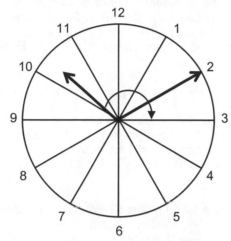

At 10:10 $\Rightarrow$ Minute hand is pointing exactly at 2 (as shown above)
                 $\Rightarrow$ Hour Hand is pointing between 10 and 11 (as shown above)
                 Note: The hour hand is not pointing exactly at 10; it was pointing exactly at 10 at 10:00.
Since the measure of each of the 12 central angles from one-hour number to the next hour number on the clock is 30° $\Rightarrow$ Angle between the Minute Hand and hour of 11 = 30° × 3 = 90°
During the one-sixth-hour between 10:00 and 10:10, the hour hand moved one-sixth of the way from 10 to 11. Since the measure of the angle between 10 and 11 is 30°, at 10:10 the hour hand has moved 1/6 of 30°, or 5° from 10 toward 11 and still has 25° to go before it touches 11.

Precisely, the hour hand has yet to go $\dfrac{25}{30} = \dfrac{5}{6}$ of the way from 10 to 11.

Angle between the hour of 11 and Hour Hand $\Rightarrow \dfrac{5}{6} \times 30° = 25°$

Total Degree Measure of Angle between Minute Hand and Hour Hand $\Rightarrow 90° + 25° = 115°$

Question #5: If it is now 7:15, what time will it be when the hour hand has moved through the angle of 10°?

Solution: The angle by which the hour hand moves every hour $\Rightarrow \dfrac{1}{12}$ of 360° = 30°

Therefore, it will move 10° in $\dfrac{1}{3}$ of an hour or 20 minutes $\Rightarrow$ 20 minutes after 7:15 is 7:35

Question #6: If it is now 9:10, what time will it be when the hour hand has moved through the angle of 20°?

Solution: The angle by which the hour hand moves every hour $\Rightarrow \dfrac{1}{12}$ of 360° = 30°

Therefore, it will move 20° in $\dfrac{2}{3}$ of an hour or 40 minutes $\Rightarrow$ 40 minutes after 9:10 is 9:50

Question #7: A watch gains 9 minutes and 5 seconds every 5 days. If the rate of gain is constant, how much does the watch gain in one day?

Solution: Amount of gain in 5 days $\Rightarrow$ 9 minutes & 5 seconds $\Rightarrow$ 9(60) + 5 = 540 + 5 $\Rightarrow$ 545 sec
Amount of gain in 1 day $\Rightarrow$ 545 seconds ÷ 5 $\Rightarrow$ 109 = 60 + 49 sec $\Rightarrow$ 1 min & 49 sec

Question #8: A watch loses 7 minutes and 12 seconds every 6 days. If the rate of loss is constant, how much does the watch lose in one day?

Solution: Amount of loss in 6 days $\Rightarrow$ 7 minutes & 12 seconds $\Rightarrow$ 7(60) + 12 = 420 + 12 $\Rightarrow$ 432 sec
Amount of loss in 1 day $\Rightarrow$ 432 seconds ÷ 6 $\Rightarrow$ 72 = 60 + 12 sec $\Rightarrow$ 1 min & 12 sec

Question #9: When a digital clock displays 5:27, the sum of the digits is 14. How many minutes after 5:27 will the sum of the digits be 20 for the first time?

Solution: In a digital clock, the largest possible sum of the digits for the minutes is 14, when it is 59 minutes after the hour. Therefore, the first time that the sum of all the digits can be 20 occurs when the hour is 6, at exactly 6:59, this is when we have the sum of the digits: 6 + 5 + 9 = 20.
The time lag between 6:59 and 5:27 $\Rightarrow$ 1 hour and 32 minutes = 60 + 32 = 92 minutes.
Therefore, the sum of 20 will occur after 92 minutes.

Question #10: When a digital clock displays 7:18, the sum of the digits is 16. How many minutes after 7:18 will the sum of the digits be 22 for the first time?

Solution: In a digital clock, the largest possible sum of the digits for the minutes is 14, when it is 59 minutes after the hour. Therefore, the first time that the sum of all the digits can be 22 occurs when the hour is 9, at exactly 8:59, this is when we have the sum of the digits: 8 + 5 + 9 = 22.
The time lag between 8:59 and 7:18 $\Rightarrow$ 1 hour and 41 minutes = 60 + 41 = 101 minutes.
Therefore, the sum of 22 will occur after 101 minutes.

Question #11: If A, B, C, and D represent distinct digits in the addition problem below, what is the value of D?

```
  AB
+ BA
 CDC
```

Solution: Two 2-digit numbers will add up to at most something in the 100's, so $C = 1$.

```
  AB
+ BA
 1D1
```

Now, B plus A in the units' column gives a 1, and since it can't simply be that $B + A = 1$ and since all digits represent distinct digits, $B + A \leq 17$, so it can't be $B + A = 21$; it must be that $B + A = 11$; so 1 gets carried. In fact, A and B can be just about any pair of digits that add up to 11 (2 and 9, 3 and 8, 4 and 7, 5 and 6, etc), but it doesn't matter what they are, they will always give you the same digit for D:

```
   29          56
 + 92        + 65
  121         121
```

Therefore, the value of D is 2.

Question #12: In the correctly worked out multiplication problem given below, each letter represents a different digit. What is the value of $A \times B \times C$?

```
  AB
×  3
 CBB
```

Solution: Since $AB < 100$, 3 times AB is less than $3 \times 100 = 300$, so C is either 1 or 2. Since 3 times B ends in B, so B is either 0 or 5. B can't be 0 because neither 100 nor 200 is a multiple of 3; so $B = 5$.

```
  A5
×  3
 C55
```

Since we already determine that C is either 1 or 2; the easiest thing to do now is test whether 155 or 255 is a multiple of 3: 155 isn't a multiple of 3, but 255 is a multiple of $3 \Rightarrow 3 \times 85 = 255$.
Now $C = 2$ and $A = 8$. Rewrite the problem again, replacing C with 2 and A with 8:

```
  85
×  3
 255
```

Value of $A \times B \times C \Rightarrow 8 \times 5 \times 2 = 80$

PART 7.0: STATISTICS – AVERAGES:

TABLE OF CONTENTS:

7.1: BASICS ABOUT AVERAGES:

The *"averages"* are generally used in statistics or data analysis for the *"Common Measures of Central Tendency"* of a discrete set of data (numerical values or measurements) which can be expressed as *"arithmetic mean"*, *"median"*, and *"mode"* – they are described as the *"middle"* or *"center"* of the data.

After a set of data has been collected, organized, and tabulated with suitable headings, we may still be confronted with a situation when it's hard to analyze or grasp the size of items in the group. Therefore, a single expression representing the whole group of data is required. For instance, the tabulated figures may show that so many students got so many scores; however, we cannot form a central idea or opinion as to the intelligence of the class. For this purpose, we have to take the aid of *"averages"* or *"measures of central tendency,"* as they are known in statistics.

A list of numbers, or numerical data, can be described by various statistical measures; some of the most common of these measures are mean, median, and mode.

In general, the word *"average"* is associated or referred to several different measures, such as: arithmetic mean, median, and mode.

7.2: ARITHMETIC MEAN:

The **"arithmetic mean"** or **"mean"** or **"average"** of a given data (consisting of n terms) is the sum of the values of all the terms in the data divided by the total number of terms in the data. In other words, the mean of a group of "n" numbers is the sum of those "n" numbers divided by "n".

Note: The word "average" is the most commonly used term for arithmetic mean. average, mean, or arithmetic mean – they all refer to the arithmetic mean.

$$\text{ARITHMETIC MEAN} \Rightarrow \frac{Total\ Sum\ of\ all\ Terms}{Total\ Number\ of\ Terms} = \frac{s}{n}$$

7.2.1: DIFFERENT RELATIONSHIPS OF MEAN:

Following are the three different relationships among mean, sum, and number of terms in the same series of data:

(A) MEAN = SUM ÷ NUMBER: To find the mean, when the sum of the terms and the number of terms are given:
To find the mean of "n" terms, divide the sum of those "n" terms by "n," the number of terms.
$\Rightarrow$ **Mean = Sum ÷ Number**

For instance: Series of Data: {10, 20, 25, 40, 45, 50, 60, 70, 80, 100}
                       Mean $\Rightarrow$ Sum ÷ Number = 500 ÷ 10 = 50

For Example: If there is a company with 5 employees who make \$6/hr., \$12/hr., \$19/hr., \$27/hr., and \$61/hr., then what is the average salary?
Solution: Mean $\Rightarrow$ Sum ÷ Number
                       $\Rightarrow$ (\$6 + \$12 + \$19 + \$27 + \$61) ÷ 5 = \$125 ÷ 5 = \$25

(B) NUMBER = SUM ÷ MEAN: To find the number of terms, when the sum of the terms and mean are given:
To find "n," the number of terms in a set of data, divide the sum of those "n" terms by the average (arithmetic mean) of those "n" terms.
$\Rightarrow$ **Number = Sum ÷ Mean**

For instance: If, Mean = 50. And, Sum of the terms = 500
                       Then, Number of terms in the series of data $\Rightarrow$ Sum ÷ Mean = 500 ÷ 50 = 10

For Example: If a student buys books with an average price of \$79 and paid a total of \$711 for all the books, then how many books did the student buy?
Solution: Mean $\Rightarrow$ \$79
             Sum $\Rightarrow$ \$711
             Number $\Rightarrow$ Sum ÷ Mean
                      $\Rightarrow$ \$711 ÷ \$79 = 9 books

(C) SUM = MEAN × NUMBER: To find the sum of the terms, when the mean and number of terms are given:
To find the sum of "n" numbers, multiply the average (arithmetic mean) of those "n" terms by "n", the number of terms.
$\Rightarrow$ **Sum = Mean × Number**
Note: It is not possible to know the actual value of any term in the set of data, or how many terms are more/less than the average; all we can know is the sum of all the terms. It's as if all the terms in the group have the average value.

For instance: If Mean = 50. And, Number of terms in the series of data = 10
                       Then, Sum of the terms $\Rightarrow$ Mean × Number = 50 × 10 = 500

For Example: If the average weight of shipment of boxes for a particular day was 99 pounds and there were 8 boxes, then what was the total weight of all the boxes?
Solution: Mean $\Rightarrow$ 99
             Number $\Rightarrow$ 8
             Sum $\Rightarrow$ Mean × Number
                      $\Rightarrow$ 99 × 8 = 792 pounds
             Note: We do not know how much any individual box weighed or how many boxes weighed more or less than 792 pounds. All we know is the total weight of all the boxes.

EZ TIP: Following are some tips for average problems:

Tip #1: To find the mean ⇒ you do not need to know each individual term in the set; you only need to know the sum of the terms and the number of terms.

Tip #2: To find the number ⇒ you do not need to know each individual term in the set; you only need to know the sum of the terms and the mean of terms.

Tip #3: To find the sum ⇒ you do not need to know each individual term in the set; you only need to know the mean of the terms and the number of terms.

Different ways of representing Mean: Some mean questions may not specify the words arithmetic mean; instead, they may use some other terminology that means the same thing as arithmetic mean. You may think of these words as synonyms of arithmetic mean. The following words/phrases are a few examples: "halfway," "midway," "midpoint," "in between," "in the center" – all these words/phrases refer to arithmetic mean.

7.2.2: MEAN OF FRACTIONS, DECIMALS, EXPONENTS, & RADICALS:

Means are not only of integers, you can also be asked to find the average (arithmetic mean) of numbers that are fractions, decimals, or exponents. You can find the mean of fractions, decimals, exponents, and radicals, just as we do with integers by applying the same formula.

Example #1: What is the number halfway between $\frac{2}{3}$ & $\frac{3}{4}$?

Solution: Mean ⇒ *Sum ÷ Number* [Write the formula for calculating arithmetic mean]

$$\Rightarrow \frac{\frac{2}{3} + \frac{3}{4}}{2}$$ [Substitute the known values]

$$\Rightarrow \frac{\frac{8}{12} + \frac{9}{12}}{2}$$ [Scale up the fractions in the numerator to their LCD]

$$\Rightarrow \frac{\frac{17}{12}}{2}$$ [Add the fractions in the numerator]

$$\Rightarrow \frac{17}{12} \div 2$$ [Divide the fraction in the numerator by the denominator]

$$\Rightarrow \frac{17}{12} \times \frac{1}{2}$$ [Switch the division to multiplication and invert the fraction]

$$\Rightarrow \frac{17}{24}$$ [Simplify the fractions]

EZ TIP: The mean of two numbers is halfway between those two numbers.

Example #2: What is the midpoint between 0.22 and 0.88?

Solution: Mean ⇒ *Sum ÷ Number* [Write the formula for calculating arithmetic mean]

$$\Rightarrow \frac{0.22 + 0.88}{2}$$ [Substitute the known values]

$$\Rightarrow \frac{1.1}{2}$$ [Do the addition]

$$\Rightarrow 0.55$$ [Do the division]

EZ TIP: The average of two numbers is the midpoint between those two numbers.

Example #3: What is the average (arithmetic mean) of 2^{10} and 2^{20}?

Solution: Mean ⇒ *Sum ÷ Number* [Write the formula for calculating arithmetic mean]

$$\Rightarrow \frac{2^{10} + 2^{20}}{2}$$ [Substitute the known values]

$$\Rightarrow \frac{2^{10}}{2^1} + \frac{2^{20}}{2^1} \qquad \text{[Divide each exponential term separately]}$$

$$\Rightarrow 2^{10-1} + 2^{20-1} \qquad \text{[Do the division by applying rules of exponents]}$$

$$\Rightarrow 2^9 + 2^{19} \qquad \text{[Simplify the exponential terms]}$$

Example #4: What is the average (arithmetic mean) of $2\sqrt{5}$ and $8\sqrt{5}$?

Solution: Mean $\Rightarrow$ *Sum ÷ Number*   [Write the formula for calculating arithmetic mean]

$$\Rightarrow \frac{2\sqrt{5} + 8\sqrt{5}}{2} \qquad \text{[Substitute the known values]}$$

$$\Rightarrow \frac{10\sqrt{5}}{2} \qquad \text{[Combine like-terms]}$$

$$\Rightarrow 5\sqrt{5} \qquad \text{[Do the division]}$$

7.2.3: MEAN OF NUMBERS IN DIFFERENT FORMATS:

It is also possible to find the average (arithmetic mean) of numbers that are in different formats, such as, integers, fractions, decimals, exponents, radicals, or percents. The mean of such numbers can be found by applying the same formula; however, before doing anything, first convert all numbers in a common format or in the same units.

For Example: Find the average (arithmetic mean) of $\sqrt{81}$, 2^3, 6.95, 85%, $\frac{1}{5}$?

Solution: Mean $\Rightarrow$ *Sum ÷ Number*   [Write the formula for calculating arithmetic mean]

$$\Rightarrow \frac{\sqrt{81} + 2^3 + 6.95 + 85\% + \frac{1}{5}}{5} \qquad \text{[Substitute the known values]}$$

$$\Rightarrow \frac{9 + 8 + 6.95 + 0.85 + 0.20}{5} = \qquad \text{[Convert all the values in terms of decimal numbers]}$$

$$\Rightarrow \frac{25}{5} \qquad \text{[Do the addition]}$$

$$\Rightarrow 5 \qquad \text{[Do the division]}$$

7.2.4: MEAN OF ALGEBRAIC EXPRESSIONS:

Algebraic expression can be averaged in the same way as any other values, by applying the same formula.

EZ RULE: To find the average (arithmetic mean) of the two or more algebraic expressions $\Rightarrow$ add all the algebraic expressions and divide them by the number of expressions.

Example #1: What is the average (arithmetic mean) of $(7x + 6)$ and $(9x + 8)$?

Solution: Mean $\Rightarrow$ *Sum ÷ Number*   [Write the formula for calculating arithmetic mean]

$$\Rightarrow \frac{(7x + 6) + (9x + 8)}{2} \qquad \text{[Substitute the known values]}$$

$$\Rightarrow \frac{16x + 14}{2} \qquad \text{[Combine like-terms]}$$

$$\Rightarrow \frac{2(8x + 7)}{2} \qquad \text{[Factor out 2 from the numerator]}$$

$$\Rightarrow 8x + 7 \qquad \text{[Cancel-out the common terms]}$$

Example #2: What is the average (arithmetic mean) of $(x^2 + 2)$ and $(7 - x^2)$ and $(15x + 9)$?

Solution: Mean $\Rightarrow$ *Sum ÷ Number*   [Write the formula for calculating arithmetic mean]

$$\Rightarrow \frac{(x^2 + 2) + (7 - x^2) + (15x + 9)}{3} \qquad \text{[Substitute the known values]}$$

$$\Rightarrow \frac{(x^2 - x^2) + (15x) + (9 + 2 + 7)}{3}$$ [Rearrange like-terms]

$$\Rightarrow \frac{15x + 18}{3}$$ [Combine like-terms]

$$\Rightarrow \frac{3(5x + 6)}{3}$$ [Factor out 3 from the numerator]

$$\Rightarrow 5x + 6$$ [Cancel-out the common terms]

7.2.5: MEAN & SUM OF CONSECUTIVE NUMBERS:

Average (arithmetic mean) can be used to find the sum of consecutive numbers.

EZ RULE: To find average (arithmetic mean) of consecutive numbers, find the mean of the terms and number of terms, and then use the following formula:

SUM OF CONSECUTIVE TERMS $\Rightarrow$ ***Mean of Consecutive Terms × Number of Consecutive Terms***

Where: Mean of Terms $\Rightarrow$ (*First Term + Last Term*) ÷ 2
Number of Terms $\Rightarrow$ (*Last Term – First Term*) + 1

Note: The mean term of a consecutive set of integers is the number that lies exactly in the middle of that set. The mean of odd number of consecutive terms will always be an integer. The mean of even number of consecutive terms will never be an integer, because there is no true middle term.

For Example: What is the sum of the integers from 70 through 90, inclusive?
Solution: Mean of Consecutive Terms $\Rightarrow$ (*First Term + Last Term*) ÷ 2
$\Rightarrow$ (70 + 90) ÷ 2 = 160 ÷ 2 = 80
Number of Consecutive Terms $\Rightarrow$ (*Last Term – First Term*) + 1
$\Rightarrow$ 90 – 70 + 1 = 21
Sum of Consecutive Terms $\Rightarrow$ (*Mean of Consecutive Terms*) × (*Number of Consecutive Terms*)
$\Rightarrow$ 80 × 21 = 1,680

7.2.6: FINDING THE MISSING TERM:

If there is a series of data with a missing term, and the average (arithmetic mean) and number of term is given $\Rightarrow$ the missing term can be found by using basic algebra and applying the following steps:

EZ STEP-BY-STEP METHOD: Apply the following step(s) to find the missing term in a sequence:

STEP 1: First, label the missing term as "*n*"

STEP 2: Next, multiply the average with the number of terms, this will give the sum of all the terms in the series of data
$\Rightarrow$ Sum of terms = Number of terms × Mean

STEP 3: Then, add the existing terms in the series of data, including "*n*" and equate that to sum of the series of data, which will result in an equation.

STEP 4: Finally, solve the resulting equation and solve for "*n*" which is the value of the missing term.

EZ RULE: **Sum of Existing Terms + Missing Term = Sum of All Terms**

For instance: Series of Data: {*n*, 20, 25, 40, 45, 50, 60, 70, 80, 100}
Mean = 50
Number of terms $\Rightarrow$ 10
Sum of the terms of existing series $\Rightarrow$ 490 + *n*
Sum = Mean × Number $\Rightarrow$ 50 × 10 = 500
Sum of Existing Terms + Missing Term = Sum of All Terms
$\Rightarrow$ 490 + *n* = 500
$\Rightarrow$ *n* = 500 – 490 = 10

For Example: In a series of six tests, a student scores 100 on the first test, 95 on the second test, 90 on the third test, 80 on the fourth test, and 70 on the fifth test. If the average over the entire six-test series test is 85, what was the score on the sixth test?

Solution: Mean $\Rightarrow 85$
Number $\Rightarrow 6$
Sum of 5 test scores $\Rightarrow 100 + 95 + 90 + 80 + 70 = 435$
Let the sixth test score $\Rightarrow n$
Sum of 6 test scores $\Rightarrow 435 + n$
Sum of 6 test scores $\Rightarrow$ Mean × Number
$\Rightarrow 85 \times 6 = 510$
EZ Problem Set Up: $\Rightarrow$ Sum of 5 test scores + n = Sum of all Tests
$\Rightarrow 435 + n = 510$
$\Rightarrow n = 510 - 435 = 75$

7.2.7: FINDING THE NEW MEAN WHEN A TERM IS ADDED/DELETED:

If there is a series of data, where the average (arithmetic mean) and number of terms are given, and a term is either added or deleted, then the new average can be found by applying the following method:

EZ STEP-BY-STEP METHOD: Apply the following step(s) to find the new average when a term is added or deleted:

STEP 1: First, find the original sum by multiplying the original mean by the original number of terms.

STEP 2: Next, add or subtract the term to get the new sum.

STEP 3: Finally, find the new mean by dividing the new sum by the new number of terms.

Example #1:   A student's average score of five tests is 70. If the student's score of 100 on the sixth test is added, what's the new average?

Solution: Original Mean $\Rightarrow 70$
Original Number $\Rightarrow 5$
Original Sum $\Rightarrow$ Original Mean × Original Number
$\Rightarrow 70 \times 5 = 350$
New Number $\Rightarrow$ Original Number + 1
$\Rightarrow 5 + 1 = 6$
New Sum $\Rightarrow$ Original Sum + Score on Sixth Test
$\Rightarrow 350 + 100 = 450$
New Average $\Rightarrow$ New Sum ÷ New Number
$\Rightarrow 450 \div 6 = 75$

Example #2:   A student's average score of six tests is 75. If the student's score of 100 on the sixth test is removed, what's the new average?

Solution: Original Mean $\Rightarrow 75$
Original Number $\Rightarrow 6$
Original Sum $\Rightarrow$ Original Mean × Original Number
$\Rightarrow 6 \times 75 = 450$
New Number $\Rightarrow$ Original Number – 1
$\Rightarrow 6 - 1 = 5$
New Sum $\Rightarrow$ Original Sum – Score on Sixth Test
$\Rightarrow 450 - 100 = 350$
New Average $\Rightarrow$ New Sum ÷ New Number
$\Rightarrow 350 \div 5 = 70$

7.2.8: FINDING A TERM THAT WAS ADDED/DELETED:

If there is a series of data, where the average (arithmetic mean) and number of terms are given, and a term is either added or deleted, after which the new mean is also given, then the term that was added or deleted can be found by applying the following method:
Use the original mean and the new mean to figure out the original sum, and the new sum to figure out the term that was added or deleted. Use the following formulas to figure out the term added or deleted:

Number Added $\Rightarrow$ New Sum – Original Sum
Number Deleted $\Rightarrow$ Original Sum – New Sum

EZ STEP-BY-STEP METHOD: Apply the following step(s) to find the term added or deleted when the average is given:

STEP 1: Since the original mean and the original number of terms are given: Find the original sum from the original mean ⇒ Original Sum = Original Mean × Original Number

STEP 2: Since the new mean and the new number of terms are given: Find the new sum from the new mean ⇒ New Sum = New Mean × New Number

STEP 3: The difference between the sum before you added or removed the number and after you added or removed the number will give you the value of the number you added or removed: i.e., apply one of the following formulas to find the term added or deleted:

    (A) If a term is added   ⇒ Term Added = New Sum – Original Sum

    (B) If a term is deleted   ⇒ Term Deleted = Original Term – New Sum

Example #1:   A student averaged a score of 80 over a series of 5 tests, and if one of the test score was added, his average goes down to 75. What was the score on the test that was added?

Solution:
    Original Mean   ⇒ 80
    Original Number ⇒ 5
    Original Sum   ⇒ *Original Mean × Original Number*
                   ⇒ 80 × 5 = 400
    New Mean   ⇒ 75
    New Number   ⇒ *Original Number + 1*
                   ⇒ 5 + 1 = 6
    New Sum   ⇒ *New Mean × New Number*
                   ⇒ 75 × 6 = 450
    Number Added   ⇒ *New Sum – Original Sum*
                   ⇒ 450 – 400 = 50
    Therefore, the test score that was added is 50

Example #2:   A student averaged a score of 75 over a series of 6 tests, and if one of the test score was removed, his average goes up to 80. What was the score on the test that was removed?

Solution:
    Original Mean   ⇒ 75
    Original Number ⇒ 6
    Original Sum   ⇒ *Original Mean × Original Number*
                   ⇒ 75 × 6 = 450
    New Mean   ⇒ 80
    New Number   ⇒ *Original Number – 1*
                   ⇒ 6 – 1 = 5
    New Sum   ⇒ *New Mean × New Number*
                   ⇒ 80 × 5 = 400
    Number Deleted ⇒ *Original Sum – New Sum*
                   ⇒ 450 – 400 = 50
    Therefore, the test score that was deleted is 50

7.2.9: KEY FACTS ABOUT MEAN:

KEY FACT #1:   If all numbers in a set of data are the same, then that number is the average (arithmetic mean) of that group.

For Example: Series of Data: {50, 50, 50, 50, 50}
    Arithmetic Mean ⇒ 250 ÷ 5 = 50

KEY FACT #2:   If the numbers in a set of data are not all the same, then the average (arithmetic mean) must be greater than the smallest number and less than the largest number, that is, it should be in between the smallest and the largest number in the set. Equivalently, at least one of the numbers is less than the average and at least one is greater.
    ⇒ Smallest Term ≤ Arithmetic Mean ≤ Largest Term

For Example: Series of Data: {10, 20, 25, 40, 45, 50, 60, 70, 80, 100}

⇒ It can be concluded that the mean must be greater than 10 (smallest term) and less than 100 (largest term).

KEY FACT #3:   The differences from the average (arithmetic mean) are called deviations. The total deviation below the average is always equal to the total deviation above the average.
⇒ Total Deviation below Average = Total Deviation above Average

For Example: Series of Data: {10, 20, 25, 40, 45, 50, 60, 70, 80, 100}
Arithmetic Mean ⇒ 500 ÷ 10 = 50

Deviation of 10 from Average of 50	= + 40
Deviation of 20 from Average of 50	= + 30
Deviation of 25 from Average of 50	= + 25
Deviation of 40 from Average of 50	= + 10
Deviation of 45 from Average of 50	= + 05
Total Deviation below Average of 50	= +110
Deviation of 60 from Average of 50	= − 10
Deviation of 70 from Average of 50	= − 20
Deviation of 80 from Average of 50	= − 30
Deviation of 100 from Average of 50	= − 50
Total Deviation above Average of 50	= −110

Total Deviation below Average = Total Deviation above Average = 110

Note: The situation in the above example is not a coincidence; in fact, the situation seen above is always true.

EZ HINT: It may be useful to try to think of the mean as the "balanced" value, that is, all the terms below the mean are less than the mean by an amount that will "balance out" the amount that the terms above the mean are greater than the mean.

KEY FACT #4:   If the average (arithmetic mean) of a set of numbers is A, and if a number, "n," is added to the set and a new average is calculated, then:

(A) The new mean will be less than A if "n" is less than A
⇒ New Mean < Original Mean

For Example: Series of Data: {10, 20, 25, 40, 45, 50, 60, 70, 80, 100}
Arithmetic Mean ⇒ 500 ÷ 10 = 50
Let's add $n = 28$ to the above series of data.
New Sum = 500 + 28 = 528
New Mean = 528 ÷ 11 = 48
Since we added 28, a number less than the mean 50, the new mean is 48, which is less than the original mean 50.
Therefore, New Mean < Original Mean

(B) The new mean will be equal to A if "n" is equal to A
⇒ New Mean = Original Mean

For Example: Series of Data: {10, 20, 25, 40, 45, 50, 60, 70, 80, 100}
Arithmetic Mean ⇒ 500 ÷ 10 = 50
Let's add $n = 50$ to the above series of data.
New Sum = 500 + 50 = 550
New Average = 550 ÷ 11 = 50
Since we added 50, a number equal to the average 50, the new average is 50, which is equal to the original average 50.
Therefore, New Average = Original Average

(C) The new mean will be greater than A if "n" is greater than A
⇒ New Mean > Original Mean

For Example: Series of Data: {10, 20, 25, 40, 45, 50, 60, 70, 80, 100}
Arithmetic Mean ⇒ 500 ÷ 10 = 50
Let's add $n = 72$ to the above series of data.

New Sum = 500 + 72 = 572
New Average = 572 ÷ 11 = 52
Since we added 72, a number greater than the average 50, the new average is 52, which is greater than the original average 50.
Therefore, New Average > Original Average

KEY FACT #5:   Average (arithmetic mean) of Evenly Spaced Terms:
If "n" numbers form an arithmetic sequence of evenly spaced numbers (one in which the difference between any two consecutive terms is the same) and:

(A) If "n" is odd, then the mean of the numbers is the mean of the smallest and the largest terms or simply the middle term in the sequence.
⇒ Mean = Mean of Smallest and Largest Terms = Middle Term

For Example: Series of Data: {10, 20, 30, 40, 50, 60, 70, 80, 90, 100, 110}
By definition, Mean = 660 ÷ 11 = 60
Mean of Smallest and Largest Terms = (10 + 110) ÷ 2 = 120 ÷ 2 = 60
Mean is the Middle Term = 60
Since "n" numbers in the above series of data forms an arithmetic sequence of evenly spaced numbers (one in which the difference between any two consecutive terms is a constant 10) and since "n" is 11 which is odd, the mean is the mean of the smallest and the largest terms or simply the middle term in the sequence.
Therefore, Mean = Mean of Smallest and Largest Terms = Middle Term

(B) If "n" is even, then the mean of the numbers is the mean of the smallest and the largest terms or mean of the two middle terms in the sequence.
⇒ Mean = Mean of Smallest and Largest Terms = Mean of the Two Middle Terms

For Example: Series of Data: {10, 20, 30, 40, 50, 60, 70, 80, 90, 100}
By definition, Mean = 550 ÷ 10 = 55
Mean of Smallest and Largest Terms = (10 + 100) ÷ 2 = 110 ÷ 2 = 55
Mean of the Two Middle Terms = (50 + 60) ÷ 2 = 110 ÷ 2 = 55
Since "n" numbers in the above series of data forms an arithmetic sequence of evenly spaced numbers (one in which the difference between any two consecutive terms is a constant 10) and since "n" is 10 which is even, the mean is the mean of the smallest and the largest terms or simply the mean of two middle terms in the sequence.
Therefore, Mean = Mean of Smallest and Largest Terms = Mean of the Two Middle Terms

Note: In an evenly spaced set of data, its mean and median are both the same number.

7.2.10: FREQUENCY DISTRIBUTION:

There are multiple ways to organize numerical data that show how the data is distributed. For some sets of data, an easy way to do so is with Frequency Distribution. It is more convenient and informative to display the values in a frequency distribution table. This is particularly useful for analyzing large amount of data that have values occurring with varying frequencies, and especially helpful while calculating weighted average.

For example, look at the following set of data: {20, 25, 25, 50, 50, 50, 50, 50, 90, 90}
This data can be grouped into a frequency distribution by listing each different value (x) and the frequency (f) with which each value of (x) occurs. The data can be organized in the following frequency distribution format:

Term (x)	Frequency (f)	Product	
20	01	20 × 1	= 20
25	02	25 × 2	= 50
50	05	50 × 5	= 250
90	02	90 × 2	= 180
Total	10		= 500

For this data, the terms (x's) can be summed up by multiplying each x by its frequency (f) and then adding the products to find the sum of all the values in the data.

EZ NOTE: The frequency distribution format not only provides a quick summary of the data, but it also simplifies the calculations of the central location and dispersion measures. With frequency distribution table, it is easier to compute descriptive statistics.

Now let's take a look at how we can use the frequency distribution table to calculate the weighted average.

7.2.11: WEIGHTED MEAN:

While calculating arithmetic mean, equal importance is given to every term or item in the group of data. However, in certain cases, items may differ in importance, and so it may become necessary to multiply each term by a suitable weight in accordance with its estimated importance. The sum total of all these products divided by the total number of weights gives the weighted arithmetic mean.

Weighted mean is the mean of two or more groups in which there are different numbers of terms in each group, or each term occur different number of times. In other words, there are more terms in one group than there are in another. Finding a combined weighted mean of a set of means is more or less like finding a simple mean, except that, to find the sum we must weigh each average by multiplying it by the number of terms it represents.

Weighted mean is an easier way of calculating the mean when the same terms in a data occur a number of times. Instead of adding all those terms individually, it is a lot easier to calculate the mean using their respective weights.

For instance: in a series of data, the term "75" may occur "19" times and another term "25" may occur "17" times. Now instead of adding the first term 19 times and the second term 17 times, it's a lot easier to use the weighting factor and find the product of 75 & 19 and 25 & 17.

Weight = number of times a quantity or term occurs, also known as *"weighting factor"* or *"frequency"*.

EZ STEP-BY-STEP METHOD: Apply the following step(s) to calculate the weighted mean of a set of numbers:
STEP 1: First, set up a table listing the quantities, their respective weights, and their respective values.
STEP 2: Next, multiply the value of each individual term in the table by its respective and corresponding weight, i.e., the number of times it appears.
STEP 3: Then, add all the products.
STEP 4: And, add all the weights.
STEP 5: Finally, divide the sum of the products by the sum of the weights.

WEIGHTED MEAN ⇒ *Sum of Products ÷ Sum of Weights* ⇒ *Sum ÷ Frequency*

EZ TIP: The correct mean has to be weighted towards the group with the greatest number.

EZ TRAP: You cannot combine means of different quantities by taking the mean of those original means. In a mean problem, if one value occurs more frequently than the others do, it is weighed more. Moreover, if you remember, the mean formula requires you to find the sum of all the terms and divide that by the total number of terms. So don't just take the mean of the means; instead work with the sums.

For Instance: Series of Data: {20, 25, 25, 50, 50, 50, 50, 50, 90, 90}

Terms (x)	Weight (f)	Product	
20	01	20 × 1	= 20
25	02	25 × 2	= 50
50	05	50 × 5	= 250
90	02	90 × 2	= 180
Total	10		= 500

Weighted Mean ⇒ *sum of products ÷ sum of weights* = 500 ÷ 10 = 50
Alternately: the above information can also be calculated in the following way:
[1(20) + 2(25) + 5(50) + 2(90)] ÷ 10 = [20 + 50 + 250 + 180] ÷ 10 = 500 ÷ 10 = 50

For Example: If in a math class of 9 students, all of them took a math test, the average score of 2 female students was 88 and the average score of the remaining 7 male students was 97. What is the average score for the entire class?

Solution:

Term (Score)	Weight (No of students)	Product (score × Students)
88	2	88 × 2 = 176
97	7	97 × 7 = 679
Total	9	= 855

Weighted Mean $\Rightarrow$ *sum of products ÷ sum of weights*   [Write the weighted mean formula]

$\Rightarrow 855 \div 9$ [Substitute the value in the formula]

$\Rightarrow 95$ [Do the division]

Alternately: the above information can also be calculated in the following way:

$\Rightarrow [2(88) + 7(97)] \div 9 = [176 + 679] \div 9 = 855 \div 9 = 95$

EZ TRAP: The answer to the above example is not 92.5, which is the average of 88 and 97. So, we can't just add 88 to 97 and divide by 2. The means of 88 and 97 were earned by different numbers of students, and so the two means had to be given different weights in the calculation. In this case, there are more male students who got a mean of 97 than female students who got a mean of 88, so the score of male students should be weighed more – they contribute more to the overall mean of the class. For this reason, 95 is called a weighted mean.

7.3: MEDIAN:

The word **"median"** means **"middle,"** so the median of a set of data arranged in ascending or descending order is the **"middle-most"** term. The median of a set of values is the value in a set below and above which there are an equal number of values. In other words, there should be an equal number of terms smaller and larger than the median. Median may also be defined as the value of that term which divides an arranged series of data into half or two equal parts.

MEDIAN $\Rightarrow$ When there are *"n"* terms, the median is the value of $\left(\dfrac{n+1}{2}\right)^{th}$ term.

EZ STEP-BY-STEP METHOD: Apply the following step(s) to find the median of a set of data:

STEP 1: Rearrange the terms in ascending or descending numerical order, i.e., from smallest to largest, or largest to smallest.

STEP 2: (A) If there is an odd number of a term in the set of data $\Rightarrow$ the Median is the exact middle term.

(B) If there is an even number of terms in the set of data (there is no single middle term) $\Rightarrow$ the Median is the average (arithmetic mean) of the two middle (innermost) terms, that is, sum of the two middle most terms divided by 2.

EZ NOTE: Especially for a large set of data, it is often true that roughly, about half of the data is less than the median and about half of the data is greater than the median, but this is not necessarily always the case. The median of a set of data can be less than, equal to, or greater than the mean.

Example #1:   Series of Data: {10, 20, 25, 40, 45, 50, 60, 65, 75, 80, 100}
Median $\Rightarrow$ *Middle Term – for odd number of terms*
$\Rightarrow$ 50   [Find the value of the middle most term]

Example #2:   Series of Data: {10, 20, 25, 40, 45, 50, 60, 65, 75, 80, 90, 100}
Median $\Rightarrow$ *Mean of Two Middle Terms – for even number of terms*
$\Rightarrow$ (50 + 60) ÷ 2   [Substitute the known values]
$\Rightarrow$ 110 ÷ 2   [Add the numbers in the parentheses]
$\Rightarrow$ 55   [Do the division]

7.4: MODE:

The *"mode"* of a set of data is the term or terms that *"occurs most frequently"* or appears the greatest number of times. The mode appears more often than any other term in the set of data. In other words, mode is the value of that term in a series of data, which occurs most predominantly and has the highest frequency.

(A) SINGLE MODE: "ONE MODE": Set of Data with One Mode:

EZ RULE: A set of data may have a *"single mode"* – which means it has only one mode – this happens when there is exactly one term that occurs most frequently.

For Example: Series of Data: {10,   25, 25, 25, 25, 50, 60, 65, 75, 80, 100}
                            Mode   ⇒ *The number(s) that occurs most frequently*
                            ⇒ 25
                            [This number appears four times, which is more times than any other number.]

(B) BIMODAL: "TWO MODES": Set of Data with Two Modes:

EZ RULE: A set of data may be *"bimodal"* – which means it has two modes – this happens when there is a tie of two terms that occurs most frequently.

For Example: Series of Data: {10,   20, 25, 25, 45, 50, 60, 65, 75, 75, 100}
                            Modes   ⇒ *The number(s) that occurs most frequently*
                            ⇒ 25 & 75
                            [Both these numbers appear two times, which is more times than the other numbers.]

(C) MULTI-MODAL: "MULTIPLE MODES": Set of Data with More Than 1 Mode:

EZ RULE: A set of data may have *"multiple modes"* – which means it has more than one mode – this happens when there is a tie of more than one term that occurs most frequently.

For Example: Series of Data: {10,   10, 25, 25, 45, 50, 50, 65, 75, 75, 100}
                            Modes   ⇒ *The number(s) that occurs most frequently*
                            ⇒ 10, 25, 50 & 75
                            [All these numbers appear two times, which is more times than the other numbers.]

(D) "NO MODE": Set of Data with No Mode:

EZ RULE: A set of data may have *"no mode"* – which means it has no mode at all – this happens when all the terms in the set of data occur equal number of times.

For Example: Series of Data: {10,   20, 25, 40, 45, 50, 60, 65, 75, 80, 100}
                            Mode   ⇒ *The number(s) that occurs most frequently*
                            ⇒ No Mode
                            [There is no number that appears more than the other numbers, all numbers appear equal number of times.]

7.5: QUARTILES:

A *"quartile"* divides a set of data into equal quarters or four equal parts.

Just like a median divides the whole set of data in half or two equal parts, a quartile divides it into quarters or four equal parts. Moreover, Quartiles are found the same way as median.

EZ STEP-BY-STEP METHOD: Apply the following step(s) to calculate the Quartiles of a set of data:
STEP 1: Arrange the series of data in ascending order of magnitude and find its median, which would be the middle most term.
STEP 2: Again find the two medians of the two resulting series – these will be the Quartiles of the original series.

MIDDLE QUARTILE: The median M and Middle Quartile or Second Quartile or Q2 are same.

UPPER QUARTILE: The median of the Upper Half of the set of data is known as Upper Quartile or First Quartile or simply Q1 ⇒ The Upper Quartile divides the upper half of the set of data into another half.
To find the Upper Quartile, only use the upper half of the data, and find its median, i.e., the middle term.

LOWER QUARTILE: The median of the Lower Half of the set of data Is known as Lower Quartile or Third Quartile or simply Q3 ⇒ The Lower Quartile divides the lower half of the set of data into another half.
To find the Lower Quartile, only use the lower half of the data, and find its median, i.e., the middle term.

Note: If there are even numbers of terms in half of the data, then take the average of the two middle terms.

For Example: Series of Data: {10, 20, 25, 40, 45, 50, 60, 65, 75, 80, 100}
Lower Quartile ⇒ 25
Middle Quartile ⇒ 50
Upper Quartile ⇒ 75

MIXED EXAMPLE: For the following series of data find its mean, median, mode, range, extremes, and the average of its median and mode: {5, 15, 20, 25, 25, 50, 72, 82, 88, 98, 125}

(A) Mean ⇒ *Sum ÷ Number*
⇒ (5 + 15 + 20 + 25 + 25 + 50 + 72 + 82 + 88 + 98 + 125) ÷ 11 = 605 ÷ 11= 55

(B) Median ⇒ *Middle Term – for odd number of terms*
⇒ 50

(C) Mode ⇒ *The number(s) that occurs most frequently*
⇒ 25

(D) Range ⇒ Largest Term – Smallest Term
⇒ 125 – 5 = 120

(E) Extremes ⇒ Lower Extreme = 5
⇒ Middle Extreme = 50
⇒ Upper Extreme = 125

(F) Mean of Median & Mode ⇒ $\dfrac{Median + Mode}{2}$

$$\Rightarrow \frac{50 + 25}{2} = \frac{75}{2} = 37.50$$

7.6: COMBINING MEAN, MEDIAN, AND MODE:

Some questions require the knowledge of mean, median, and mode.

Example #1:   If the mode of the following set of numbers is 15, then what is the average (arithmetic mean) and median of the set of numbers?
$\{11, 12, 18, 19, 15, n\}$

Solution: Since the mode of the set of numbers is 15, the value of n must be 15 for it to be the mode (the number that occurs most frequently).

Mode	$\Rightarrow$ *Number(s) that occurs most frequently*	[Write the appropriate formula]
	$\Rightarrow 15$	[Find the term(s) that occurs most frequently]

Arrange the set of numbers in increasing order $\Rightarrow \{11, 12, 15, 15, 18, 19\}$

Mean	$\Rightarrow$ *Sum $\div$ Number*	[Write the appropriate formula]
	$\Rightarrow (11 + 12 + 18 + 19 + 15 + 15) \div 6$	[Substitute the known values]
	$\Rightarrow 90 \div 6$	[Add the numbers in the parentheses]
	$\Rightarrow 15$	[Do the division]
Median	$\Rightarrow$ *Mean of Two Middle Terms* (*even terms*)	[Write the appropriate formula]
	$\Rightarrow (15 + 15) \div 2$	[Substitute the known values]
	$\Rightarrow 30 \div 2$	[Add the numbers in the parentheses]
	$\Rightarrow 15$	[Do the division]

Example #2:   If the average (arithmetic mean) of the following set of numbers is 12, then what is the median and mode?
$\{2, 11, 15, 16, n\}$

Solution:

Mean	$\Rightarrow \dfrac{2+11+15+16+n}{5} = 12$	[Equate the mean formula with the actual mean]
	$\Rightarrow \dfrac{44+n}{5} = 12$	[Substitute the known values]
	$\Rightarrow 44 + n = 60$	[Cross-multiply]
	$\Rightarrow n = 16$	[Subtract 44 from both sides]

Arrange the set of numbers in increasing order $\Rightarrow \{2, 11, 15, 16, 16\}$

Median	$\Rightarrow$ *Middle Term – for odd number of terms*	[Write the appropriate formula]
	$\Rightarrow 15$	[Find the value of the middle most term]
Mode	$\Rightarrow$ *Number(s) that occurs most frequently*	[Write the appropriate formula]
	$\Rightarrow 16$	[Find the term(s) that occurs most frequently]

7.7: MEASURES OF DISPERSION:

The **"measures of dispersion,"** or **"spread,"** for a discrete set of data (numerical values or measurements) is the degree to which numerical data is dispersed or spread out, and it can take many forms in data analyses and can be measured in many ways. Let's take a closer look at each one of the measures of dispersion.

7.7.1: RANGE:

The simplest or the most basic measure of dispersion is called the **"range"**. The Range of a set of data is defined as the difference or distance between the largest or highest term and the smallest or lowest term in the numerical data. In other words, range of a group of numbers is the greatest number minus the least number.
Note: Since distance is always positive, the range must always be a positive value.
RANGE ⇒ **Largest Term – Smallest Term**

For Example: Series of Data: {10,   20, 25, 40, 45, 50, 60, 65, 75, 80, 100}
                            Range   ⇒ $100 - 10 = 90$
                            Note how the range depends on only two values in the given set of data.

7.7.2: EXTREMES:

The Extremes of a set of data are the highest term also known as the **"upper extreme"** and the lowest term also known as the **"lower extreme"**.
Note: If both extremes are equal, then all the terms in the set of data are equal.
UPPER EXTREME ⇒ Highest or Biggest Term
LOWER EXTREME ⇒ Lowest or Smallest Term

For Example: Series of Data: {10,   20, 25, 40, 45, 50, 60, 65, 75, 80, 100}
                            Lower Extreme ⇒ 10   &   Upper Extreme ⇒ 100

7.7.3: STANDARD DEVIATION:

Since the range is affected by only the two most extreme values in the set of measurements, other measures of dispersion have been developed that are affected by every value. The most commonly used of these other measures is the **"standard deviation"**. Just like mean, median, mode, quartiles, and range, standard deviation is just another term used to describe sets of numbers. As we have already seen, to find the range of a set of n numbers, we take the smallest number and subtract it from the largest number in the given set of data. This measures how widely the numbers in the set of data are dispersed.
For instance: The range of 5, 9, 11, 12, 19, 20, and 27 = $27 - 5 = 22$.
Another way to measure the dispersion or deviation of a set of numbers is by using the concept of standard deviation, which measures the distance or the gap between the arithmetic mean and the set of numbers. Therefore, the standard deviation can be generally interpreted as the average distance from the arithmetic mean for the n values

For Example: If the mean of a set of data is 185 and the standard deviation is 10, what is the range of scores that fall
                            within the standard deviation of the mean?
Solution: The range of scores that fall within the standard deviation is ($185 - 10 = 175$) to ($185 + 10 = 195$).

Standard deviation is a measure of how **"spread-out"** a set of data numbers is in a data distribution, that is, how much the numbers **"deviate"** from the mean. In other words, the standard deviation is a number that expresses the degree to which the set of numbers vary from the mean, either above it or below it.

EZ STEP-BY-STEP METHOD: Apply the following steps, to calculate the Standard Deviation of a set of n numbers:
STEP 1: Find the average (arithmetic mean) of the numbers in the set of data.
STEP 2: Find the differences between that average and each value of the numbers in the set of data
STEP 3: Square each of the differences.
STEP 4: Find the average of the squared differences by summing the squared values and dividing the sum by the number of values.
STEP 5: Take the positive square root of that average.

EZ NOTE: Although you are not likely to deal with or actually calculate standard deviation on your test, but it will always be helpful to have a basic understanding about standard deviation. Moreover, looking at the steps involved in finding the standard deviation may help you better understand its meaning. Occasionally you may be asked to compare standard deviations between sets of data, or otherwise demonstrate that you at least understand what standard deviation means.

EZ TIP: Most questions on your test about standard deviation are more likely to concern the difference between standard deviation and the mean. Standard deviation usually comes down to a single number such as 2.5 or 7.0.

Example #1: Find the standard deviation for the following set of data: {1, 5, 10, 16, 18}
Solution: Mean of the set of data $\Rightarrow$ (1 + 5 + 10 + 16 + 18) ÷ 5 = 50 ÷ 5 = 10
Organize the information in the following table:

n	$(n - 10)$	$(n - 10)^2$
1	−9	81
5	−5	25
10	0	00
16	+6	36
18	+8	64
		206

Standard Deviation $\Rightarrow \sqrt{\dfrac{206}{5}}$ = 6.4 (approx.)

RELATIONSHIP BETWEEN THE SPREAD AND STANDARD DEVIATION:

The standard deviation cannot be negative, and when two sets of data are compared, the one with the larger dispersion will have the larger standard deviation.

- The lesser the spread (a set of data in which most of the points are close to the mean), the lower the standard deviation, and the lower the degree of variation. {1, 2, 5, 7, 9 }
- The greater the spread (a set of data in which most of the points are away from the mean), the higher the standard deviation, and the higher the degree of variation. {1, 18, 27, 57, 69 }

Note that standard deviation depends on every data value; however, it depends most on values that are farthest away from the mean. This is the reason why a distribution with data grouped closely around the mean has a smaller standard deviation than the data spread far away from the mean.

To illustrate this fact, let's compare another set of data, which also has the same mean (10).

Example #2: Find the standard deviation for the following set of data: {6, 9, 10, 11, 14}
Solution: Mean of the set of data $\Rightarrow$ (6 + 8 + 10 + 12 + 14) ÷ 5 = 50 ÷ 5 = 10
Organize the information in the following table:

n	$(n - 10)$	$(n - 10)^2$
6	−4	16
9	−1	01
10	0	00
11	+1	01
14	+4	16
		34

Standard Deviation $\Rightarrow \sqrt{\dfrac{34}{5}}$ = 2.6 (approx.)

Observe that the numbers in the second set of data are grouped more closely around the mean (10) than the numbers in the first set of data. Finally, note the standard deviation, which is less for the second set (2.6) than for the first set (6.4).

PRACTICE EXERCISE – QUESTIONS AND ANSWERS WITH EXPLANATIONS: STATS – AVERAGES:

Question #1: If there is a company with 5 employees who make $6/hr., $8/hr., $10/hr., $16/hr., and $20/hr., what is the average salary?

Solution:

Mean $\Rightarrow$ *Sum ÷ Number*   [Write the formula for calculating arithmetic mean]

$\Rightarrow \dfrac{6 + 8 + 10 + 16 + 20}{5}$ [Substitute the known values]

$\Rightarrow \dfrac{60}{5}$ [Do the addition]

$\Rightarrow \$12$ [Do the division]

Question #2: If a student buys books with an average price of $69, and paid a total of $621 for all the books, how many books did the student buy?

Solution:

Mean $\Rightarrow \$69$ [Given]

Sum $\Rightarrow \$621$ [Given]

Number $\Rightarrow$ *Sum ÷ Mean*   [Write the formula for calculating the number of terms]

$\Rightarrow \$621 ÷ \$69$ [Substitute the known values]

$\Rightarrow 9$ books   [Do the division]

Question #3: If the average weight of shipment of boxes for a particular day was 88 pounds, and there were 7 boxes, what was the total weight of all the boxes?

Solution:

Mean $\Rightarrow 88$ [Given]

Number $\Rightarrow 7$ [Given]

Sum $\Rightarrow$ *Mean × Number*   [Write the formula for calculating the sum of terms]

$\Rightarrow 88 × 7$ [Substitute the known values]

$\Rightarrow 616$ pounds   [Do the multiplication]

Question #4: What is the average (arithmetic mean) of the following numbers: {1/2, 1/4, 1/8}?

Solution:

Mean $\Rightarrow$ *Sum ÷ Number*   [Write the formula for calculating arithmetic mean]

$\Rightarrow \dfrac{\frac{1}{2} + \frac{1}{4} + \frac{1}{8}}{3}$ [Substitute the known values]

$\Rightarrow \dfrac{\frac{4}{8} + \frac{2}{8} + \frac{1}{8}}{3}$ [Scale up the fractions in the numerator to their LCD]

$\Rightarrow \dfrac{\frac{7}{8}}{3}$ [Add the fractions in the numerator]

$\Rightarrow \dfrac{7}{8} ÷ 3$ [Divide the fraction in the numerator by the denominator]

$\Rightarrow \dfrac{7}{8} × \dfrac{1}{3}$ [Switch the division to multiplication and invert the fraction]

$\Rightarrow \dfrac{7}{24}$ [Simplify the fractions]

Question #5: What is the average (arithmetic mean) of the following numbers: {11.25, 12.25, 15.75, 16.75, 17.5, 18}?

Solution:

Mean $\Rightarrow$ *Sum ÷ Number*   [Write the formula for calculating arithmetic mean]

$\Rightarrow \dfrac{11.25 + 12.25 + 15.75 + 16.75 + 17.5 + 18}{6}$ [Substitute the known values]

$\Rightarrow \dfrac{91.5}{6}$ [Do the addition]

$\Rightarrow 15.25$ [Do the division]

Question #6:   What is the average (arithmetic mean) of 2^{15} and 2^{25}?

Solution: Mean $\Rightarrow$ *Sum ÷ Number*   [Write the formula for calculating arithmetic mean]

$\Rightarrow \dfrac{2^{15} + 2^{25}}{2}$ [Substitute the known values]

$\Rightarrow \dfrac{2^{15}}{2^{1}} + \dfrac{2^{25}}{2^{1}}$ [Divide each exponential term separately]

$\Rightarrow 2^{15-1} + 2^{25-1}$ [Do the division by applying rules of exponents]

$\Rightarrow 2^{14} + 2^{24}$ [Simplify the exponential terms]

Question #7:   What is the average (arithmetic mean) of $6\sqrt{11}$ and $8\sqrt{11}$?

Solution: Mean $\Rightarrow$ *Sum ÷ Number*   [Write the formula for calculating arithmetic mean]

$\Rightarrow \dfrac{6\sqrt{11} + 8\sqrt{11}}{2}$ [Substitute the known values]

$\Rightarrow \dfrac{14\sqrt{11}}{2}$ [Combine like-terms]

$\Rightarrow 7\sqrt{11}$ [Do the division]

Question #8:   What is the average (arithmetic mean) of the following numbers: $\sqrt{64}$, 2^4, 10.85, 75%, $\dfrac{2}{5}$, 24?

Solution: Mean $\Rightarrow$ *Sum ÷ Number*   [Write the formula for calculating arithmetic mean]

$\Rightarrow \dfrac{\sqrt{64} + 2^4 + 10.85 + 75\% + \dfrac{2}{5} + 24}{6}$ [Substitute the known values]

$\Rightarrow \dfrac{8 + 16 + 10.85 + 0.75 + 0.40 + 24}{6}$ [Convert all the values in terms of decimal numbers]

$\Rightarrow \dfrac{60}{6}$ [Do the addition]

$\Rightarrow 10$ [Do the division]

Question #9:   What is the average (arithmetic mean) of $(6x + 7)$ and $(8x + 9)$?

Solution: Mean $\Rightarrow$ *Sum ÷ Number*   [Write the formula for calculating arithmetic mean]

$\Rightarrow \dfrac{(6x + 7) + (8x + 9)}{2}$ [Substitute the known values]

$\Rightarrow \dfrac{14x + 16}{2}$ [Combine like-terms]

$\Rightarrow \dfrac{2(7x + 8)}{2}$ [Factor out 2 from the numerator]

$\Rightarrow 7x + 8$ [Cancel-out the common terms]

Question #10:   What is the average (arithmetic mean) of $(x^2 + 2)$ and $(8 - x^2)$ and $(18x + 11)$?

Solution: Mean $\Rightarrow$ *Sum ÷ Number*   [Write the formula for calculating arithmetic mean]

$\Rightarrow \dfrac{(x^2 + 2) + (8 - x^2) + (18x + 11)}{3}$ [Substitute the known values]

$\Rightarrow \dfrac{(x^2 - x^2) + (18x) + (8 + 2 + 11)}{3}$ [Rearrange common terms]

$\Rightarrow \dfrac{18x + 21}{3}$ [Combine like-terms]

$$\Rightarrow \frac{3(6x + 7)}{3}$$ [Factor out 3 from the numerator]

$\Rightarrow 6x + 7$ [Cancel-out the common terms]

Question #11: What is the sum of the integers from 50 through 70, inclusive?
Solution: Mean of Consecutive Terms $\Rightarrow$ (*First Term* + *Last Term*) ÷ 2   [Write the formula]
                                                     $\Rightarrow$ (50 + 70) ÷ 2 = 120 ÷ 2 = 60   [Substitute the values in formula]
                   Number of Consecutive Terms $\Rightarrow$ (*Last Term* – *First Term*) + 1   [Write the formula]
                                                     $\Rightarrow$ 70 – 50 + 1 = 21   [Substitute the values in formula]
                   Sum of Consecutive Terms $\Rightarrow$ (Mean of Consecutive Terms) × (Number of Consecutive Terms)
                                                     $\Rightarrow$ 60 × 21 = 1,260

Question #12: A student averaged a score of 59 over a series of 5 tests, and if he scored 26 in the first test, 52 in the second test, 69 in the third test, 72 in the fourth test, how much did he score in the fifth test?
Solution: Mean of 5 Tests $\Rightarrow$ 59
                   Number of Tests $\Rightarrow$ 5
                   Sum of 5 Tests $\Rightarrow$ 59 × 5 = 295
                   Sum of 4 tests $\Rightarrow$ 26 + 52 + 69 + 72 = 219
                   Let the score of fifth Test $\Rightarrow$ n
                   EZ Problem Set Up $\Rightarrow$ Sum of 4 Tests + Score of Fifth Test = Sum of 5 Tests
                                       $\Rightarrow$ 219 + n = 295   [Set up the equation]
                                       $\Rightarrow$ n = 76   [Subtract 219 from both sides]

Question #13: A student's average score of four tests is 75. If the student's score of 100 on the fifth test is added, what's the new average?
Solution: Original Mean $\Rightarrow$ 75
                   Original Number $\Rightarrow$ 4
                   Original Sum $\Rightarrow$ *Mean* × *Number*
                                    $\Rightarrow$ 4 × 75 = 300
                   New Sum $\Rightarrow$ *Original Sum* + *New Value*
                                    $\Rightarrow$ 300 + 100 = 400
                   New Number $\Rightarrow$ *Original Number* + 1
                                    $\Rightarrow$ 4 + 1 = 5
                   New Mean $\Rightarrow$ *Sum* ÷ *Number*
                                    $\Rightarrow$ 400 ÷ 5 = 80

Question #14: A student's average score of five tests is 80. If the student's score of 100 on the fifth test is removed, what's the new average?
Solution: Original Mean $\Rightarrow$ 80
                   Original Number $\Rightarrow$ 5
                   Original Sum $\Rightarrow$ *Mean* × *Number*
                                    $\Rightarrow$ 5 × 80 = 400
                   New Sum $\Rightarrow$ *Original Sum* – *New Value*
                                    $\Rightarrow$ 400 – 100 = 300
                   New Number $\Rightarrow$ *Original Number* – 1
                                    $\Rightarrow$ 5 – 1 = 4
                   New Mean $\Rightarrow$ *Sum* ÷ *Number*
                                    $\Rightarrow$ 300 ÷ 4 = 75

Question #15: A student averaged a score of 97 over a series of 6 tests, and if one more test score was added, his average goes down to 75. How much did he score on the test that was added?
Solution: Original Mean $\Rightarrow$ 97
                   Original Number $\Rightarrow$ 6
                   Original Sum $\Rightarrow$ *Mean* × *Number*
                                    $\Rightarrow$ 97 × 6 = 582
                   New Number $\Rightarrow$ *Original Number* + 1

$\Rightarrow$ 6 + 1 = 7

New Mean $\Rightarrow$ 75

New Sum $\Rightarrow$ *Mean × Number*

$\Rightarrow$ 75 × 7 = 525

Number Added $\Rightarrow$ *Original Sum – New Sum*

$\Rightarrow$ 582 – 525 = 57

Therefore, the test score that was added is 57

Question #16: A student averaged a score of 60 over a series of 6 tests, and if one of the test score was removed, his average goes down to 55. What was the score on the test that was removed?

Solution: Original Mean $\Rightarrow$ 60

Original Number $\Rightarrow$ 6

Original Sum $\Rightarrow$ *Mean × Number*

$\Rightarrow$ 60 × 6 = 360

New Number $\Rightarrow$ *Original Number – 1*

$\Rightarrow$ 6 – 1 = 5

New Mean $\Rightarrow$ 55

New Sum $\Rightarrow$ *Mean × Number*

$\Rightarrow$ 55 × 5 = 275

Number Added $\Rightarrow$ *Original Sum – New Sum*

$\Rightarrow$ 360 – 275 = 85

Therefore, the test score that was removed is 85

Question #17: If a man drives the first five hours of his trip at 90 miles per hour and the last two hours at 55 miles per hour due to some traffic delays, what is his average speed for the entire trip?

Solution: Weighted Mean $\Rightarrow$ *sum of products ÷ sum of weights*   [Write the formula to calculate weighted mean]

$\Rightarrow$ [5(90) + 2(55)] ÷ [5 + 2]   [Substitute the known values]

$\Rightarrow$ 560 ÷ 7   [Simplify within the brackets]

$\Rightarrow$ 80   [Do the division]

Question #18: If a man drives the first 2 hours of his trip at 95 miles per hour and the last 5 hours at 88 miles per hour due to some traffic delays, what is his average speed for the entire trip?

Solution: Weighted Mean $\Rightarrow$ *sum of products ÷ sum of weights*   [Write the formula to calculate weighted mean]

$\Rightarrow$ [2(95) + 5(88)] ÷ [2 + 5]   [Substitute the known values]

$\Rightarrow$ 630 ÷ 7   [Simplify within the brackets]

$\Rightarrow$ 90   [Do the division]

Question #19: What is the median of the following numbers: {1, 17, 5, 15, 7}?

Solution: Arrange the terms in ascending order $\Rightarrow$ {1, 5, 7, 15, 17}

Number of terms $\Rightarrow$ 5 (odd number of terms)

Median $\Rightarrow$ *Middle Term*   [Write the formula for calculating median]

$\Rightarrow$ 7   [Find the value of the middle most term]

Question #20: What is the median of the following numbers: {8, 1, 18, 5, 17, 9}?

Solution: Arrange the terms in ascending order $\Rightarrow$ {1, 5, 8, 9, 17, 18}

Number of terms $\Rightarrow$ 6 (even number of terms)

Median $\Rightarrow$ *Mean of the Two Middle Terms*   [Write the formula for calculating median]

$\Rightarrow \dfrac{8+9}{2}$ [Find the mean of the two middle most terms]

$\Rightarrow \dfrac{17}{2}$ [Do the addition]

$\Rightarrow$ 8.5   [Do the division]

Question #21: What is the mode of the following numbers: {12, 19, 15, 19, 16, 17}?

Solution: Mode $\Rightarrow$ *Number(s) that occurs most often*   [Write the formula for calculating mode]

$\Rightarrow$ 19   [Find the term(s) that occurs most frequently]

Question #22: What is the mode of the following numbers: {7, 17, 11, 19, 7, 12, 11, 15}?
Solution: Mode   ⇒ *Number(s) that occurs most often*   [Write the formula for calculating mode]
                    ⇒ 7 and 11   [Find the term(s) that occurs most frequently]

Question #23: If the mode of the following set of numbers is 20, then what is the average (arithmetic mean) and median of the set of numbers?
{12, 13, 18, 19, 20, n}
Solution: Since the mode of the set of numbers is 20, the value of *n* must be 20 for it to be the mode (the number that occurs most frequently).
Now the set of numbers looks like this: {12, 13, 18, 19, 20, 20}
     Mean   ⇒ *Sum ÷ Number*   [Write the appropriate formula]
                  ⇒ (12 + 13 + 18 + 19 + 20 + 20) ÷ 6   [Substitute the known values]
                  ⇒ 102 ÷ 6   [Simplify within parentheses]
                  ⇒ 17   [Do the division]
     Median ⇒ *Mean of Two Middle Terms* (even terms)   [Write the appropriate formula]
                  ⇒ (18 + 19) ÷ 2   [Substitute the known values]
                  ⇒ 37 ÷ 2   [Simplify within parentheses]
                  ⇒ 18.5   [Do the division]

Question #24: If the average (arithmetic mean) of the following set of numbers is 15, then what is the median and the mode?
{11, 12, 16, 18, n}
Solution: Mean   ⇒ *Sum ÷ Number* = 15   [Equate the mean formula with the actual mean]
$$\Rightarrow \frac{11+12+16+18+n}{5} = 15 \qquad \text{[Substitute the known values]}$$
$$\Rightarrow \frac{57+n}{5} = 15 \qquad \text{[Simplify the left side]}$$
                  ⇒ 57 + n = 75   [Cross-multiply]
                  ⇒ n = 18   [Subtract 57 from both sides]
Set of numbers in increasing order ⇒ {11, 12, 16, 18, 18}
     Median ⇒ *Middle Term – for odd number of terms* [Write the appropriate formula]
                  ⇒ 16   [Find the value of the middle most term]
     Mode   ⇒ *Number(s) that occurs most often*   [Write the appropriate formula]
                  ⇒ 18   [Find the term(s) that occurs most frequently]

Question #25: What is the range of the following numbers: {7, 9, 18, 26, 57, 68, 85}?
Solution: Range   ⇒ Largest Term – Smallest Term
                  ⇒ 85 – 7 = 78

Question #26: What are the extremes of the following numbers: {7, 9, 18, 26, 57, 68, 85}?
Solution: Lower Extreme   ⇒ 7
     Upper Extreme   ⇒ 85

Question #27: What is the standard deviation of the following set of data: {1, 2, 10, 11, 14, 15, 17}?
Solution: Average of the set of data = (1 + 2 + 10 + 11 + 14 + 15 + 17) ÷ 7 = 70 ÷ 7 = 10
Organize the information in the following table:

n	$(n - 10)$	$(n - 10)^2$
1	−9	81
2	−8	64
10	0	00
11	+1	01
14	+4	16
15	+5	25
17	+7	49
		236

Standard Deviation $\Rightarrow \sqrt{\dfrac{236}{7}}$ = 5.8 (approx.)

Question #28: What is the standard deviation of the following set of data: {1, 5, 8, 9, 10, 11, 12, 16, 18}?

Solution: Average of the set of data = (1 + 5 + 8 + 9 + 10 + 11 + 12 + 16 + 18) ÷ 9 = 90 ÷ 9 = 10

Organize the information in the following table:

n	$(n - 10)$	$(n - 10)^2$
1	−9	81
5	−5	25
8	−2	04
9	−1	01
10	0	00
11	+1	01
12	+2	04
16	+6	36
18	+8	64
		216

Standard Deviation $\Rightarrow \sqrt{\dfrac{216}{9}}$ = 4.9 (approx.)

Question #29: In a certain normal distribution, the arithmetic mean is 87.25 and standard deviation is 1.25. What value is exactly 2 standard deviations more than the mean?

Solution: Arithmetic Mean $\Rightarrow$ 87.25
One Standard Deviation $\Rightarrow$ 1.25
Two Standard Deviations $\Rightarrow$ 2(1.25) = 2.5
Two Standard Deviations more than the Arithmetic Mean $\Rightarrow$ 87.25 + 2.5 = 89.75

Question #30: In a certain normal distribution, the arithmetic mean is 89.5 and standard deviation is 1.5. What value is exactly 5.5 standard deviations less than the mean?

Solution: Arithmetic Mean $\Rightarrow$ 89.5
One Standard Deviation $\Rightarrow$ 1.5
Two Standard Deviations $\Rightarrow$ 5.5(1.5) = 8.25
Two Standard Deviations less than the Arithmetic Mean $\Rightarrow$ 89.5 − 8.25 = 81.25

PART 8.0: STATISTICS – GRAPHS:

TABLE OF CONTENTS:

8.1: BASICS ABOUT GRAPHS:

The *"data interpretation"* or *"graph"* questions involve the analysis of data displayed in graphical or tabular formats. These questions essentially require you to read, interpret, analyze, and logically interpret the data supplied in terms of a set of tables or graphs. The good part about these questions is that no new topics are tested, they test your ability to work with the same topics such as, simple arithmetic, percents, ratios, averages, etc., in a different context; however, the basic fundamentals and principles remain to be the same. A basic graph question may require a simple arithmetic calculation (addition, subtraction, multiplication, and division); where as a more complex graph question may require calculation of percent, average, or ratio. Graph questions require a strong understanding of basic mathematical operations and functions, and a good attention to details. Each question can be answered by selecting the appropriate information and applying various mathematical techniques. It is important that you are able to understand the information presented in a table or in the various types of graphs.

Part-Whole Relationship: Almost every set of graph questions involve the part and whole relationship in some way. Whenever a question involves a fraction, percent, ratio, or proportion, it is actually referring to the relationship between the parts and wholes. So make sure you understand the part-whole relationship; if you're not clear with it, you must review the basics.

Format and Concept: In general, there is nothing conceptually difficult about graphs, tables, and charts; in fact, they're just different ways of presenting the same information that you may see in a regular math problem. Thus, if you are having trouble with these questions, you must try to determine whether the problem is with the format, or with the concepts involved. If the problem is with the concepts involved, you must go back and review the basics from our other review modules, and again try these problems.

Inference Questions: The inference questions are a little different from the other questions. In these questions, you have to determine whether a statement or information can be inferred from the graph. These types of questions are similar to the logical reasoning questions, and it usually comes down to understanding the scope of the graph. In order to answer the inference questions correctly, first of all, you must understand the scope of the graph and be able to differentiate between what MUST be true and what MIGHT be true. Next, check for each statement, and determine if it is *inferable* or not from the information given in the graphs.

READING AND ANALYZING THE DATA:
Data Analysis questions may require you to do more than just read the data presented in the form of a graph or chart, they may even require you to analyze the data.
(A) Reading the Data: One part of this section tests the ability to read the data given in the table or graph.
(B) Analyzing the Data: The other part of this section tests the ability to use the data presented and perform data interpretation, analysis, inference, deduction, conclusion, application, manipulation, identification, comparison, and/or future predictions of trends.

DIFFERENT FORMS IN WHICH DATA CAN BE PRESENTED:
Data are facts and information. By analyzing data, we can make predictions, draw inferences or conclusions, and solve problems. To be useful, data must be organized in the form of a table/chart or it can be presented in a graph. The same data or information can be summarized and presented in various forms, including tables, charts, or graphs.

There are several different kinds of tables and graphs; however, some of the most common ones are listed below:
- Table/Chart/Grid
- Pictograph
- Single Line Graph
- Double Line Graph
- Single Bar Graph
- Double Bar Graph
- Scatter Plot Graph
- Circle Graph or Pie Chart

WHAT DATA INTERPRETATION QUESTIONS TEST:

Data interpretation questions may test your ability or require you to perform some of the following tasks:

- **Reading & Comprehension:** Ability to accurately read and comprehend the data presented in tables or graphs.
- **Identification:** Ability to identify specific pieces of information or data.
- **Interpretation:** Ability to interpret and analyze information presented in tables, charts, or graphs.
- **Comparison:** Ability to compare data or quantities from different parts of the table or graph.
- **Forming Relationships:** Ability to form relationships among different data presented in different parts of the table or graph.
- **Recognition:** Ability to recognize trends and changes in the data.
- **Calculations:** Ability to perform calculations based on the information presented or deduced.
- **Manipulation:** Ability to manipulate the data.
- **Forecasts & Predictions:** Ability to make future forecasts and predictions.
- **Inference & Conclusion:** Ability to draw inferences and conclusions to solve problems.

All Types of Graphs, Tables, Charts, and Grids are Accurate – Trust Them: All math problems, that use any types of graphs, tables, charts, or grids are always drawn accurately and can be trusted. Usually no modifications are needed on them, but you may have to label them. All you have to do is to interpret the data given, and analyze it.

Units Given in Tables or Graphs: The units of the table or graph are usually given with the title, or underneath the title, or on the relevant scale on the axes of the graph, or on the row or column of the table or chart. The units are generally given in parentheses or quotation marks. It is important to make sure you understand the units (hundreds, thousands, etc.) before you even try to answer the questions. First, figure out the units the table or graph is using and the units in which the question is asking for the answer, and then make sure to express your answer in the correct units. Be careful of phrases such as "sales in millions of dollars" or "population in hundreds of thousands", etc. You should always be on a look out for such type of phrases, they are very common to appear on the tables or graphs, and extremely easy to miss!

Scales given in Graphs: The scale is usually located along the vertical or horizontal axis of a line or a bar graph, and indicates how many units each tick-mark along the line signifies. Be careful, the scale may not necessarily start at zero, so check to see where it actually starts and see how the information is measured.

Zeros of Scales: The scale may not necessarily start at zero, so make sure to note whether the scale starts at zero or somewhere other than zero. Such graphs present the same information, but now you cannot estimate as wildly as you did when the scale starts at zero. Nevertheless, you can still tell at a glance if one value is greater or less than the other is, but you cannot quickly estimate the relative ratios.

TIPS FOR GRAPH QUESTIONS:

While working with data interpretation questions, make sure to do the following:

- Read the title(s), labels and keys very carefully
- Understand the row and column headings if it's a chart or a table, or the x-axis and y axis labels if it's a graph.
- Mark and label key information on the graphs, such as each coordinate point, axis, etc, if they are not already labeled.
- Look at the entire table or graph and not just a small part of it.
- Understand how the data is displayed and which data is relevant to the question.
- Know how to process the relevant data to solve the problem and answer the question correctly.
- Understand the type of information being presented or displayed in the table or graph clearly.
- Understand what happens to the data as you move through the table or graph.
- Look for sudden increases or decreases.
- Look for trends or patterns formed.
- Ignore extraneous information and zero-in on what the question is asking for or what you are looking for.
- Don't get intimidated by the complex visual presentation of data – take some time to figure out what information is displayed in the table, graph, or chart, before you read the accompanying questions.
- Don't confuse decimals with percentages and vice versa – if the units are percentages, then an entry of 0.5 means 0.5%, which is equal to 0.005.
- Make sure not to make any false assumptions.
- In inference questions, only the information that is given can be used.

- On line or bar graphs, it may be sometimes helpful to use the edge of your answer sheet as a straightedge so that you can line up the points on the graph with their corresponding numerical values on the x-axis or the y-axis (scale) of the graph. Make sure the edge of your answer sheet is completely parallel to the corresponding axis.
- Read any accompanying notes underneath the table, chart, or graph, if there is any.
- If there are multiple lines or bars on the graph, make sure to refer to the key that explains the distinction between them.
- Finally, make sure to completely familiarize yourself with the graphs before going ahead and tackling the questions, and check and see if your chosen answer makes sense.

APPROXIMATIONS ON GRAPH QUESTIONS:

On graph questions, you should always try to approximate wherever possible. No matter how difficult a graph question may appear at first glance, it can usually be made easier if you take advantage of the large spread that is typically found among the quantities in the answer choices – by approximating instead of calculating wherever possible. Moreover, since many questions only ask for an approximate answer, it may be possible to save some valuable time by rounding off. So you can often estimate on graph problems, but first check to see how close the answer choices are – that will tell you how accurate you need to be. Moreover, since graph questions generally take more time to solve than other math questions, approximating on a difficult graph question can be especially useful, if you want to take a guess and move on, or don't have enough time to be more specific. In most cases, you won't be required to find a precise value. As a rule, try to find precise values only as a last resort. Always remember, you're not being tested on whether you can tell if a value is 9.17 or 9.18, what you are being actually tested on is whether you are able to understand the basic concepts behind graphs.

DOUBLE GRAPHS:

Double Tables/Graphs: Sometimes graph questions come in sets consisting of one or more graphs accompanied by several questions. In such cases, you may be presented with a pair of tables or graphs, or one table and one graph for the same set of questions. It can be in the form of two line graphs or two bar graphs or two pie charts, or any other combination. The two tables or graphs given will be related in one way or the other. These questions require you to take data from both graphs and combine the information to answer the question. Make sure to use both graphs while answering these questions.

Double: Table + Graph: Sometimes, you may get a combination of a graph and a table, in which case, the table covers one aspect, while the accompanying graph breaks the information further down.

Double Scale Graphs: It can often get more confusing when there are two tables or graphs occupying the same space with either a common scale or two different scales. Sometimes there will be only one scale, in which case, both graphs will refer to the same vertical or horizontal scale; and at other times, there will be two scales, in which case, one graph will refer to the scale on the left-hand-side, the other graph to the scale on the right-hand-side. Make sure not to mix up the scales and to double-check that you are using the correct scale when working with double graphs.

Two Scales: There may be more than one line or set of bars on one graph, if so, they may have different scales. Check the right-hand side of the graph to make sure – because that's where a second scale would be placed.

Double Pie Charts: Pie charts can also come in pairs of two. In that case, make sure that you do not attempt to compare slices from one pie with slices from another one because the size of the whole in each pie will most likely be different. A quick glimpse might suggest that one slice of one pie is bigger than another slice of the other pie; however, that may not necessarily be true. A slice of one pie may have a greater percentage of the whole than another slice of the other pie; however, the second slice may have a higher dollar value than the first pie because the second pie probably has a bigger whole than the first pie. Since the totals for two pie charts may be different, the pieces of the two pies are not directly comparable.

COMPARING TABLES/GRAPHS WITH OTHER THINGS:

COMPARISON BETWEEN TABLES AND GRAPHS:

All different types of tables and graphs follow the same fundamentals and principles; although, the values are presented in different formats, such as, rows, columns, lines, bars, etc. Graphs can be used to show virtually all the information that could otherwise appear in a table and vice versa. Therefore, the same information can be presented in the form of a table or graph. Following is the comparison between tables and graphs:

(A) PRECISION: Table is a much more **precise** and **accurate** way of presenting data than graphs, since in a table, exact numbers can be shown. On the other hand, graphs are not very precise, and they do not show the exact numbers, at least not the way a table does.

(B) CONCISION: Graphs are a much more **concise** and **succinct** way of presenting data than tables, since in a graph, short and to-the-point information can be shown. On the other hand, tables are not very concise and it's often difficult to show short and to-the-point information.

(C) SIMPLICITY: Graphs are a much **simpler** and **straightforward** way of presenting data. On the other hand, tables can be often complex and massive with multiple columns and rows; however, the basic structure is always the same – it only has columns and rows.

(D) ESTIMATION: With graphs, it's often quite easy to **estimate** and **approximate** values from just looking at them. On the other hand, with tables, it's often hard to estimate or approximate values from just looking at them, at least not the way you can by just looking at a graph. On your test, it would be very rare that you'll need an exact value, so don't bother about getting a very precise value; usually, you will only have to get a rough estimation.

(E) VISUAL EFFECTS: Graphs have a visual feature, it's a lot easier to make the comparison and see the **trends** than in a table, since in a graph you can show the upward or downward **movements**. On the other hand, in tables it's virtually impossible to show the visual movement the way a graph does.

(F) ONE GLIMPSE IS WORTH A THOUSAND WORDS: The best part about a graph is that we can see the relative value of each item by simply looking at their positions. Just a simple glance at the graph can provide a lot of useful information. We can see the relative value of the given point on the line simply by looking at their heights.
For instance, just by glancing at the graph, it's easy to see that one value is almost half or double of the other.

Therefore, it's clear that in many respects, both tables and graphs have different advantages and disadvantages; they both have similarities and differences as they share many of the same characteristics. One must be careful in picking a table or a graph to present their data depending on the type of data they want to present.

DIFFERENCES BETWEEN GRAPHS AND GEOMETRY DIAGRAMS:
Graphs are unlike geometry diagrams as there are many differences between the two. Generally, when you are provided with a geometry diagram, you are usually not given information unless you need it in order to answer the question. In other words, you are given only the pertinent information without anything that is extra or unwanted.

However, in a table or graph, you may be given a lot of extraneous and irrelevant information that you probably don't need in order to answer the question, or it may even include something that you are not being tested on. In this way, graphs are unlike diagrams, since the graphs include a lot of unwanted and extra information.

SIMILARITIES BETWEEN GRAPHS AND READING COMPREHENSION PASSAGES:
Graphs have a lot in common with the reading passages; in both, not all the detailed information is needed or is important, but only the information that they question you about. So a graph is more comparable to a reading passage. In fact, one of the main skills you are being tested on is the ability to distill and extract the relevant information from the clutter that they provide you. You should be able to pull out and zero-in the required information that is needed to answer the given question.

Because of the similarities of graphs with reading passages, it may be a good idea to apply some of the same strategies you use for answering reading passages. For instance, you should briefly skim over the graph and then look at the questions. When you quickly look over the graph, try to figure out the main idea of the graph, i.e., what kind of central information does the graph presents. Similarly, when you start answering a question, first try to figure out what you need to know in order to answer that question, and then go back to the graph and look for that information. For more in-depth knowledge, refer to our review on reading comprehension.

8.2: TABLES & CHARTS:

HIGHLIGHTS OF TABLE/CHART:
- A table is the most basic form of representing any type of collection of data.
- A table uses rows and columns to represent or organize the collection of data in an easy to read tabular form.
- The data represented in a table can also be represented in a form of a graph, or vice versa.

USES OF TABLE/CHART:
- Tables are useful to compare increase and/or decrease in quantities over periods of time.
- Tables are also useful to quickly compare relative changes in quantities and to find specific quantities at a specific time.

PARTS OF TABLE/CHART:
Title of Table/Chart: The title of the table tells us the topic of the table and what the information means. It also explains or describes what the table represents and makes it easier to read and interpret the table. The title is usually clear and concise. One should always make sure to read it first.

Rows: The Rows of a table are the horizontal sections that are generally read from left to right. The first row of the table is generally the Row Heading. The rows of a table can be used to show the period of time, such as, days, weeks, months, years etc or range of quantities, such as sales, production, growth, temperature, average salary etc.

Columns: The Columns of a table are the vertical sections that are generally read from top to bottom. The first column of the table is generally the Column Heading. The columns of a table can be used to show the period of time, such as, days, weeks, months, years etc or range of quantities, such as sales, production, growth, temperature, average salary etc.

READING TABLE/CHART:
To read the table, first look for a specific unit on the row heading and then match that row with the corresponding unit on the column heading.

Note: A table that represents data is also sometime referred to as a matrix or a grid.

8.3: PICTOGRAPHS:

HIGHLIGHTS OF PICTOGRAPH:
- A Pictograph uses pictorial symbols or pictures to represent the collection of data on a graph.
- There are no numbers to examine in pictographs, except in the key or the labels on the graph.
- Each picture or symbol represents a real number of a particular item.

USES OF PICTOGRAPH:
- Pictographs are an important source to represent data because it is easier to visualize and then analyze or compare the data that is represented in the form of pictures/symbols.

PARTS OF PICTOGRAPH:
Title of Pictograph: The title of the pictograph tells us the topic of the pictograph and what the information means. It also explains or describes what the pictograph represents and makes it easier to read and interpret the pictograph. The title is usually clear and concise. One should always make sure to read it first.

Key: The Key is a list of words, numbers, symbols, or combination of these that helps in the identification of the items in a pictograph or in interpretation of the pictograph. It explains what number each picture or symbol represents and what the conversion factor is, that is, it tells how to convert a picture/symbol to a real number. If each picture/symbol is labeled with what it represents, then it may not be necessary to create a key.

Row Headings: The Row Headings explain what the data given in the form or pictures/symbols represent.

READING PICTOGRAPH:
To read the pictograph, first look at a specific row, and then compute its value based on the conversion factor given in the key. Each symbol represents a fixed number of items as indicated in the key.

8.4: Single Line Graphs:

Highlights of Single Line Graph:
- Single Line Graphs use lines to represent the collection of data on a graph.
- Points are plotted on the graph according to the different values of the horizontal and vertical axis. These points are then connected by a line, which makes it a Single Line Graph.
- In single line graphs, quantities can be compared by the height of the point on the line.
- In single line graphs, the height of each point on the line shows its value on the corresponding axis.
- The elevation of the points on a single line graph depends on the amount of quantity it represents. The higher the point on the line, the higher the quantity it represents; the lower the point on the line, the lower the quantity it represents.

EZ Hint: To measure the height of a point on the single line graph, use your pencil or a piece of paper, such as, the edge of your test booklet, or the admission card to the test, as a straight edge.

Uses of Single Line Graph:
- Single Line Graphs are useful to show how a quantity changes continuously.
- Single Line Graphs are useful to show trends or compare increase and/or decrease in quantities over periods of time.
- Single Line Graphs are also useful to quickly compare relative changes in quantities over a period of time and to find specific quantities at a specific time period. By analyzing the rise and fall of the line, one can tell whether something is increasing, decreasing, or staying the same.

Parts of Single Line Graph:
Title of Single Line Graph: The title tells us the topic of the single line graph and what the information means. It also explains or describes what the single line graph represents and makes it easier to read and interpret it. The title is usually clear and concise. One should always make sure to read it first.
Vertical Axis: The Vertical Axis of the Single Line Graph shows the range of quantities, such as, sales, production, growth, temperature, average salary etc. It is read from bottom (which is usually zero) to top.
Horizontal Axis: The Horizontal Axis of the Single Line Graph usually shows the period of time in regular time intervals, such as, days, weeks, months, years etc. It is read from left (which is usually zero) to right.
Origin: The vertical axis and horizontal axis intersects at the origin or zeros of the graph, and as we move from left to right or bottom to top, the value increases.
Key: The Key is a list of words, numbers, symbols, or combination of these that helps in the identification of the items in a graph or in interpretation of the graph. It explains what each of the lines represents. If the line is labeled with what it represents, then it may not be necessary to create a key.

Reading Single Line Graph:
To read the Line Graph, first look for a specific time period on the horizontal axis and then match the height of the point on the line with the number on the vertical axis which is the actual quantity for that specific time period.
In order to find a specific numerical value of a particular point on the line from a line graph, find the correct point on the line, and move horizontally across from that point on the line to the value on the scale on the left. The vertical distance from the bottom of the graph to the point on the line is the value of that point.
Note: This is different from a table, where we are given exact values.

Slope of Line: We can tell a lot about the information in a line graph without even looking at the exact values. Just by examining the slope of the line that connects the points, we can tell whether there was an increase, decrease, or no change, from one time period to the next. Sometimes, the quantity is measured as time changes. Since, time period on the horizontal axis usually increases from left to right and the scale on the vertical axis usually increases from bottom to top, the following can be concluded:
Upward Sloping: A line that slopes up from left to right, shows an increase in the quantity during that time period.
Downward Sloping: A line that slopes down from left to right, shows a decrease in the quantity during that time period.
Flat Sloping: A line that slopes horizontally (flat line), shows no change in the quantity during that time period.

Steepness of Line: The steepness of a line can also be informative. A steeper line indicates a faster rate of change than a flatter line. This can also be confirmed by actually reading off the values and comparing them.

8.5: DOUBLE LINE GRAPHS:

HIGHLIGHTS OF DOUBLE LINE GRAPH:
- Double Line Graphs use double lines to represent the collection of data on a graph, with each line representing a different item.
- Points are plotted on the graph according to the different values of the horizontal and vertical axis. These points are then connected by a line, which makes it a Double Line Graph.
- The two lines can be differentiated by making one of the lines solid and the other dotted – The first line represents the first variable and the second line represents the second variable.
- In Double Line Graphs, different quantities can be compared by the height of the points on the line on the corresponding axis.
- The elevation of the points on a double line graph depends on the amount of quantity it represents. The higher the point on the line, the higher the quantity it represents; the lower the point on the line, the lower the quantity it represents.

EZ HINT: To measure the height of a point on the single bar graph, use your pencil or a piece of paper, such as, the edge of your test booklet, or the admission card to the test, as a straight edge.

USES OF DOUBLE LINE GRAPH:
- Double Line Graphs are useful to show how different quantities change continuously.
- Double Line Graphs are useful to show trends or compare increase and/or decrease in quantities in two variables over periods of time. One can compare different quantities or the same quantity at different times.
- Double Line Graphs are also useful to quickly compare relative changes in quantities of two variables and to find specific quantities of each variable at a specific time period. By analyzing the rise and fall of the line, one can tell whether something is increasing, decreasing, or staying the same.

PARTS OF DOUBLE LINE GRAPH:
Title of Double Line Graph: The title tells us the topic of the double line graph and what the information means. It also explains or describes what the double line graph represents and makes it easier to read and interpret it. The title is usually clear and concise. One should always make sure to read it first.
Vertical Axis: The Vertical Axis of the Double Line Graph shows the range of quantities, such as, sales, production, growth, temperature, average salary etc. It is read from bottom (which is zero) to top.
Horizontal Axis: The Horizontal Axis of the Double Line Graph shows the periods of time, such as, days, weeks, months, years etc. It is read from left (which is zero) to right.
Origin: The vertical axis and horizontal axis intersect at the origin or zeros of the graph, and as we move from left to right or bottom to top, the value increases.
Key: The Key is a list of words, numbers, symbols, or combination of these that helps in the identification of the items in a graph or in interpretation of the graph. It explains what each of the two lines represent. The two lines can be differentiated by making one of the lines solid and the other dotted or with different patterns/colors. If each line is labeled with what it represents, then it may not be necessary to create a key.

READING DOUBLE LINE GRAPH:
To read the Double Line Graph, first look for a specific time period on the horizontal axis and then match the height of the point on the line with the number on the vertical axis which is the actual quantity of that specific variable for that specific time period.

8.6: SINGLE BAR GRAPHS:

HIGHLIGHTS OF SINGLE BAR GRAPH:
- Single Bar Graphs use bars to represent the collection of data on a graph.
- Points are plotted on the graph according to the different values of the horizontal and vertical axis. These points are then connected by bars, which makes it a Single Bar Graph.
- In single bar graphs, quantities can be compared by the height or length of a bar.
- In single line graphs, the height of each bar shows its value on the corresponding axis.
- The elevation of the points on a single line graph depends on the amount of quantity it represents. The higher the height of the bar, the higher the quantity it represents; the lower the height of the bar, the lower the quantity it represents.
- Bar Graphs can have either vertical or horizontal bars.
- On a bar graph, the height of each column shows its value on the corresponding axis.

EZ HINT: To measure the height of a point on the single bar graph, or to compare bars that are not adjacent to each other or to the axis, use your pencil or a piece of paper, such as, the edge of your test booklet, or the admission card to the test, as a straight edge.

USES OF SINGLE BAR GRAPH:
- Single Bar Graphs are useful to show how quantities change continuously.
- Single Bar Graphs are useful to show trends or compare increase and/or decrease in quantities over periods of time.
- Single Bar Graphs are also useful to quickly compare relative changes in quantities over a period of time and to find specific quantities at a specific time period. By analyzing the rise and fall of the line, one can tell whether something is increasing, decreasing, or staying the same.

PARTS OF SINGLE BAR GRAPH:
Title of Single Bar Graph: The title tells us the topic of the single bar graph and what the information means. It also explains or describes what the single bar graph represents and makes it easier to read and interpret it. The title is usually clear and concise. One should always make sure to read it first.
Vertical Axis: The Vertical Axis of the Single Bar Graph shows the range of quantities, such as, sales, production, growth, temperature, average salary etc. It is read from bottom (which is zero) to top.
Horizontal Axis: The Horizontal Axis of the Single Bar Graph shows the labels for the bars or periods of time, such as, days, weeks, months, years etc. It is read from left (which is zero) to right.
Origin: The vertical axis and horizontal axis intersect at the origin or zeros of the graph, and as we move from left to right or bottom to top, the value increases.
Key: The Key is a list of words, numbers, symbols, or combination of these that helps in the identification of the items in a graph or in interpretation of the graph. It explains what the bar represents. If the bar is labeled with what it represents, then it may not be necessary to create a key.

READING BAR GRAPH:
To read the Single Bar Graph and estimate what value each bar represents, first look for a bar label or specific time period on the horizontal axis and then match the height of the bar with the number on the vertical axis which is the actual quantity for that specific bar or time period.
In order to find a specific numerical value of a particular bar from a bar graph, find the correct bar, and move horizontally across from the top of the bar that points on the line to the value on the scale on the left. The vertical distance from the bottom of the graph to the point on the line is the value of that point. Note: This is different from a table, where we are given exact values.

8.7: DOUBLE BAR GRAPHS:

HIGHLIGHTS OF DOUBLE BAR GRAPH:

- Double Bar Graphs use double bars to represent the collection of data on a graph, with each bar representing a different item.
- Points are plotted on the graph according to the different values of the horizontal and vertical axis. These points are then connected by bars, which makes it a Double Bar Graph.
- The two bars can be differentiated by making one of the bars lightly shaded and the other darkly shaded – The first bar represents the first variable and the second bar represents the second variable.
- In Double Bar Graphs, different quantities can be compared by the height or length of the bars on the corresponding axis.
- The elevation of the bars on the double bar graph depends on the amount of quantity it represents. The higher the height of the bar, the higher the quantity it represents; the lower the height of the bar, the lower the quantity it represents.
- Double Bar Graphs can have either vertical or horizontal bars.

EZ HINT: To measure the height of a point on the double bar graph, or to compare bars that are not adjacent to each other or to the axis, use your pencil or a piece of paper, such as, the edge of your test booklet, or the admission card to the test, as a straight edge.

USES OF DOUBLE BAR GRAPH:

- Double Bar Graphs are useful to show how different quantities change continuously.
- Double Bar Graphs are useful to show trends or compare increase and/or decrease in quantities in two variables over periods of time. One can compare different quantities or the same quantity at different times.
- Double Bar Graphs are also useful to quickly compare relative changes in quantities of two variables and to find specific quantities of each variable at a specific time period. By analyzing the rise and fall of the bar, one can tell whether something is increasing, decreasing, or staying the same.

PARTS OF DOUBLE BAR GRAPH:

Title of Double Bar Graph: The title tells us the topic of the double bar graph and what the information means. It also explains or describes what the double bar graph represents and makes it easier to read and interpret it. The title is usually clear and concise. One should always make sure to read it first.

Vertical Axis: The Vertical Axis of the Double Bar Graph shows the range of quantities, such as, sales, production, growth, temperature, average salary etc. It is read from bottom (which is zero) to top.

Horizontal Axis: The Horizontal Axis of the Double Bar Graph shows the periods of time, such as, days, weeks, months, years etc. It is read from left (which is zero) to right.

Origin: The vertical axis and horizontal axis intersect at the origin or zeros of the graph, and as we move from left to right or bottom to top, the value increases.

Key: The Key is a list of words, numbers, symbols, or combination of these that helps in the identification of the items in a graph or in interpretation of the graph. It explains what each of the two bars represent. The two bars can be differentiated by making one of the bars lightly shaded and the other darkly shaded or with different patterns/colors. If each bar is labeled with what it represents, then it may not be necessary to create a key.

READING DOUBLE BAR GRAPH:

To read the Double Bar Graph, first look for a specific time period on the horizontal axis and then match the height of each of the bars with the number on the vertical axis which is the actual quantity of that specific variable for that specific time period.

8.8: SCATTER PLOT GRAPHS:

HIGHLIGHTS OF SCATTER PLOT GRAPH:

- A Scatter Plot Graph uses grid and points to represent the collection of data on a graph.
- Points are plotted on the graph according to the different values of the horizontal and vertical axis. These points are scattered all around the graph, which makes it a Scatter Plot Graph.
- Scatter Plots are useful to compare a relationship or variation between two types of quantities or characteristics of the same group of people or things.
- To measure the location of a point on the graph, use your pencil or a piece of paper, such as, the edge of your test booklet, or the admission card to the test, as a straight edge.

USES OF SCATTER PLOT GRAPHS:

- Scatter Plot graphs are useful to represent types of data, such as, Height – Weight; Area – Perimeter; Height – Shadow; Distance – Time, etc.

PARTS OF SCATTER PLOT GRAPH:

Title of Scatter Plot Graph: The title tells us the topic of the scatter plot graph and what the information means. It also explains or describes what the scatter plot graph represents and makes it easier to read and interpret it. The title is usually clear and concise. One should always make sure to read it first.

Vertical Axis: The Vertical Axis of the Scatter Plot shows the range of the first quantity, such as, height, weight, age, etc. It is read from bottom (which is zero) to top.

Horizontal Axis: The Horizontal Axis of the Scatter Plot shows the range of the second quantity, such as, height, weight, age, etc. It is read from left (which is zero) to right.

Origin: The vertical axis and horizontal axis intersect at the origin or zeros of the graph, and as we move from left to right or bottom to top, the value increases.

Key: The Key is a list of words, numbers, symbols, or combination of these that helps in the identification of the items in a graph or in interpretation of the graph. It explains what each of the parts/sectors represent. Each point can be differentiated by making them in different shades or with different patterns/colors. If each point is labeled with what it represents, then it may not be necessary to create a key.

READING SCATTER PLOT GRAPH:

To read the Scatter Plot, first look for the first quantity on the horizontal axis and the second quantity of the vertical axis, the point of intersection of these two values is the point that represents those two quantities.

8.9: CIRCLE GRAPHS / PIE CHARTS:

HIGHLIGHTS OF CIRCLE GRAPHS:
- Circle Graph is also known as a Pie Chart.
- Circle Graphs use circles to represent the collection of data on graph.
- Circle Graphs are divided into parts known as sectors, where each sector represents a different quantity.
- The size of each sector in a circle graph is exactly proportional to the quantity it represents – the bigger the section, the higher the quantity it represents; the smaller the section, the lower the quantity it represents.
- The sections of a circle graph are often labeled with percents, fractions, or decimals. The size of each section corresponds to the percent or fraction it represents. For example, a section labeled 25% will be ¼ of the circle.
- A circle graph shows how things are distributed – the part or fraction of a circle occupied by each piece or slice of the "pie" indicates what fraction or part of the whole it represents. Usually, the pie chart will identify what percent of the whole pie each piece represents.
- If the sectors are given in percentages, then the sum of all the sections should always equal 100%. If the sectors are given in fractions or decimals, then the sum of all the sections must equal 1. For this reason, Circle Graphs are useful to represent different parts of the same whole.
- The amounts given in numerical form on the circle graph always add up to the total amount being referred to.
- Since percents are often used in circle graphs, the 360 degrees of the circle represent 100 percent.
- The total value or size of the whole pie is usually given over or under the graph; either as "TOTAL" or "100%".

USES OF CIRCLE GRAPHS:
- Circle Graphs are useful to quickly compare what percentage each part is of the whole and what is the break up of each section that makes the whole.
- A circle graph is used to show how a whole amount is broken into parts.
- Circle graphs are used to show the relationship of various parts of a quantity to each other and to the whole quantity
- Circle graphs are used to show how various sectors share in the whole amount. Circle graphs usually give the percentage that each sector receives.

STYLES OF CIRCLE GRAPHS:
There are several styles of Circle Graphs. In one of the most common style, the sectors are labeled directly on the graph either inside the sectors or with the help of arrows. In the other style, there is a key that describes what each sector represents. Both these styles represent the same data in slightly different styles.

PARTS OF CIRCLE GRAPH/ PIE CHART:
Title of Circle Graph: The title tells us the topic of the circle graph and what the information means. It also explains or describes what the circle graph represents and makes it easier to read and interpret it. The title is usually clear and concise. One should always make sure to read it first.
Vertical Axis: There is no Vertical Axis in a Circle Graph.
Horizontal Axis: There is no Horizontal Axis in a Circle Graph.
Origin: The center of the circle/pie is the origin of the Circle Graph.
Sectors: The circle is divided into parts or sectors, where each sector represents a different category. The size of each sector is exactly proportional to the quantity it represents. The bigger the section, the higher the quantity it represents; the smaller the section, the lower the quantity it represents. The sum of all the sections should always equal 100%.
Key: The Key is a list of words, numbers, symbols, or combination of these that helps in the identification of the items in a graph or in interpretation of the graph. It explains what each of the parts/sectors represents. Each part/sector can be differentiated by making them in different shades or with different patterns/colors. If each part/sector is labeled with what it represents, then it may not be necessary to create a key.

READING CIRCLE GRAPH:
To read the Circle Graph, use the following tips:

TIP #1: First look at a specific sector and then identify the category and the quantity it represents.

TIP #2: To find the value of a particular piece of the pie, multiply the appropriate percent by value of the whole pie.
For instance, to find the value of a particular item, find the slice labeled with that item, and see what percent of the whole pie it represents. Then multiply the value of that item by the whole.

PRACTICE EXERCISE – QUESTIONS AND ANSWERS WITH EXPLANATIONS: STATS – GRAPHS:

TABLE/CHART:

Table/Chart – Calorie Table/Chart – (Different Types of Oils):

Type of Oil	Amount	Calories
Olive Oil	1 oz	150
Sunflower Oil	2 oz	200
Vegetable Oil	1 oz	200
Corn Oil	2 oz	150
Fish Oil	0.5 oz	125

(Note: The above grid is strictly made up only for the purpose of this problem, and does not represent actual calories.)

Refer to the Table/Chart above while answering the following questions:

Question #1: How many calories are there in 5 oz. of olive oil?
Solution: 1 oz of olive oil   ⇒ 150 calories
              5 oz of olive oil   ⇒ 150 × 5 = 750 calories

Question #2: How many calories are there in 1 oz of sunflower oil?
Solution: 2 oz of sunflower oil ⇒ 200 calories
              1 oz of sunflower oil ⇒ 200 ÷ 2 = 100 calories

Question #3: One ounce of vegetable oil has how many more calories than one ounce of olive oil?
Solution: 1 oz of vegetable oil   ⇒ 200 calories
              1 oz of olive oil   ⇒ 150 calories
              1 oz of vegetable oil – 1 oz of olive oil ⇒ 200 – 150 = 50 calories
              Therefore, 1 oz of vegetable oil has 50 more calories than 1 oz of olive oil.

Question #4: One ounce of sunflower oil has how many more calories than one ounce of corn oil?
Solution: 1 oz of sunflower oil = 200 ÷ 2   ⇒ 100 calories
              1 oz of corn oil   = 150 ÷ 2   ⇒ 75 calories
              1 oz of sunflower oil – 1 oz of corn oil ⇒ 100 – 75 = 25 calories
              Therefore, 1 oz of sunflower oil has 25 more calories than 1 oz of corn oil.

Question #5: What is the total number of calories in 5 oz of olive oil and 2 oz of vegetable oil?
Solution: 1 oz of olive oil   ⇒ 150 calories
              5 oz of olive oil   = 5 × 150   ⇒ 750 calories
              1 oz of vegetable oil   ⇒ 200 calories
              2 oz of vegetable oil   = 2 × 200   ⇒ 400 calories
              5 oz of olive oil + 2 oz of vegetable oil ⇒ 750 + 400 = 1,150 calories

Question #6: What is the total number of calories in 8 oz of sunflower oil and 9 oz of corn oil?
Solution: 1 oz of sunflower oil = 200 ÷ 2   ⇒ 100 calories
              8 oz of sunflower oil = 100 × 8   ⇒ 800 calories
              1 oz of corn oil   = 150 ÷ 2   ⇒ 75 calories
              9 oz of corn oil   = 75 × 9   ⇒ 675 calories
              8 oz of sunflower oil + 9 oz of corn oil ⇒ 800 + 675 = 1,475 calories.

Question #7: What is the ratio of calories in 1 oz olive oil to calories in 1 oz of sunflower oil?
Solution: 1 oz of olive oil   ⇒ 150 calories
              1 oz of sunflower oil ⇒ 100 calories
              Ratio ⇒ 1 oz of olive oil : 1 oz of sunflower oil ⇒ 150:100 = 3:2

Question #8: Which oil has the highest number of calories per ounce?

Solution:

1 oz of olive oil		$\Rightarrow$ 150 calories
1 oz of sunflower oil	= 200 ÷ 2	$\Rightarrow$ 100 calories
1 oz of vegetable oil		$\Rightarrow$ 200 calories
1 oz of corn oil	= 150 ÷ 2	$\Rightarrow$ 75 calories
1 oz of fish oil	= 125 × 2	$\Rightarrow$ 250 calories

Therefore, fish oil has the highest number of calories per ounce.

Question #9: Which oil has the least number of calories per ounce?

Solution:

1 oz of olive oil		$\Rightarrow$ 150 calories
1 oz of sunflower oil	= 200 ÷ 2	$\Rightarrow$ 100 calories
1 oz of vegetable oil		$\Rightarrow$ 200 calories
1 oz of corn oil	= 150 ÷ 2	$\Rightarrow$ 75 calories
1 oz of fish oil	= 125 × 2	$\Rightarrow$ 250 calories

Therefore, corn oil has the least number of calories per ounce.

Question #10: What is the average no of calories in 1 oz of olive, sunflower, vegetable, corn, and fish oil?

Solution:

1 oz of olive oil		$\Rightarrow$ 150 calories
1 oz of sunflower oil	= 200 ÷ 2	$\Rightarrow$ 100 calories
1 oz of vegetable oil		$\Rightarrow$ 200 calories
1 oz of corn oil	= 150 ÷ 2	$\Rightarrow$ 75 calories
1 oz of fish oil	= 125 × 2	$\Rightarrow$ 250 calories
Total		$\Rightarrow$ 775 calories
Average	= 775 ÷ 5	$\Rightarrow$ 155 calories

PICTOGRAPH:

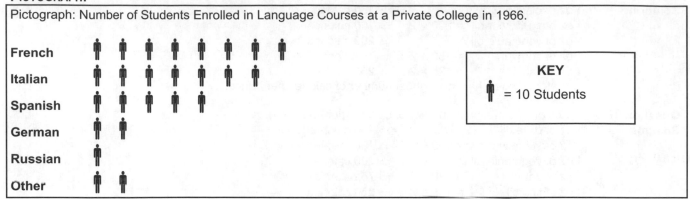

Pictograph: Number of Students Enrolled in Language Courses at a Private College in 1966.

French
Italian
Spanish
German
Russian
Other

KEY

= 10 Students

Refer to the pictograph above while answering the following questions:

Question #1: Which one of the five language courses has the highest enrollment?
Solution: French
(Its clear from the pictograph above that French language course has the highest enrollment since it has the most number of symbols).

Question #2: Which one of the five-language course has the lowest enrollment?
Solution: Russian (Its clear from the pictograph above that Russian language course has the lowest enrollment since it has the least number of symbols).

Question #3: How many students are enrolled in French course?
Solution: French course = 8 × 10 = 80 (Since there are 8 symbols for French course and each symbol represents 10 students, to find the total enrollment for French course, multiply 8 by 10.)

Question #4: How many students are enrolled in Russian course?
Solution: Russian course = 1 × 10 = 10 (Since there is 1 symbol for Russian course and each symbol represents 10 students, to find the total enrollment for Russian course, multiply 1 by 10.)

Question #5: How many students are enrolled in Italian and German courses?
Solution:
Italian   = 7 × 10   ⇒ 70
German = 2 × 10   ⇒ 20
Italian + German = 70 + 20   ⇒ 90

Question #6: What is the total number of students enrolled in language courses?
Solution:
French   = 8 × 10   ⇒ 80
Italian   = 7 × 10   ⇒ 70
Spanish   = 5 × 10   ⇒ 50
German   = 2 × 10   ⇒ 20
Russian   = 1 × 10   ⇒ 10
Other   = 2 × 10   ⇒ 20
Total   ⇒ 250
Therefore, the total number of students enrolled in language courses is 250.

Question #7: How many more students are taking French course than German course?
Solution:
French   = 8 × 10   ⇒ 80
German   = 2 × 10   ⇒ 20
French – German = 80 – 20   ⇒ 60
Therefore, there are 60 more students who are taking French courses than German courses.

Question #8: How many more students are taking Italian course than Spanish course?
Solution: Italian   = 7 × 10   ⇒ 70

Spanish   = 5 × 10   ⇒ 50
French – German = 70 – 50   ⇒ 20
Therefore, there are 20 more students who are taking Italian courses than Spanish courses.

Question #9:   What is ratio of students taking French course to students taking Italian course?

Solution: French   = 8 × 10   ⇒ 80
Italian   = 7 × 10   ⇒ 70
Ratio ⇒ French : Italian   ⇒ 80:70 = 8:7

Question #10:   If the "Other" category includes five languages, what is the average (arithmetic mean) number of students taking each language course offered at the college?

Solution: French   = 8 × 10   ⇒ 80
Italian   = 7 × 10   ⇒ 70
Spanish   = 5 × 10   ⇒ 50
German   = 2 × 10   ⇒ 20
Russian   = 1 × 10   ⇒ 10
Other   = 2 × 10   ⇒ <u>20</u>
Total   ⇒ <u>250</u>
Average   = 250 ÷ 10   ⇒ 25
Therefore, the average number of students taking each language course at the college is 25.

SINGLE LINE GRAPH:

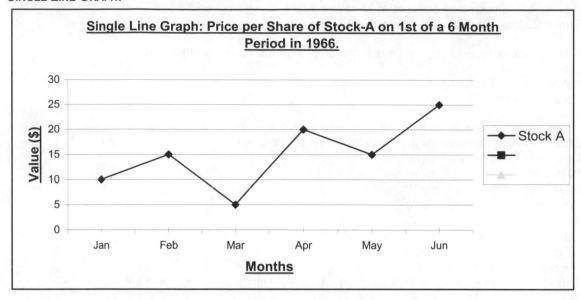

Single Line Graph: Price per Share of Stock-A on 1st of a 6 Month Period in 1966.

Refer to the Single Line Graph above while answering the following questions:

Question #1: In what month was the value of Stock-A the highest?
Solution: Highest value of Stock-A ⇒ $25 in June
(Simply read the graph and look for the highest value of Stock-A ⇒ Follow the line representing Stock-A to its highest point, and then check the corresponding month at the bottom of the graph.)

Question #2: In what month was the value of Stock-A the lowest?
Solution: Lowest value of Stock-A ⇒ $5 in March
(Simply read the graph and look for the lowest value of Stock-A ⇒ Follow the line representing Stock-A to its lowest point, and then check the corresponding month at the bottom of the graph.)

Question #3: What was the value of Stock-A in the month of January?
Solution: Value of Stock-A in the month of January ⇒ $10
(Simply read the graph and look for the stock value in the month of January ⇒ Locate the month of January on the horizontal axis and look for its corresponding value on the vertical axis.)

Question #4: What was the value of Stock-A in the month of June?
Solution: Value of Stock-A in the month of June ⇒ $25
(Simply read the graph and look for the stock value in the month of June ⇒ Locate the month of June on the horizontal axis and look for its corresponding value on the vertical axis.)

Question #5: By how much did the value of Stock-A increase between February and April?
Solution: Value of Stock-A in February ⇒ $15
Value of Stock-A in April ⇒ $20
Increase in the value of Stock-A between February and April ⇒ $20 – $15 = $5

Question #6: What is the difference between the highest and lowest value of a share of Stock-A?
Solution: Highest value of Stock-A ⇒ $25
Lowest Value of Stock-A ⇒ $5
Highest Value of Stock-A – Lowest Values of Stock-A ⇒ $25 – $5 = $20

Question #7: What is the ratio of highest to the lowest value of Stock-A?
Solution: Highest value of Stock-A ⇒ $25
Lowest Value of Stock-A ⇒ $5
Ratio ⇒ Highest Value of Stock-A : Lowest Values of Stock-A ⇒ $25:$5 = 5:1

Question #8:   What is the average price of Stock-A during the six-month period?
Solution: Value of Stock-A in January $\Rightarrow$ $10
               Value of Stock-A in February $\Rightarrow$ $15
               Value of Stock-A in March $\Rightarrow$ $5
               Value of Stock-A in April $\Rightarrow$ $20
               Value of Stock-A in May $\Rightarrow$ $15
               Value of Stock-A in June $\Rightarrow$ $25
               Total $\Rightarrow$ $90
               Average Value of Stock-A $\Rightarrow$ $90 ÷ 6 = $15

Question #9:   What is the average six-monthly increase in the value of Stock-A?
Solution: Increase in the value of Stock-A during the six-monthly period, from $10 in January to $25 in June = $25 – $10 = $15
               Average six-monthly increase $\Rightarrow$ $15 ÷ 6 = $2.50

Question #10:   If from June to December the value of stock-A increases at the same rate as it did from January to June, what should be the predicted value of a share of stock-A on December 31st?
Solution: The value of Stock-A increased from $10 in January to $25 in June, which is a 150% increase or 2.5 times as much.
               At the same rate, in December the value of stock-A should be:
               [(150% of $25) + $25] = $62.50 or $25 × 2.5 = $62.50

Question #11:   In what period was the percent increase in the value of a share of stock-A the greatest?
Solution: March
               (The increase (or decrease) in value can easily be determined by the steepness or slope of the graph $\Rightarrow$ since the slope of the graph is steepest in the period of March, therefore the rate of growth or percent increase in the value of stock-A was then the greatest.)
               (Mathematically: the price of stock-A went up from $5 in March to $20 in April, which is an increase of 300%, which was the greatest percent increase in the value of stock-A).

Question #12:   In what period was the percent increase in the value of a share of stock-A the least?
Solution: January
               (The increase (or decrease) in value can easily be determined by the steepness or slope of the graph $\Rightarrow$ Since the slope of the graph is flattest in the period of January and therefore the rate of growth or percent increase in the value of stock-A was then the least.)
               (Mathematically: the price of stock A went up from $10 in January to $15 in February, which is an increase of 50%, which was the least percent increase in the value of stock-A.)

DOUBLE LINE GRAPH:

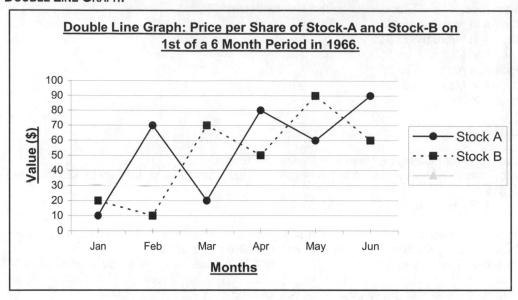

Double Line Graph: Price per Share of Stock-A and Stock-B on 1st of a 6 Month Period in 1966.

Refer to the Double Line Graph above while answering the following questions:

Question #1: On the first of what month was the difference in the value of a share of Stock-A and a share of Stock-B the greatest? Or the ratio of Stock-A to Stock-B was the greatest?

Solution: Greatest difference in the value of Stock-A and Stock-B = $60 in February.
(Simply read the graph and look for the greatest difference between the value of stock-A and stock-B ⇒ Compare one stock to the other, month by month. The month in which the dots are farthest apart is the one in which there is the greatest difference between the value of share of the two stocks.)

Question #2: On the first of what month was the difference in the value of a share of Stock-A and a share of Stock-B the least? Or the ratio of Stock-A to Stock-B was the least?

Solution: Least difference in the value of Stock-A and Stock-B = $10 in January.
(Simply read the graph and look for the least difference between the value of stock-A and stock-B ⇒ Compare one stock to the other, month by month. The month in which the dots are closest is the one in which there is the least difference between the value of share of the two stocks.)

Question #3: What is the difference, in dollars, between the highest value of Stock-A and lowest value of Stock-B?
Solution: Highest Value of Stock-A ⇒ $90
Lowest Value of Stock-B ⇒ $10
Highest Value of Stock-A – Lowest Value of Stock-B ⇒ $90 – $10 = $80

Question #4: What is the difference, in dollars, between highest value of Stock-B to the lowest value of Stock-A?
Solution: Highest Value of Stock-B ⇒ $90
Lowest Value of Stock-A ⇒ $10
Difference = Highest Value of Stock-B – Lowest Value of Stock-A ⇒ $90 – $10 = $80

Question #5: What is the ratio of the average value of Stock-A to the average value of Stock-B?

Solution:

	Stock-A	Stock-B
Stock Value in January	$10	$20
Stock Value in February	$70	$10
Stock Value in March	$20	$70
Stock Value in April	$80	$50
Stock Value in May	$60	$90
Stock Value in June	$90	$60
Total	$330	$300
Average Value	⇒ $ 330 ÷ 6	⇒ $ 300 ÷ 6

$\Rightarrow$ \$55 $\Rightarrow$ \$50

Ratio $\Rightarrow$ Average Value of Stock-A : Average Value of Stock-B = \$55:\$50 = 11:10

Question #6: If from June to December the value of each stock increases at the same rate as it did from January to June, then on December 31st of the same year, what will be the ratio of the value of a share of stock-A to the value of a share of stock-B?

Solution: The value of Stock-A increased from \$10 in January to \$90 in June, which is a 800% increase or 9 times as much

At the same rate, in December the value of stock-A should be:

[(800% of \$90) + \$90] = \$810 or 90 × 9 = \$810

The value of Stock-B increased from \$20 in January to \$60 in June, which is a 200% increase or 3 times as much.

At the same rate, in December the value of stock-A should be:

[(200% of \$60) + \$60] = \$180 or 60 × 3 = \$180.

Stock-A $\Rightarrow$ \$10 in Jan -to- \$90 in June -to- \$810 in Dec

Stock-B $\Rightarrow$ \$20 in Jan -to- \$60 in June -to- \$180 in Dec

Ratio $\Rightarrow$ Value of Stock-A in Dec : Value of Stock-B in Dec = \$810:\$180 = 9:2

SINGLE BAR GRAPH:

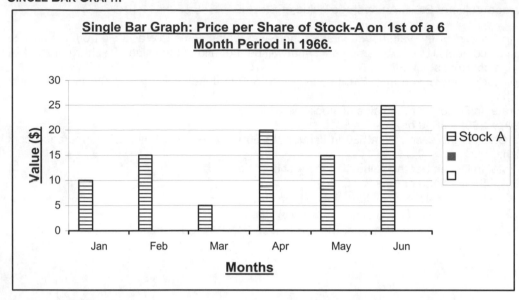

Refer to the Single Line Graph above while answering the following questions:

Question #1: In what month was the value of Stock-A the highest?
Solution: Highest value of Stock-A = $25 in June
(Simply read the graph and look for the highest value of Stock-A ⇒ Follow the line representing Stock-A to its highest point, and then check the corresponding month at the bottom of the graph.)

Question #2: In what month was the value of Stock-A the lowest?
Solution: Lowest value of Stock-A = $5 in March
(Simply read the graph and look for the lowest value of Stock-A ⇒ Follow the line representing Stock-A to its lowest point, and then check the corresponding month at the bottom of the graph.)

Question #3: What was the value of Stock-A in the month of January?
Solution: Value of Stock-A in the month of January = $10
(Simply read the graph and look for the stock value in the month of January ⇒ Locate the month of January on the horizontal axis and look for its corresponding value on the vertical axis.)

Question #4: What was the value of Stock-A in the month of June?
Solution: Value of Stock-A in the month of June = $25
(Simply read the graph and look for the stock value in the month of June ⇒ Locate the month of June on the horizontal axis and look for its corresponding value on the vertical axis.)

Question #5: By how much did the value of Stock-A increase between February and April?
Solution: Value of Stock-A in February ⇒ $15
Value of Stock-A in April   ⇒ $20
Increase in the value of Stock-A between February and April ⇒ $20 – $15 = $5

Question #6: What is the difference between the highest and lowest value of a share of Stock-A?
Solution: Highest value of Stock-A   ⇒ $25
Lowest Value of Stock-A   ⇒ $5
Highest Value of Stock-A – Lowest Values of Stock-A ⇒ $25 – $5 = $20

Question #7: What is the ratio of highest to the lowest value of Stock-A?
Solution: Highest value of Stock-A   ⇒ $25
Lowest Value of Stock-A   ⇒ $5
Ratio = Highest Value of Stock-A : Lowest Values of Stock-A = $25:$5 = 5:1

Question #8: What is the average price of Stock-A during the six-month period?
Solution: Value of Stock-A in January   ⇒ $10
Value of Stock-A in February ⇒ $15
Value of Stock-A in March   ⇒ $5
Value of Stock-A in April   ⇒ $20
Value of Stock-A in May   ⇒ $15
Value of Stock-A in June   ⇒ $25
Total   ⇒ $90
Average Value of Stock-A   ⇒ $90 ÷ 6 = $15

Question #9: What is the average six-monthly increase in the value of Stock-A?
Solution: Increase in the value of Stock-A during the six-monthly period, from $10 in January to $25 in June =
$25 – $10 = $15
Average six-monthly increase ⇒ $15 ÷ 6 = $2.50

Question #10: If from June to December the value of stock-A increases at the same rate as it did from January to June, what should be the predicted value of a share of stock-A on December 31st?
Solution: The value of Stock-A increased from $10 in January to $25 in June, which is a 150% increase or 2.5 times as much.
At the same rate, in December the value of stock-A should be:
[(150% of $25) + $25] = $62.50 or $25 × 2.5 = $62.50

Question #11: In what period was the percent increase in the value of a share of stock-A the greatest?
Solution: March
(The increase (or decrease) in value can easily be determined by the steepness or slope of the graph ⇒ since the slope of the graph is steepest in the period of March, therefore the rate of growth or percent increase in the value of stock-A was then the greatest.)
(Mathematically: the price of stock-A went up from $5 in March to $20 in April, which is an increase of 300%, which was the greatest percent increase in the value of stock-A).

Question #12: In what period was the percent increase in the value of a share of stock-A the least?
Solution: January
(The Increase (or decrease) in value can easily be determined by the steepness or slope of the graph ⇒ Since the slope of the graph is flattest in the period of January and therefore the rate of growth or percent increase in the value of stock-A was then the least.)
(Mathematically: the price of stock A went up from $10 in January to $15 in February, which is an increase of 50%, which was the least percent increase in the value of stock-A).

DOUBLE BAR GRAPHS:

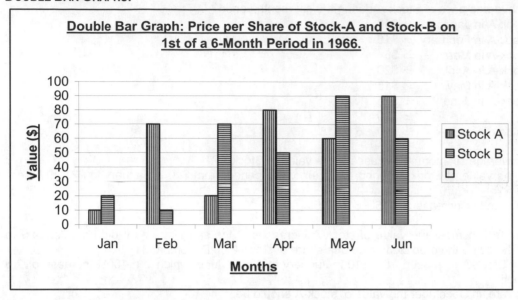

Double Bar Graph: Price per Share of Stock-A and Stock-B on 1st of a 6-Month Period in 1966.

Refer to the Double Bar Graph above while answering the following questions:

Question #1: On the first of what month was the difference in the value of a share of Stock-A and a share of Stock-B the greatest? Or the ratio of Stock-A to Stock-B was the greatest?

Solution: Greatest difference in the value of Stock-A and Stock-B = $60 in February.
(Simply read the graph and look for the greatest difference between the value of stock A and stock-B ⇒ Compare one stock to the other, month by month. The month in which the dots are farthest apart is the one in which there is the greatest difference between the value of share of the two stocks.)

Question #2: On the first of what month was the difference in the value of a share of Stock-A and a share of Stock-B the least? Or the ratio of Stock-A to Stock-B was the least?

Solution: Least difference in the value of Stock-A and Stock-B = $10 in January.
(Simply read the graph and look for the least difference between the value of stock-A and stock-B ⇒ Compare one stock to the other, month by month. The month in which the dots are closest is the one in which there is the least difference between the value of share of the two stocks.)

Question #3: What is the difference, in dollars, between the highest value of Stock-A and lowest value of Stock-B?

Solution: Highest Value of Stock-A   ⇒ $90
Lowest Value of Stock-B   ⇒ $10
Highest Value of Stock-A – Lowest Value of Stock-B ⇒ $90 – $10 = $80

Question #4: What is the difference, in dollars, between highest value of Stock-B to the lowest value of Stock-A?

Solution: Highest Value of Stock-B   ⇒ $90
Lowest Value of Stock-A   ⇒ $10
Difference ⇒ Highest Value of Stock-B – Lowest Value of Stock-A ⇒ $90 – $10 = $80

Question #5: What is the ratio of the average value of Stock-A to the average value of Stock-B?

Solution:

	Stock-A	Stock-B
Stock Value in January	$10	$20
Stock Value in February	$70	$10
Stock Value in March	$20	$70
Stock Value in April	$80	$50
Stock Value in May	$60	$90
Stock Value in June	$90	$60
Total	$330	$300
Average Value of Stock-A	⇒ $ 330 ÷ 6	⇒ $ 300 ÷ 6

$\Rightarrow$ $55 $\Rightarrow$ $50

Ratio $\Rightarrow$ Average Value of Stock-A : Average Value of Stock-B = $55:$50 = 11:10

Question #6:   If from June to December the value of each stock increases at the same rate as it did from January to June, then on December 31st of the same year, what will be the ratio of the value of a share of stock-A to the value of a share of stock-B?

Solution: The value of Stock-A increased from $10 in January to $90 in June, which is a 800% increase or 9 times as much

At the same rate, in December the value of stock-A should be:

[(800% of $90) + $90] = $810 or 90 × 9 = $810

The value of Stock-B increased from $20 in January to $60 in June, which is a 200% increase or 3 times as much

At the same rate, in December the value of stock-A should be:

[(200% of $60) + $60] = $180 or 60 × 3 = $180

Stock-A $\Rightarrow$ $10 in Jan -to- $90 in June -to- $810 in Dec

Stock-B $\Rightarrow$ $20 in Jan -to- $60 in June -to- $180 in Dec

Ratio $\Rightarrow$ Value of Stock-A in Dec : Value of Stock-B in Dec $\Rightarrow$ $810 : $180 = 9:2

SCATTER PLOT GRAPH:

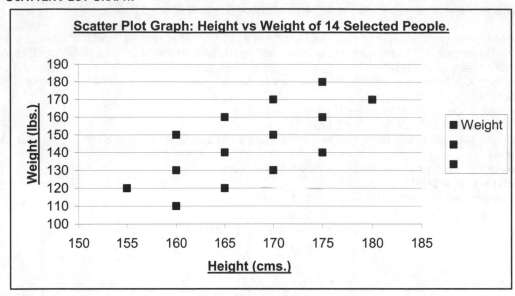

Refer to the Scatter Plot Graph above while answering the following questions:

Question #1: According to the scatter plot graph above, what is the weight of a person whose height is 180 cm?
Solution: Weight of a person whose height is 180 cm ⇒ 170 lbs
(Simply read the graph and look for the weight of the person who is 180 cm.)

Question #2: According to the scatter plot graph above, what is the height of a person who weighs 180 pounds?
Solution: Height of a person who is 180 lbs ⇒ 175 cm
(Simply read the graph and look for the height of the person who is 180 lbs.)

Question #3: According to the scatter plot graph above, what is the weight of the tallest person?
Solution: Weight of the tallest person ⇒ 170 lbs
(Simply read the graph and look for the weight of the tallest person.)

Question #4: According to the scatter plot graph above, what is the height of the lightest person?
Solution: Height of the lightest person ⇒ 160 cm
(Simply read the graph above for the height of the lightest person.)

Question #5: According to the scatter plot graph above, what is the difference between the height of the tallest and the shortest person?
Solution: Height of the tallest person   ⇒ 180 cm
Height of the shortest person ⇒ 155 cm
Difference between the height of the tallest and the shortest person
= Height of the tallest person – Height of the shortest person = 180 cm – 155 cm = 25 cm

Question #6: What is the difference between the weight of the heaviest and the lightest person?
Solution: Weight of the heaviest person   ⇒ 180 lbs
Weight of the lightest person   ⇒ 110 lbs
Difference between the weight of the heaviest and the lightest person
= Weight of the heaviest person – Weight of the lightest person = 180 lbs – 110 lbs = 70 lbs

Question #7: According to the scatter plot graph above, how many people are shorter than 175 cm and weigh less than 150 pounds.
Solution: 6 People
First, find all the points on the graph that represent people who are shorter than 175 cm, this results in 10 such points. Then out of these 10 points, find all points on the graph that represent men who weigh

less than 150 pounds, this results in 6 points. Therefore, there are 6 points that are left. These 6 points represent people who are shorter than 175 cm and who weigh less than 150 pounds.

Alternate Method: Use process of elimination to find the answer. First eliminate all points on the graph that represent people who are 175 cm and taller, this results in elimination of 4 out of 14 points, which leaves 10 points. Then eliminate all points on the graph that represent people who weigh 150 pounds or more, this results in further elimination of 4 points, which leaves 6 points. Therefore, all but 6 points have been eliminated. These 6 points represent people who are shorter than 175 cm and who weigh less than 150 pounds.

Question #8: According to the scatter plot graph above, how many people are taller than 160 cm and weigh more than 150 pounds?

Solution: 5 People

First, find all the points on the graph that represent people who are taller than 160 cm, this results in 10 such points. Then out of these 10 points, find all points on the graph that represent people who weigh more than 150 pounds, this results in 5 points. Therefore, there are 5 points that are left. These 5 points represent people who are taller than 160 cm and who weigh more than 150 pounds.

Alternate Method: Use process of elimination to find the answer. First eliminate all points on the graph that represent people who are 160 cm and taller, this results in elimination of 4 out of 14 points, which leaves 10 points. Then eliminate all points on the graph that represent people who weigh 150 pounds or more, this result in further elimination of 5 points, which leaves 5 points. Therefore, all but 5 points have been eliminated. These 5 points represent people who are taller than 160 cm and who weigh more than 150 pounds.

Question #9: According to the scatter plot graph above, what is the average weight of the 14 selected people?

Solution: Total Weight $\Rightarrow$ 110 + 120 + 120 + 130 + 130 + 140 + 140 + 150 + 150 + 160 + 160 + 170 + 170 + 180
$\Rightarrow$ 2,030 lbs

Average Weight $\Rightarrow$ 2,030 lbs. ÷ 14 = 145 lbs

Question #10: According to the scatter plot graph above, what is the average height of the 14 selected people?

Solution: Total Height $\Rightarrow$ 155 + 160 + 160 + 160 + 165 + 165 + 165 + 170 + 170 + 170 + 175 + 175 + 175 + 180
$\Rightarrow$ 2,345 cm

Average Height $\Rightarrow$ 2,345 cm ÷ 14 = 167.50 cm

Question #11: According to the scatter plot graph above, what is the ratio of the height of the tallest to the height of the shortest person?

Solution: Height of the tallest person $\Rightarrow$ 180 cm

Height of the shortest person $\Rightarrow$ 155 cm

Ratio = Height of the tallest person : Height of the shortest person = 180:155 = 36:31

Question #12: According to the scatter plot graph above, what is the ratio of the weight of the heaviest to the weight of the lightest person?

Solution: Weight of the heaviest person $\Rightarrow$ 180 lbs

Weight of the lightest person $\Rightarrow$ 110 lbs

Ratio $\Rightarrow$ Weight of the heaviest person : Weight of the lightest person = = 180:110 = 18:11

CIRCLE-GRAPH/PIE-CHARTS:

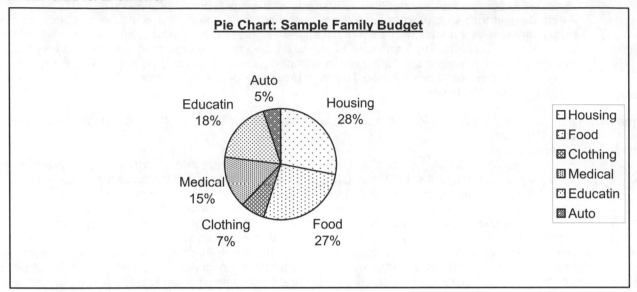

Refer to the Circle-Graph/Pie-Chart above while answering the following questions:

Question #1:   According to this sample budget, which category accounts for most amount of money spent?
Solution: Housing
                    (Simply look for the biggest sector in the circle graph; housing is the biggest sector with 28% share.)

Question #2:   According to this sample budget, which category accounts for the least amount of money spent?
Solution: Auto
                    (Simply look for the smallest sector in the circle graph; auto is the smallest sector with 5% share.)

Question #3:   According to the sample budget shown above, a family with a monthly income of $1,500 should expect
                    to spend how much on clothing?
Solution: Net Monthly Income ⇒ $1,500
                    Clothing Expense   ⇒ 7% of 1,500 = 0.07 × 1,500 = $105

Question #4:   According to the sample budget shown above, a family with a monthly income of $1,500 should expect
                    to spend how much on auto?
Solution: Net Monthly Income ⇒ $1,500
                    Auto Expense   ⇒ 5% of 1,500 = $75

Question #5:   According to the sample budget shown above, a family with a monthly income of $2,000 should expect
                    to spend how much on housing and food?
Solution: Net Monthly Income   ⇒ $2,000
                    Housing Expense   = 28% of 2,000 ⇒ $560
                    Food Expense   = 27% of 2,000 ⇒ $540
                    Housing + Food Expense   ⇒ $1,100

Question #6:   According to the sample budget shown above, a family with a monthly income of $2,000 should expect
                    to spend how much on education and medical?
Solution: Net Monthly Income   ⇒ $2,000
                    Education Expense = 18% of 2,000 ⇒ $360
                    Medical Expense   = 15% of 2,000 ⇒ $300
                    Education + Medical Expense   ⇒ $660

Question #7:   According to the sample budget shown above, a family with a monthly income of $2,500 would spend
                    how much more on housing than on food?

Solution: Net Monthly Income $\Rightarrow$ $2,500
Housing Expense   = 28% of 2,500 $\Rightarrow$ $700
Food Expense   = 27% of 2,500 $\Rightarrow$ $675
Housing Expense – Food Expense $\Rightarrow$ $700 – $675 = $25

Question #8:   According to the sample budget shown above, a family with a monthly income of $2,500 would spend how much more on education than on medical?

Solution: Net Monthly Income $\Rightarrow$ $2,500
Education Expense   = 18% of 2,500 $\Rightarrow$ $450
Medical Expense   = 15% of 2,500 $\Rightarrow$ $375
Education Expense – Medical Expense $\Rightarrow$ $450 – $375 = $75

Question #9:   According to this sample budget, what is the ratio of amount spent on education to amount spent on medical?

Solution: Education Expense $\Rightarrow$ 18%
Medical Expense $\Rightarrow$ 15%
Ratio $\Rightarrow$ Education : Medical $\Rightarrow$ 18:15 = 6:5

Question #10:   A family with a monthly income of $5,000 spends $1,100 a month on education; by how much will they exceed the sample budget?

Solution: Net Monthly Income $\Rightarrow$ $5,000
Actual Education Expense $\Rightarrow$ $1,100
Education Expense (according to the budget) $\Rightarrow$ 18% of 5,000 = 0.18 × 5,000 = $900
Actual Education Expense – Education Expense $\Rightarrow$ $1,100 – $900 = $200

Question #11:   If the areas of the sectors in the circle graph are drawn in proportion to the percent shown, what is the measure, in degrees, of the central angle of the sector representing the percent of auto expenses?

Solution: Since the sum of the central angles for the six sectors is 360°, the central angle for the sector representing auto expenses is $\Rightarrow$ 5% of 360° = (0.05) (360°) = 18°

Question #12:   If the areas of the sectors in the circle graph are drawn in proportion to the percent shown, what is the measure, in degrees, of the central angle of the sector representing the percent of medical expenses?

Solution: Since the sum of the central angles for the six sectors is 360°, the central angle for the sector representing medical expenses is $\Rightarrow$ 15% of 360° = (0.15) (360°) = 54°

THIS PAGE HAS BEEN INTENTIONALLY LEFT BLANK

EZ BOOK STORE: ORDERS & SALES:

ORDERS & SALES INFORMATION: EZ Solutions books can be ordered via one of the following methods:

🖥 ON-LINE ORDERS:
On-line Orders can be placed 24/7 via internet by going to: www.EZmethods.com

✉ E-MAIL ORDERS:
E-Mail Orders can be placed 24/7 via internet by emailing: orders@EZmethods.com

☎ PHONE ORDERS:
Phone Orders can be placed via telephone by calling: ++301.622.9597

📠 FAX ORDERS:
Fax Orders can be placed via fax by faxing: ++301.622.9597

🖳 MAIL ORDERS:
Mail Orders can be placed via regular mail by mailing to the address given below:
EZ Solutions
Orders Department
P.O. Box 10755
Silver Spring, MD 20914
USA

OTHER OPTIONS: EZ Solutions books are also available at most major bookstores.

Institutional Sales: For volume/bulk sales to bookstores, libraries, schools, colleges, universities, organization, and institutions, please contact us. Quantity discount and special pricing is available.

EZ BOOK LIST:

LIST OF EZ TEST PREP SERIES OF BOOKS:

EZ Test Prep Series books are available for the following sections:
- EZ Solutions – Test Prep Series – General Test Taking Strategies
- EZ Solutions – Test Prep Series – Math Strategies
- EZ Solutions – Test Prep Series – Math Review – Arithmetic
- EZ Solutions – Test Prep Series – Math Review – Algebra
- EZ Solutions – Test Prep Series – Math Review – Applications
- EZ Solutions – Test Prep Series – Math Review – Geometry
- EZ Solutions – Test Prep Series – Math Review – Word Problems
- EZ Solutions – Test Prep Series – Math Review – Logic & Stats
- EZ Solutions – Test Prep Series – Math Practice – Basic Workbook
- EZ Solutions – Test Prep Series – Math Practice – Advanced Workbook
- EZ Solutions – Test Prep Series – Verbal Section – Reading Comprehension
- EZ Solutions – Test Prep Series – Verbal Section – Sentence Correction/Completion
- EZ Solutions – Test Prep Series – Verbal Section – Critical Reasoning
- EZ Solutions – Test Prep Series – Verbal Section – Vocabulary
- EZ Solutions – Test Prep Series – Verbal Section – Grammar
- EZ Solutions – Test Prep Series – Verbal Section – Writing Skills

Note: Some of these books have already been published and others will be released shortly.

EZ Test Prep Series books are available for the following standardized tests:
- EZ Solutions GMAT Test Prep Series of Books
- EZ Solutions GRE Test Prep Series of Books
- EZ Solutions SAT Test Prep Series of Books
- EZ Solutions ACT Test Prep Series of Books
- EZ Solutions PRAXIS Test Prep Series of Books
- EZ Solutions POWER MATH Test Prep Series of Books